WHAT THE
BIBLE SAYS
ABOUT

GRACE

WHAT THE
BIBLE SAYS
ABOUT
GRACE

William Pile

College Press Publishing Company, Joplin, Missouri

BT
751.2
.P44
1990

Printed and Bound in the
United States of America
All Rights Reserved

Library of Congress Catalog Card Number: 89-081454
International Standard Book Number: 0-89900-264-1

DEDICATION

To God's greatest fleshly gift to me,
and the one who may not be as
"full of grace and truth"
as her Savior is, but she's close,
my wife of more than thirty years,
Carmelita.

Table of Contents

ACKNOWLEDGMENTS

Behind this volume is a personal pilgrimage (from legalism to grace) made by its author during a nearly thirty-year period. That trip would not have been possible without the following individuals:

• An anonymous man in Tulsa, Oklahoma in the early 1960s who first caused me to question my conditionality concept of salvation. I met him at his door. I never got his name, but I got his message. I went away worried and searching for a Christian lifestyle that had more security in it. I'll probably never see him again except in eternity, where I hope to thank him personally.

•My wife of more than 30 years, Carmelita, who, though she has not been personally involved in my theological studies, demonstrated "grace living" to me before we either one knew what the term meant.

•Edwin DeVries, who first asked me to articulate my findings on grace to a national forum at Nationwide Youth Roundup on August 5, 1976.

• A host of Christians and Christian leaders who have been encouraged to taste what was for them the "new wine" of Christian grace under my preaching. They liked it, begged for more, and validated it with their lives. People like Don and Joyce Brewer, LeRoy and Roxanne Brennfoerder, Arch Word, Ron Hunt, Victor Knowles, Walt Fagan (deceased), Dr. Sterling Lacy, Dixie and LaVoy Johnson, and dozens of others whose lives have blossomed under the warm sunshine of God's grace.

• Bruce Larson, prolific author, whose book *No Longer Strangers*, gave me the permission and showed me how to live the grace I discovered in God's Word.

And then there are those people and organizations without which the actual production of a volume such as this would be impossible. People like my Dad and Mother, Sam and Helen Pile, who not only gave me my mind and my spiritual heritage, but also proofread for intelligibility; Ralph and Margaret Bell, who listened patiently with their octogenarian ears as I tested out some of my conclusions; Carl Ketcherside, spiritual patriarch of the Restoration Movement in the last half of the twentieth century, who advised and encouraged; and hosts of nameless but patient people who let me test my findings on their spiritual minds. And then there were the libraries at Fuller Theological Seminary, Pasadena, California, Westminster Theological Seminary of California, Escondido, California, and St. Louis Christian College, Florissant, Missouri, which made available scores of books for my research. And there were the good folk at Paradise Springs, Palyermo, California who made their "Noah's Ark" cabin available to me when I couldn't find solitude for studying and writing in Los Angeles. No book is written by one person. This one is no exception. And I thank God for all these helpers He sent my way.

INTRODUCTION

What you are about to read is not the stuff of dusty books and stuffy libraries. For twenty-four years I have dressed the Lord's vineyard in the inner-city. There, people don't care how much you know until they know how much you care. Churches in general, and churches in our movement in particular, have pretty well failed in the crucible of Downtown, USA. Our message has too often only healed the wounds of these people slightly (Jer. 6:14). During those years I have read plenty of dusty books as I've sought to have something substantial and life-changing to take to people who are victims, cynics, powerless, and hopeless. What I'm saying is that I didn't learn grace in grad school or seminary. I learned it on the streets of Northeast Los Angeles, among addicts, gang-bangers, homosexuals, illegal aliens, the abandoned, the homeless and hungry. God taught me grace. That's the vantage point from which I write.

For insightful theology on grace and its cognates I highly endorse Dr. Virgil Warren's contribution to this series entitled, *What the Bible Says About Salvation.* The work you are holding in your hand is not so much a textbook for theologians as it is a workbook for Christians in pulpit and pew. Even workbook is not the best term. Maybe we should coin a new term: lifebook.

The theology section (Part One) is certainly not heavyweight. Rather than try to run up and down all the pathways theologians have taken over the centuries, like a hound sniffing a trail, I have tried to let the Word present its own system of theology as pertains to grace. That does not mean that I have not consorted with theologians on occasion, but I have tried very much to keep their role secondary. I believe Part One presents a reasonable, liveable, and Biblical view of God's giving disposition, demonstrated in the cross, which is most desperately needed by us sinners.

Because I believe grace is the most liberating aspect of the good news, I have tried to demonstrate its practicality in the everyday life of the Christian in Part Two. If is sounds like I see grace as a panacea for all human problems, you read me right. It certainly has answers for the throwaways who live downtown. Let me tell you more about that. Carmelita and I recently sat in an inner-city gathering in South St. Louis, Mo. It was the last day of a series of studies on grace held at the Cornerstone. Each participant was invited to share what benefit he or she had received from the course. One by one they told stories of how God's grace had revolutionized their lives: from alcoholism to sobriety, from schizophrenia to mental health, from phobia to fellowship, from cynicism to hope, from dead religion to living faith, from prostitution to productive employment. I told Bro. Carl Ketcherside, who in his eightieth year was leading them, "Today I've understood grace. I've seen and heard it. If John saw the 'One and Only, who came from the Father, full of grace and truth' (John 1:14), I've seen recipients of grace and truth." As an aside, I might add that the comprehension those simple people had of grace was better than I've heard explained from most pulpits.

More about the design of Part Two. Following each discussion is a section entitled "Into the Life," which is designed to animate that particular subject for the reader. It is my hope that this device will cause readers to come away not saying, "I learned something," but, "That's something I can use beginning today." Hopefully, Bible class teachers will study Part One carefully on their own, and then use the thirteen chapters of Part Two in a class setting. The same format could work for Christian parents with teenagers.

You get the idea. I do not want this volume only to be informational, to make readers smarter, but also instructional and motivational, to make our lives everything Jesus Christ went to the cross to make them.

W.P.

PART ONE
THE
THEOLOGY
OF GRACE

1

THE PROBLEM OF SIN

Sin is a problem for everyone. It is no less a problem for a sinless God than it is for sinful mortals. It was a risk He took when He created us with moral freedom. We chose loving ourselves instead of Him (which is the philosophical basis of sin), thus creating the dilemma called sin. Sin is a two-edged dilemma: it destroys the sinner, and it destroys his relationship with His Creator.

The beginning of solving any problem lies in the direction of clear definitions. Three new covenant passages pretty well define sin. It is "lawlessness," i.e. breaking God's laws, according to I John 3:4; it is "wrongdoing" according to I John 5:17; and it is failure to do what we know is right to do according to James 4:17. A "sleeper" definition is found in Romans 3:23 where Paul equates sin with "fall(ing) short of the glory of God." These are the classical Biblical definitions and volumes have been written on these verses alone.

When sinners themselves try to define their negative behavior, the soup thickens. A.H. Strong defines sin as "lack of conformity to the moral law of God, either in act, disposition or state."[1] Koehler defines and illustrates it in much greater detail. "The Bible defnes sin as 'the transgression of the law,' as 'anomia,' lawlessness (I John 3:4). No deed, word, thought, or desire are in themselves sin, but become sin by being at variance with the Law of God. To eat the fruit of a tree seems to us a rather innocent matter, but since God had forbidden it, it was a sin to Adam and Eve (Gen. 2:17). When Saul spared Agag, the king of Amalek, and the best of the sheep and oxen for sacrifice, it looked like a humane and pious thing; yet God had commanded him to destroy Amalek utterly, and so it was a sin to spare them (I Sam. 15). When at the exodus from Egypt the children of Israel borrowed jewels of silver and gold from the Egyptians (Exod. 12:35-36), without returning them, it was not a sin, because God expressly commanded them to do this (Exqd. 3:22). Whether or not anything is a sin is not determined by what we think or how we feel about it, but solely by this: does it or does it not agree with the Word of God? Sin is not a physical, but a moral condition, and it consists in this, that a given act, behaviour, or condition of man is not what God wants it to be; it is nonconformity with the will of God. Thus, to sin means to do what God forbids (Gen. 2:17), or not to do what He enjoins (James 4:17), or not to be as He wants us to be (Lev. 19:2). Hence, with respect to the Law, sin is a departure from its rule; with respect to God, sin is disobedience to His will.

"Every departure from the Law is sin, whether this be great or small, known or unknown, intended or accidental, or even when it is against our will (Rom. 7:19). The question whether anything is or is not sin, is not determined by our personal opinion, our knowledge, our intention, or our will, but solely by this one fact, whether or not it is in agreement with the will of God. Our personal attitude may aggravate or mitigate our guilt, but it does not change the nature of the act or the conduct as a transgression of the Law. Even the good intention and purpose one may have, will not change an unlawful act into a lawful one (I Sam. 15:1-26). We cannot sin to the glory of God (Rom. 6:1,2)."[2]

Enough "thick soup." We know what the word means when it is used in Scripture.

PAUL'S UGLY AND DISCOMFORTING PICTURE IN ROMANS 1-3

Most Bible students are aware that Romans 1:18-3:18 is the Apostle Paul's discourse on the universality of sin. The section climaxes with the dreadful declaration that "all have sinned and fall short of the glory of God" (3:23). But the passage is also a fairly exhaustive study on the nature of sin. Romans 1:18-32 discusses the sins to which Gentiles were particularly susceptible; Romans 2:1-3:8 addresses the sins of the Jews; and Romans 3:9-18 is Paul's broad brush stroke which indicts anyone who might have felt left out in the previous verses.

Sins of the Gentiles (heathen, pagans) tended to fall into the broad categories of perversion, depravity and debauchery — the kinds of sins that horrify "decent people." Sins of the Jews were generally quite opposite, the kind that hardly threaten a society — the sins of believers, of the religious, of "nice" people. But both categories were equally abhorrent to God. "What shall we conclude then? Are we any better? Not at all! We have already made the charge that Jews and Gentiles alike are all under sin" (Rom. 3:9). As incredible as that sounds to the person who finds himself "not nearly as bad as" hosts of other sinners, it is Biblical. Perhaps a closer look at the sins mentioned in these chapters will make it a little easier for us to accept this truth. (The following is only a cursory study. Most good commentaries will provide Greek definitions and examinations of grammatical constructions that you may desire for deeper study.)

THE UGLY

Sin is the choice to do wrong — Romans 1:18-20. The wrath of God is being revealed from heaven against all the godlessness and wickedness of men who suppress the truth by their wickedness, since what may be known about God is plain to them, because God has made it plain to them. For since the creation of the world God's invisible qualities — his eternal power and divine nature — have been clearly seen, being understood from what has been made, so that men are without excuse.

We have exercised our right to ignore, suppress, or postpone dealing with the evidence of God in nature ("godlessness") in order to practice "unrighteousness." That has been our choice and we are "without excuse."

Sin is the refusal to glorify and thank God — Romans 1:21. For although they knew God, they neither glorified him as God nor gave thanks to him, but their thinking became futile and their foolish hearts were darkened.

God deserves both glory and thanks, but we chose a path which dishonors him and robs him of the thanks he deserves. The result? God gets His honor and thanks from someone else and we sink into futile thinking and living.

Sinners exchange the immortal for the mortal — Romans 1:22-25. Although they claimed to be wise, they became fools and exchanged the glory of the immortal God for images made to look like mortal man and birds and animals and reptiles. Therefore God gave them over in the sinful desires of their hearts to sexual impurity for the degrading of their bodies with one another. They exchanged the truth of God for a lie, and worshiped and served created things rather than the Creator — who is forever praised. Amen.

With minds beclouded by self-will man becomes the center of his own world. We give our affections to created things instead of the Creator. This triggers a kind of abandonment by God in order that the folly of our exchange might be fully felt by us.

The sexual implications of sin — Romans 1:26,27. Because of this, God gave them over to shameful lusts. Even their women exchanged natural relations for unnatural ones. In the same way the men also abandoned natural relations with women and were inflamed with lust for one another. Men committed indecent acts with other men, and received in themselves the due penalty for their perversion.

Freud may have been right when he concluded that just about all human behavior has sexual connections. For sure sinning does. It has in its very nature not only habituation, but degradation. We seldom curtail sin, or taper off. Once it has severed our relationship with God, God's image, in which we were created (Gen. 1:26), seems to dim, and we become more like animals than people, driven more by instinct than intellect. Put another way, once we have misused moral freedom by making wrong choices about God, our moral nature is overtaken by our bestial nature and we seek satisfaction in perverting our own sexuality. "Sexual perversion will give us the meaning we have been missing in life," we tell ourselves. In such obvious misuse of our sexuality we attempt to shake God off and justify our choice of self over Him. But abused sexuality has its own judgments, some of which are almost immediate (venereal disease, unwanted pregnancy, and jealousy and murder, for instance). Thus sexuality, which God designed to offer great meaning to life, when sin enters into it, loses its meaning, and in some instances even becomes a shortcut to death.

The moral and spiritual implications of sin — Romans 1:28-31. Furthermore, since they did not think it worthwhile to retain the knowledge of God, he gave them over to a depraved mind, to do what ought not to be done. They have become filled with every kind of wickedness, evil, greed and depravity. They are full of envy, murder, strife, deceit and malice. They are gossips, slanderers, God-haters, insolent, arrogant and boastful; they invent ways of doing evil; they disobey their parents, they are senseless, faithless, heartless, ruthless.

The original wrong choice and its subsequent wrong choices start a spiritual chain reaction which ends in total spiritual bankruptcy. Sin has created a moral and spiritual environment which is virtually hostile to life itself.

The final subjugation of conscience to sin — Romans 1:32. Although they know God's righteous decree that those who do such things deserve death, they not only continue to do these very things, but also approve of those who practice them.

We become so overwhelmed by the power we have given sin in our lives that the conviction of broken laws and consequent punishment recedes into the background of our minds. We sin almost without conscience. To increase our ease we encourage others to make the same wrong choices. Why should we care about others if we don't care about ourselves? Sin makes us want nothing better than to go down the drain and pull the rest of the world down with us. Could there be any worse degradation of God's crowning creative act?

THE DISCOMFORTING

The Jews (who might have been blushing in embarrassment at the depravity of the Gentiles as Paul lifted the garbage-can lid on their sins in Romans 1) now come under Paul's stinging indictment in Romans 2:1-3:8. This passage contains some very surprising, and discomforting insights into the nature of sin.

22

Sin inflicts on us a judgmental view of the sins of others and a peculiar blindness about our own — Romans 2:1-3. You, therefore, have no excuse, you who pass judgment on someone else, for at whatever point you judge the other, you are condemning yourself, because you who pass judgment do the same things. Now we know that God's judgment against those who do such things is based on truth. So when you, a mere man, pass judgment on them and yet do the same things, do you think you will escape God's judgment?

What a blind spot sin gives us! We somehow think that by loudly announcing the sins of others, our own will go unnoticed, even though they may be the very same sins. The reality is that our underlining someone else's sin, underlines our own at the same time. It does even more. It makes us especially contemptible when we are found out. And it has us defying God's justice, as if our sins will go unpunished because we tipped Him off about someone else's. Is that distorted thinking, or what?

Sin discounts the justice of God — Romans 2:4-16. Or do you show contempt for the riches of his kindness, tolerance and patience, not realizing that God's kindness leads you toward repentance? But because of your stubbornness and your unrepentant heart, you are storing up wrath against the day of God's wrath, when his righteous judgment will be revealed. God 'will give to each person according to what he has done.' To those who by persistence in doing good seek glory, honor and immortality, he will give eternal life. But for those who are self-seeking and who reject the truth and follow evil, there will be wrath and anger. There will be trouble and distress for every human being who does evil: first for the Jew, then for the Gentile; but glory, honor and peace for everyone who does good: first for the Jew, then for the Gentile. For God does not show favoritism. All who sin apart from the law will also perish apart from the law, and all who sin under the law will be judged by the law. For it is not those who hear the law who are righteous in God's sight, but it is those who obey the law who will be declared righteous. (Indeed, when Gentiles, who do not have the law, do by nature things required by the law, they are a law for themselves, even though they do not have the law, since they show that the requirements of the law are written on their hearts, their consciences also bearing witness, and their thoughts now accusing, now even defending them.) This will take place on the day when God will judge men's secrets through Jesus Christ, as my gospel declares.

Speaking of the blind spots, here's another one. God doesn't zap us every time we sin. Instead, He exercises patience, not because we deserve it, but because He believes in us, that we will turn from sin. But sin is so blinding that somehow we come to believe that God is not ever going to get around to balancing the scales. Thus we sin on blithely, tipping the scales more and more against ourselves. But justice is God's character. It will be meted out, both to blatant sinners and to bland. We who have had the special privilege of knowing God's will firsthand (from the Bible), will experience God's justice first because of our privilege. Now that's quite a different view than sin and Satan give us!

Sin makes the sinner arrogant — Romans 2:17-3:2. Now you, if you call yourself a Jew; if you rely on the law and brag about your relationship to God; if you know his will and approve of what is superior because you are instructed by the law; if you are convinced that you are a guide for the blind, a light for those who are in the dark, an instructor of the foolish, a teacher of infants, because you have in the law the embodiment of knowledge and truth — you, then, who teach others, do you not teach yourself? You who preach against stealing, do you steal? You who say that people should not commit adultery, do you commit adultery? You who abhor idols, do you rob temples? You who brag about the law, do you dishonor God by breaking the law? As it is written: 'God's name is blasphemed among the Gentiles because of you.'

Circumcision has value if you observe the law, but if you break the law, you have become as though you had not been circumcised. If those who are not circumcised keep the law's requirements, will they not be regarded as though they were circumcised? The one who is not circumcised physically and yet obeys the law will condemn you who, even though you have the written code and circumcision, are a lawbreaker.

A man is not Jew if he is only one outwardly, nor is circumcision merely outward and physical. No, a man is a Jew if he is one inwardly; and circumcision is circumcision of the heart, by the Spirit, not by the written code. Such a man's praise is not from men, but from God.

What advantage, then, is there in being a Jew, or what value is there in circumcision? Much in every way! First of all, they have been entrusted with the very words of God.

The Jews continue being our model of the blinding deceit of sin. They felt superior to others because of their special covenant relationship with God, and resting in that feeling they fell victim to the same sins as everyone else. Their arrogance was the ladder from which they toppled. This is precisely how sin attacks decent people and professing Christians today. Whatever special benefits we have only have meaning if we live up to the expectations of the Benefactor. Otherwise those benefits condemn us. We Christians have the sacred scriptures. We know them and quote them. But they will condemn us if we don't live up to them.

Sin is not some grand theological game — Romans 3:5-8. But if our unrighteousness brings out God's righteousness more clearly, what shall we say? That God is unjust in bringing his wrath on us? (I am using a human argument.) Certainly not! If that were so, how could God judge the world? Someone might argue, "If my falsehood enhances God's truthfulness and so increases his glory, why am I still condemned as a sinner?" Why not say — as we are being slanderously reported as saying and some claim that we say — "Let us do evil that good may result"? Their condemnation is deserved.

This has to be the ultimate insult aimed at God. It has to come from the pits of hell and the mind of Satan. That God deserves the ultimate blame for sin. That He somehow comes out the better for our sinning. Follow this convoluted reasoning: the ugliness of our sins makes the righteousness of God shine all the more brightly; therefore we should sin more so He shines more brightly; and we can feel free to do this because, after all, God is just, and He will not condemn us for doing what glorifies Him. Sin becomes a move in a cosmic chess game. We are pawns, moved at His will, sometimes sacrificed, whatever it takes to win the game and gain the glory. Surely no more elaborate fantasy has ever been concocted to attempt to legitimize our choice to disobey God!

Sin can hardly be hyperbolized — Romans 3:9-18. What shall we conclude then? Are we any better? Not at all! We have already made the charge that Jews and Gentiles alike are all under sin. As it is written: "There is no one righteous, not even one; there is no one who understands, no one who seeks God. All have turned away, they have together become worthless; there is no one who does good, not even one." "Their throats are open graves; their tongues practice deceit." "The poison of vipers is on their lips." "Their mouths are full of cursing and bitterness." "Their feet are swift to shed blood; ruin and misery mark their ways, and the way of peace they do not know." "There is no fear of God before their eyes."

This collage of Old Testament passages obviously exaggerates the sinfulness of humanity. But not by a lot. Sin is pandemic, especially when you realize that there is a whole category of sins committed by righteous people who are loathe to admit them (Rom. 2:1-3:9). Satan is indeed the "prince of this world" (John 12:31) and "the whole world is under the control of the evil one" (I John 5:19b).

ONE SIZE FITS ALL

This is not just Paul's theology of sin. What Paul said in hundreds of words, Jesus said in one stinging challenge: "If any one of you is without sin, let him begin stoning her" (John 8:7). That unanswered challenge has such a solid ring of truth that it has become proverbial of the universality of sin.

Because the recurring theme of Paul's letters to Christians was grace, he occasionally repainted the background against which grace shines so beautifully. "For all have sinned and fall short of the glory of God" (Rom. 3:23). "Therefore, just as sin entered the world through one man, and death through sin, and in this way death came to all men, because all sinned" (Rom. 5:12). "For God has bound all men over to disobedience so that he may have mercy on them all" (Rom 11:32). "But the scripture declares that the whole world is a prisoner of sin, so that what was promised, being given through faith in Jesus Christ, might be given to those who believe" (Gal. 3:22). In Romans 5:6-11 the frightening spiral of our degradation is contained in his description of us as "powerless" (v. 6), "sinners" (v. 8), and "enemies" (v. 10). A few observations about the nature of sin from these passages:

— The issue of God's glory is an interesting one, deserving of a separate study, no doubt. Scores of passages mention it. However, it is obvious from Romans 3:23 that God's glory is diminished to some degree when man sins (at least in the eyes of men). Sin is an attack on His character, not just ours. Since God's ultimate purpose is His own glorification (Exod. 14:4; Rev. 19:1), and since He created us for that very purpose (Isa. 43:7), when we choose to disobey God, His plans (at least in our case) are thwarted, and His glory is diminished. If each of us is a shining star which He has cast into the firmament to illuminate His glory, and even one of us falls, the heavens are just a bit darker and His glory a bit dimmer. To maintain His honor He must judge sin, comdemn sinners to eternal banishment, or provide atonement for their sins. All this He has done.

— The effects of the first sin were awesome. Not only did Adam and Eve suffer a reduction in the level of their relationship with God, physical death began its work in them. The effects of every sin committed since are exactly the same: sin separates us from God and guarantees our mortality.

— Sin has to be declared universal in order that God can put into motion His solution — mercy. If one person were found to be sinless, we would hold out hope for ourselves, and would push God away until we had exhausted every human effort at perfection or had deceived ourselves to the point of believing we had achieved sinlessness. In either case God would be denied the demonstration of His mercy.

— Sin is not something you just shake off, like a pesky viral infection. It is enslaving, immobilizing. We are helpless against it. Until we recognize this aspect of it, we will continue trying to break its chains with human strength. We will keep plotting our escape (without success, of course), while God offers to *give* us our freedom.

— Sin is quick-sand, always pulling you downward. And the more you struggle to get out on your own the deeper you go.

"FLAYED, TORN AND MANGLED"

As mentioned earlier, some sins carry physical consequences (besides death, which is the ultimate physical consequence), and some of those are rather immediate. Catalogs of sins (I Cor. 6:9,10; Gal. 5:19-21; Eph. 4:25-32) certainly suggest some of those consequences: sexually transmitted diseases, physical disability, imprisonment, financial bankruptcy, and premature death, for example. No matter how sophisticated medical science becomes the physical consequences of sin will never be eradicated.

The spiritual consequences, however, are even more serious. Matthew says that Jesus saw crowds of sinners as being "harassed and helpless" (Matt. 9:36). "The Greek word here for 'harassed' literally means 'flayed, torn, and mangled.' Sin does leave its victims full of wounds and bruises and festering sores."[3] When the spirit of man is raped and ravished by sin he is very much like the victim of a physical assault. There are serious doubts that he can ever be whole again.

Paul's word picture in Colossians 1:13 is equally frightening.

Sin puts us in the "dominion of darkness." To convince people of how sinister sin is, he pictures it as a kingdom shrouded in darkness. We are held in darkness by unseen powers. We can't fight them because we can't see them. We pace up and down corridors of darkness, never knowing whether we're deeper in darkness or closer to the light. Escaping is out of the question because we walked in voluntarily and now we're subjects. All that is left for us is to hope that the King of Light will storm the walls of the Dominion of Darkness and free us. Paul says He will, and so does Peter (I Pet. 2:9), but in the meantime our darkness is more pervasive than the air we breathe.

We live in an age when every moral flaw of humankind is labeled an illness: alcoholism, overeating, drug addiction, gambling, spouse abuse, child abuse, etc. Without passing judgment on the use and abuse of that label, it is significant that Jesus likened sin to sickness: "It is not the healthy who need a doctor, but the sick. I have not come to call the righteous, but sinners" (Mark 2:17.(Don't misunderstand. Jesus used sickness metaphorically here. He is not saying that sin is just another form of sickness.) This is a sickness of the spirit of man. The spirit isn't functioning properly. Just as when one part of the physical body is ill other parts sometimes don't work as well, so it is with the spirit. A "broken spirit" affects the mind and body. Oh, the ravages of physical illness! How disabling it can be! How awful the pain! Sin does the same thing to our spirits.

FROM SPIDER WEBS TO ROPES

It may seem redundant to keep emphasizing the habituation aspect of sin, but the Bible does. Is there any consequence that is more ignored in our times? " . . . That we should be slaves to sin" is the way Paul put it in Romans 6:6. When we sin we give up a piece of our autonomy. The body abuser often avows that he can "quit any time I want," yet he doesn't. Doesn't he ever want to? Of course, but he finds the thin spider web has wound around him so many times it has turned into an unbreakable cord.

This is not to say that people don't ever break the ropes on their own. But once we have conquered one vice a host of others stand in the wings leering at us, daring us to come after them. And even if we conquer several, new ones seem to march into place like endless rows of a marching band. This phenomenon is certainly obvious in life's passages. When the fiery lust of youth cools in middle age, Satan has a portfolio of new sins waiting — envy, jealousy, greed, materialism, rebellion, evil speaking, and distrust.

THE HELL THERE IS

What seems to be the most serious consequence of sinning is also the hardest for us sinners to process: eternal condemnation. We have so little to compare it to. "Then they will go away into eternal punishment," Jesus said in Matthew 25:46. Whatever else hell is, it is separation from God forever. This is a condition even the vilest of sinners has never experienced while alive. Not even for a split second has God abandoned His creation. The prospects of even a split second separated from God are horrifying. What of time without end?

"GET THIS MONKEY OFF MY BACK"

Every person, sometime in his life, senses a need to do something about sin. Lifestyles are determined by one's answer to the question, "What shall I do about my sin?" Hardly ever is the question faced so directy, however. More often we answer the question without facing it. We simply move in the direction of a lifestyle without really examining it. We hardly realize that the lifestyle is our way of dealing with the nagging problem of sin.

For purposes of this study we will attempt to give names to these answers, some of which are the concoction of the author. And some may be oversimplifications, perhaps, but most of us can find ourselves somewhere in them.

1. *The stoic, monastic, gnostic answer.* "The flesh is inherently evil. Sin can only be coped with by withdrawal from this sinful world system, so I'll withdraw." This is not a really popular lifestyle these days.

2. *The Epicurean answer.* "There is nothing I can do about sin so I'll just try to enjoy it." Few people reason this deeply about sin, like the ancient Greek philosopher did, but it seems to be the prevailing lifestyle in modern western civilization.

3. *The hedonist answer.* "True personal fulfillment is found in the enjoyment of pleasure, including sinful pleasure. So, I'll enjoy to the fullest." The "playboy" philosophy, we call it in the U.S. But it predates Hugh Hefner, and will still be going strong long after Hugh can't play anymore.

4. *The pious religionist answer.* "I'll be religious enough so that I can compare favorably with the citizenry as a whole and thereby feel comfortable in my sin." This was the philosophy of those who questioned Jesus in Luke 13:1-5.

5. *The self-righteous Christian answer.* "I'll fashion for myself (or my church will do it for me) a classification system for sins, and so long as I avoid the basest sins, I'll be justified (at least in my own and/or my church's eyes). This philosophy was voiced by the Pharisee in Luke 18: " 'God, I thank you that I am not like other men — robbers, evildoers, adulterers — or even like this tax collector. I fast twice a week and give a tenth of all I get' " (vv. 11,12). He had his good works scale too. It makes the sin scale seem so sensible!

6. *The "cheap grace" answer.* "Now that I am a Christian and have God's grace, the blood of Jesus will cleanse me from all my sin. So I don't even think much about sin any more. Whatever I do, God will forgive." This is how the bulk of profess-

ing Christians deal with sin.

7. *The perfectionist answer.* "I don't sin any more, now that I'm saved. After all, isn't that what I John 3:9 says?" We all cut a wide path around this fellow.

8. *The Roman Catholic answer.* "If I do more righteous acts than sinful ones, God will accept me for heaven." Many besides Roman Catholics believe this. They're going to get on God's Great Judgment Scales, and hope they can tip them toward heaven.

9. *The neo-moralist answer.* "The whole concept of sin is just a religious guilt trip and I refuse to take it. Sin is only when someone is hurt by what you do. I recognize no other definition." This has invaded American thinking heavily since the 1960's. A gift of the hippies and flower-children, this comes with ample validation by academia and religion.

There may be eight more ways mortals try to rationalize sin out of moral and spiritual importance. But there is a striking difference between these rationalizations and the attitude taken by spiritual giants of the Bible as they faced their own sinfulness. At this juncture we shall look only at that difference, leaving the reasons for it to the next section.

David — I have sinned against the Lord (II Sam. 12:13).

Ezra and Israel — Then, at the evening sacrifice, I rose from my self-abasement, with my tunic and cloak torn, and fell on my knees with my hands spread out to the Lord my God and prayed: 'O my God, I am too ashamed and disgraced to lift up my face to you, my God, because our sins are higher than our heads and our guilt has reached to the heavens' (Ezra 9:5,6).

The prodigal son — When he came to his senses, he said, 'How many of my father's hired men have food to spare, and here I am starving to death! I will set out and go back to my father and say to him, Father, I have sinned against heaven and against you. I am no longer worthy to be called your son; make me like one of your hired men' (Luke 15:17-19).

The apostle Paul — I thank Christ Jesus our Lord, who has given me strength, that he considered me faithful, appointing me to his service. Even though I was once a blasphemer and a persecutor and a violent man, I was shown mercy because I acted in ignorance and unbelief. The grace of our Lord was poured out on me abundantly, along with the faith and love that are in full acceptance: Christ Jesus came into the world to save sinners — of whom I am the worst" (I Tim. 1:12-15).

THAT SMELLY, SOOTY ALTAR

When you read Leviticus 1 (and similar descriptions of offerings Jews were required to present on the altar of burnt offering) with your senses, and not just your intellect, you discover that that piece of furniture must have been exceedingly vile looking and smelling. Animal heads, fat, entrails, hide, hair, feathers, and blood were burned on it. It must have been quite an eyesore! (Nose-sore?) And I think I know why. God wanted the ghastliness of sin to be seen and smelled. He wanted the acrid smoke from the altar to burn its way into the eyes and noses of all Israel. He didn't want anybody thinking sin was trivial, or inconsequential — just a gravel in God's sandal.

Have we presented a ghastly enough picture of sin? But not overblown one iota! Only when sin is seen in all its horror does grace appear next to it in all its splendor. Viewing God's gracious gift of our salvation against any backdrop other than our hopelessness does it a disservice. "Give the devil his due," Christian preachers, so people will appreciate "God's unspeakable gift."

I visited recently a businessmen's early morning Bible study where the first part of Romans was under discussion. When the moderator came to the description of the sins of the Gentiles he spoke of how offensive and inappropriate such language seemed to be in such a sublime letter. When he opened up the verses for discussion, it was as if we were studying some aberrant human behavior practiced only by cavemen. It never occurred to him that "they" in Romans 1 are "us." Right then I realized that this group was preparing to perform the great drama of grace without first setting up the scenery. And I predicted (within my own heart, of course) that they would come away with less than a command performance.

Endnotes

1. *Systematic Theology*, Judson Press, Valley Forge, 1886, 1976, p. 549.
2. Edward W.A. Koehler, *A Summary of Christian Doctrine*, p. 62,63.
3. James M. Tolle, *The Grace of God*, Tolle Publication, San Fernando, 1971, p. 11.

2

GOD'S REMEDY FOR SIN: GRACE

The eight answers to the sin problem mentioned in Chapter One are of course no answers at all. Sin is still there. They are simply rationalizations which attempt to make the most of an impossible situation. It is the impossibility of the human predicament which the Mosaic Law system so successfully demonstrated. "Therefore no one will be declared righteous in his sight by observing the law; rather, through the law we become conscious of sin" (Rom. 3:20). The same thought is stated even more forcefully in Galatians 3:10: "All who rely on observing the law are under a curse, for it is written: 'Cursed is everyone who does not continue to do everything written in the book of the Law.' "

Man's helplessness in the face of sin is stated succinctly in Galatians 3:22a: "But the Scripture declares that the whole world is a prisoner of sin." This reality must be faced for two reasons:

1. So that no one can feel exempted from sin and its penalty; and

2. So everyone will be ready to hear God's remedy which is

stated in the rest of that verse: "So that what was promised, being given through faith in Jesus Christ, might be given to those who believe" (Gal. 3:22b). What was promised was "justification" (v. 24) and sonship (v. 26). Both of these words are part of the Biblical concept of grace.

UNINSPIRED DEFINITIONS

While there are several uses in the New Testament of the Greek word *charis*, we focus only on its soteriological use, namely passages and definitions that relate to the place of grace in salvation.

"Grace is that peculiar disposition in the heart of God to favor those who deserve only condemnation . . . . Sinners deserve nothing; yet there is nothing God will not do for them. Calvary proves that. God will go to any length to heap favors on sinners; and the worse they are, the more He favors them. He offers them the highest place in heaven, the nearest position to the throne. The parable of the prodigal son reveals the grace of the Father. He looks for us *while we are in our filthy rags*. He puts the robe of righteousness on us *after embracing us*. He does not clean us up first so that He can embrace us with more relish. He wants us to know that our rightful place is in His presence — in His bosom. If we can accept this place by faith, we will experience it in fact."[1]

Charles C. Ryrie defines grace as "that which awakens pleasure or secures joy." Defining it soteriologically he says, "In this sense, then, grace is the favor of God in giving His Son and the benefit to men of receiving that Son."[2] Ryrie offers complete listings and definitions of both Old and New Testament words that are rendered by our English word "grace" in the first chapter of his work.

W.E. Vine defines it both objectively ("that which bestows or occasions pleasure, delight or causes favourable regard") and subjectively ("on the part of the bestower, the friendly dispostion from which the kindly act proceeds, graciousness, lovingkindness, goodwill generally").[3]

And then there's this charming, and surprisingly comprehensive definition: "Grace is the gift of Christ, who exposes the gulf which separates God and man, and, by exposing it, bridges it."[4]

There is the clever (albeit imperfect) alliterative definition that is popular today: God's Riches at Christ's Expense (G.R.A.C.E.).

The simplest, most widely accepted definition of grace is: *the unmerited favor of God*. This writer can offer no improvement on that.

JESUS SHOWS US WHAT GRACE IS

Charis is seldom used in the Gospels. It belongs more to the writings of Paul. However, there is no more powerful expositor of grace than He who was God's Grace Personified. Besides demonstrating grace living, Jesus gave us some simple discourses illustrating it. Of several He spoke, I have chosen two which have had special impact in my life. The complete reproduction of the passages is absolutely necessary to be able to see the beauty of grace. (We don't wish to produce a "Paint by Number" canvas and hope the reader will add the colors.)

Luke 7:36-50 — Now one of the Pharisees invited Jesus to have dinner with him, so he went to the Pharisee's house and reclined at the table. When a woman who had lived a sinful life in that town learned that Jesus was eating at the Pharisee's house, she brought an alabaster jar of perfume, and as she stood behind him at his feet weeping, she began to wet his feet with her tears. Then she wiped them with her hair, kissed them and poured perfume on them.

When the Pharisee who had invited him saw this, he said to himself, "If this man were a prophet, he would know who is touching him and what kind of woman she is — that she is a sinner."

37

Jesus answered him, "Simon, I have something to tell you."

"Tell me, teacher," he said.

"Two men owed money to a certain moneylender. One owed him five hundred denarii, and the other fifty. Neither of them had the money to pay him back, so he canceled the debts of both. Now which of them will love him more?"

Simon replied, "I suppose the one who had the bigger debt canceled."

"You have judged correctly," Jesus said.

Then he turned toward the woman and said to Simon, "Do you see this woman? I came into your house. You did not give me any water for my feet, but she wet my feet with her tears and wiped them with her hair. You did not give me a kiss, but this woman, from the time I entered, has not stopped kissing my feet. You did not put oil on my head, but she has poured perfume on my feet. Therefore, I tell you, her many sins have been forgiven — for she loved much. But he who has been forgiven little loves little."

Then Jesus said to her, "Your sins are forgiven."

The other guests began to say among themselves, "Who is this who even forgives sins?"

Jesus said to the woman, "Your faith has saved you; go in peace."

Whew! What a story. Just about everything we need to know about sin, sinners, and grace is here. Let's see some highlights at least. First a look at the characters in the drama, according to their appearance, then the story Jesus told.

Simon the Pharisee — a member of a religious group which found its standing with God to rest in compliance with all the rules and regulations of the Old Testament and the Torah. You don't think of people like this partying much, or if they did, you can't imagine them having a very good time. Life is too serious, what with all these laws to keep track of. Whatever, Simon surely never planned a party like this one! Simon and his cronies were grace-poor, grace-ignorant. They were self-righteous, smug, and religiously arrogant (the worst arrogance of all). They had "dotted all their jots, and crossed all their tittles." They really didn't need God, much less Jesus. Simon's party, to which Jesus came by invitation, was the perfect setting for a lesson on grace. It was the perfect setting for a *real party!*

Jesus — Grace on two legs. Walking, talking, breathing, living. "For the grace of God that brings salvation has appeared to all men" (Titus 2:11). He appeared that day at Simon's door. He was the guest. We don't know why Simon invited Him, but we do know why he accepted the invitation. Not to argue or upbraid, but to bless. He came to a have a *real* good time. That's what grace is — God having a real good time, blessing us lavishly! The question of the day: can a man like Simon, who feels he is rich and doesn't need a thing, but is actually "wretched, pitiful, poor, blind and naked" (Rev. 3:17) have a really good time? Stay tuned in . . .

The Woman — "One of those women," obviously a prostitute. She crashed the party because that's what you do when you don't have a ticket, when you're desperate. She was either going to get thrown out or it was going to be the best party of her life. Risky? Sure, but going to bed every night was risky too. She knew who was having fun there. And she went straight to Him. So what if He was the Guest of Honor? So what that she was the only one there without a ticket, and the only one crying? So what if the host was horrified and the guests gasped? She had to have relief. Nothing else was working. She represents all of us who discover that we are helplessly, hopelessly lost. We're not invited to the Really Big Party, called life. We've tried to get prettied up for it, but we're still misfits. Morals, religion, rationalizations, resolutions, good deeds, concoctions, connections — nothing has worked. We can't buy any real fun, but maybe someone will *give* us some. She and we are the 500 denarii debtors.

Other Guests — Obviously they were fellow Pharisees, birds of a feather with Simon. They came for a godly good time. It was a BYOR (Bring Your Own Righteousness) party, and what was this woman of the street doing there? They thought they were having fun until she came in. They lost their appetites when they took one look at her. Some may have made a quick exit for fear

39

they would be recognized as her customers. Whatever, the color must have drained from their cheeks and their smiles somersaulted into smirks. And when the real moment of joy arrived, when Jesus announced that "her many sins have been forgiven," they couldn't handle it. That wasn't their idea of fun. To give somebody forgiveness when they didn't deserve it? So, they reverted to what they had always considered fun — arguing over words: "Who is this man who even forgives sins?" (v. 49). They were the 50 denarii debtors. No big deal. Even if they did admit to some minor infractions or indiscretions, they were not to be compared to this, this slut!

The Story — All of us are in debt to God because of our sins. But it's our perception of the amount that matters. That perception determines how we approach God, how we live our lives. Some might say, "I'm hopelessly in debt. No way out." Others: "Well, I'm a little behind in my payments, but . . . . " The truth of the matter, as Chapter One delineated, is that we are all 500 denarii debtors, there's no way we can pay the debt our sins have incurred, and when we realize it we come to God like this woman came to Jesus. We empty ourselves of any self-value, fall at His feet like the paupers we are. All we have to give is ourselves, and empty selves at that. We weep when we realize that He hasn't turned us away. He has accepted our nothingness, loved us anyway, and miracle of miracles — our sins are forgiven!

The bigger the debt forgiven the bigger is our love. The more unselfish is our service. And the better the quality. More lavish. What the Pharisees thought they were giving God through their elaborate system of do's and don'ts would flow naturally from grace-saturated hearts that were bursting with love.

Jesus sent the woman home in peace (v. 50). The party was over. The Pharisees left in turmoil. Simon vowed to watch his door more closely next time. After all, hadn't the only one without a ticket won the Grand Prize? That's the way grace is. It blesses those who need it, and irritates those who think they don't. Those who need it find, and go away in peace. Those who don't need it don't find it, and they just go away.

A GOD WHO HATES TO LOSE

Luke 15 — Now the tax collectors and "sinners" were all gathering around to hear him. But the Pharisees and the teachers of the law muttered, "This man welcomes sinners and eats with them."

Then Jesus told them this parable: "Suppose one of you has a hundred sheep and loses one of them. Does he not leave the ninety-nine in the open country and go after the lost sheep until he finds it? And when he finds it, he joyfully puts it on his shoulders and goes home. Then he calls his friends and neighbors together and says, 'Rejoice with me; I have found my lost sheep.' I tell you that in the same way there will be more rejoicing in heaven over one sinner who repents than over ninety-nine righteous persons who do not need to repent.

"Or suppose a woman has ten silver coins and loses one. Does she not light a lamp, sweep the house and search carefully until she finds it? And when she finds it, she calls her friends and neighbors together and says, 'Rejoice with me; I have found my lost coin.' In the same way, I tell you, there is rejoicing in the presence of the angels of God over one sinner who repents."

Jesus continued: "There was a man who had two sons. The younger one said to his father, 'Father, give me my share of the estate.' So he divided his property between them.

"Not long after that, the younger son got together all he had, set off for a distant country and there squandered his wealth in wild living. After he had spent everything, there was a severe famine in that whole country, and he began to be in need. So he went and hired himself out to a citizen of that country, who sent him to his fields to feed pigs. He longed to fill his stomach with the pods that the pigs were eating, but no one gave him anything.

"When he came to his senses, he said, 'How many of my fathers's hired men have food to spare, and here I am starving to death! I will set out and go back to my father and say to him: 'Father, I have sinned against heaven and against you. I am no longer worthy to be called your son; make me like one of your hired men.' So he got up and went to his father.

41

"But while he was still a long way off, the father saw him and was filled with compassion for him; he ran to his son, threw his arms around him and kissed him.

"The son said to him, 'Father, I have sinned against heaven and against you. I am no longer worthy to called your son.'

"But the father said to his servants, 'Quick! Bring the best robe and put it on him. Put a ring on his finger and sandals on his feet. Bring the fattened calf and kill it. Let's have a feast and celebrate. For this son of mine was dead and is alive again; he was lost and is found.' So they began to celebrate.

"Meanwhile, the older son was in the field. When he came near the house, he heard music and dancing. So he called one of the servants and asked him what was going on. 'Your brother has come,' he replied, 'and your father has killed the fattened calf because he has him back safe and sound.'

"The older brother became angry and refused to go in. So his father went out and pleaded with him. But he answered his father, 'Look! All these years I've been slaving for you and never disobeyed your orders. Yet you never gave me even a young goat so I could celebrate with my friends. But when this son of yours who has squandered your property with prostitutes comes home, you kill the fattened calf for him!'

" 'My son,' the father said, 'you are always with me, and everything I have is yours. But we had to celebrate and be glad, because this brother of yours was dead and is alive again; he was lost and is found.' "

These three stories are like sparkling diamonds, beautiful any way you look at them, radiating marvelous truths from almost any perspective. To debate over what was the most basic lesson our Lord intended to convey in telling these stories would surely obscure their multi-faceted beauty. Let us see them as an elementary introduction to grace.

One third of the audience that day (tax collectors and "sinners") could hardly have failed to see themselves as the lost sheep, lost coin and lost son in Jesus' stories. They must have felt a strong surge of hope. Another third of the audience (the Pharisees and teachers) might never learn their meaning, inasmuch as they were already committed to salvation by self-righteousness (v. 2). The final third (the twelve disciples) might have only the smallest seed of grace planted in them, but it would grow. To us living this side of the cross, to us who have read the apostle Paul's marvelous treatises on the subject, and to us who have felt the incredible thrill of grace, these stories are pregnant with the beauty of this disposition of our Heavenly Father.

Contrary to what the headings of your Bible may say, these are not stories about lost things and people. These are stories about our Heavenly Father. His disposition toward us is manifest in the shepherd, the woman, and the father. Just how is our Heavenly Father disposed toward us?

He gives us our freedom, despite the risk of losing us. Though we are His by virtue of creation, He will not make us slaves. We are free to lose ourselves, because He doesn't intend that we stay lost.

He acknowledges our intrinsic value, even though our extrinsic value may be nil. How much is a lost sheep worth while it's lost? How much wool does it give? Or a lost coin? How many ice cream cones will it buy? Or a lost son? How many smiles can he give you? Or hugs? God's gift of eternal life makes sense when we understand His value system. He's a real "futures" investor!

He goes after us. He doesn't sit back and wait until we come around. True, the prodigal's father didn't go down to the whore houses or pig pens, but "while he was still a long way off, his father saw him." He had probably looked down that road every morning! God didn't leave us, we left Him. And yet He actively seeks us. His gracious work through His Spirit in the hearts of all sinners who are away from Him is celebrated both in Scripture and in life. Now that's grace!

He seeks until He finds. It was no perfunctory glance by any of them: shepherd, woman, father. God intends to find us and all His efforts are aimed in that direction. "He is . . . not wanting anyone to perish, but everyone to come to repentance" (II Pet. 3:9b).

He gives us a free ride home. We paid the fare to our destruction but He pays the return fare. The picture of the shepherd carrying the lost sheep on his shoulders is a poignant one. We might have been driving that animal home in front of a peach switch — for all the trouble it caused us. "While we were still sinners Christ died for us" (Rom. 5:8b). It's at this juncture that we wonder if God isn't soft-headed, or at least soft-handed in his dealing with sinners. He is neither. Other passages teach His judgment against sin. This one depicts His grace. Perhaps our discomfort with this picture of God arises because we can't see ourselves with such an unselfish disposition toward sinners. That's what set the Pharisees' and teachers' teeth on edge (Luke 15:2). God's gracious disposition will always be somewhat theoretical to us because we simply are incapable of reproducing it ourselves. May it always remain a little mysterious to us!

God rejoices when we come, no matter the circumstances of our return. The sheep and coin had to be searched out; the profligate son came back on his own. There's no prescription with God. He's just glad to have us back. Once again God's grace clashes with ours. We'd like to push every repentant sinner through our mold. We might like to prescribe probation, or penance. The issue with God is our restoration, not the means. He wants to have a party celebrating our return.

He never has enough of us until He has all of us. Ninety-nine sheep weren't enough. Nor were nine coins. Nor one son. We've learned too easily to look at the lostness of our family and friends in statistical terms. Ninety-nine percent; ninety percent; even fifty percent — those aren't bad numbers really. But God's grace isn't centered in statistics. He intends to give until there are no more in need. Don't you get the feeling from the good news story that even if there had been only one lost sinner in the world, God would still have given His son?

Moreover, we find that, even in our ugliness, God is approachable, and more. The young wastrel dared to think that his father might again allow him in his presence and maybe even hear his plaintive cry. When he finally cleared that last hill he was

44

met with compassion, hugs, and kisses. God's predisposition is to be accepting and forgiving. It is as though no account is kept of our ugliness once we move in the direction of repentance. How's that for grace?

The compassion seen in the shepherd and the father can only be understood in the context of grace. God is heavily invested in us, and so passion may be expected. But why not the passion of anger? Disappointment? Exasperation? No, it's compassion because we are never separated entities (until the moment of our eternal condemnation). God sees a bit of himself invested in all of us, and how can He hate us? And then there's His investment on the cross. How can He hate those for whom Christ died? No, there's no surprise in compassion, really.

He will accept us back so long as we are able to come back. All the mythology connected to the so-called "unpardonable sin" notwithstanding, the Bible pictures the door always open. Some of us, in our moments of self-righteous exclusivism, try to find evidence that God has shut the door, but under the covenant of grace there is no such evidence. The sin against the Holy Spirit (Matt. 12:31) is man slamming the door on God's agent for his salvation, not vice versa. And Hebrews 6:4-6 is not a picture of God barring the door, but man. Let not man deny God this aspect of His grace. We would be derelict though, if we didn't note the limitation of God's grace that is implied in this story. The sheep, coin and son were still intact, still alive. A dead sheep, destroyed coin, and dead son would have ended the stories. Likewise, death ends God's graciousness toward us, since we can no longer respond to it.

In the parable of the lost son, there were actually two lost sons: one lost in profligate sin; one lost in self-righteous sin. The older brother is Jesus' "P.S." to the lesson, designed to teach the Pharisees and teachers of Jewish law, and us who read today, that the concept of the grace of God is difficult to accept. We can see in his behavior and words all the difficulties we face with grace. *Grace doesn't seem fair.* If people choose to mess up their lives they should have to live with the mess. The truth is, we all mess up our lives, some in ugly ways, some in tidy ways, and God provides a way out for all of us. *The economics of grace seem a bit askew.* Leave ninety-nine to look for one? Have a party for the spendthrift, but not the hard worker? It doesn't make much sense unless you are the one lost sheep, or the repentant spendthrift. The economics of grace are God's business. *The joyful atmosphere of grace* is disturbing to us too. Sin was too serious for such frivolity, the older son must have thought. If the prodigal's brother had gone into the party he would have immediately discovered that what was being celebrated there was not so much his brother's return as his father's generosity. A quality he might have need of on his behalf some day. Grace is about forgiveness, and restoration and celebration. Grace doesn't elevate sin, nor ignore it. Grace celebrates love. *"Are all our good deeds and faithfulness for nought?"* the older brother asked. We can surely feel his frustration, can't we? We've been so loyal and now the playboy gets the attention. Grace will always get short shrift in our hearts so long as we identify with the ninety-nine, the nine, and the older son. We don't need much grace ourselves and hence we're parsimonious in extending it to others. Yes, our good deeds are for nought in establishing our worth to God. And if we try to obtain righteousness by them they are less than nought. They may be the cause of our condemnation!

The grace of God is just like those three stories: it is the path to salvation for self-confessed, repentant sinners; but a rock of offense to those who trust in their own righteousness.

"BUT GOD, IT JUST AIN'T FAIR!"

Jesus isn't going to be finished with us until we get a little angry about grace. That seems to be what this final story is designed to do.

Matthew 20:1-16 — "The kingdom of heaven is like a landowner who went out early in the morning to hire men to work in his vineyard. He agreed to pay them a denarius for the day and sent them into his vineyard.

"He went out again about the sixth hour and the ninth hour and did the same thing. About the eleventh hour he went out and found still others standing around. He asked them, 'Why have you been standing here all day long doing nothing?'

" 'Because no one hired us,' they answered.

"He said to them, 'You also go and work in my vineyard.'

"When evening came, the owner of the vineyard said to his foreman, 'Call the workers and pay them their wages, beginning with the last ones hired and going on to the first.'

"The workers who were hired about the eleventh hour came and each received a denarius. So when those came who were hired first, they expected to receive more. But each one of them also received a denarius. When they received it, they began to grumble against the landowner. 'These men who were hired last worked only one hour,' they said, 'and you have made them equal to us who have born the burden of the work and the heat of the day.'

"But he answered one of them, 'Friend, I am not being unfair to you. Didn't you agree to work for a denarius? Take your pay and go. I want to give the man who was hired last the same as I gave you. Don't I have the right to do what I want with my own money? Or are you envious because I am generous?'

"So the last will be first, and the first will be last."

So this is how grace works? Neither labor unions nor legislative labor committees would think much of it, would they? Neither would some Christians if this story means what it seems to. Hold on for some more shocks.

God is the employer and the giver. There is nothing new about this except that He is both in the same setting, and to the same group of people. If we're talking about forgiveness of sins and eternal life we'd like Him to be one or the other. Either we earn salvation or it's a gift. What the 12-hour employees didn't recognize was that their very chance to earn a denarius was a gift too. They thought they had earned it. But in reality they got to spend twelve hours looking forward to it, the 1-hour men only one hour. The view of the 12-hour men was as distorted as was the older brother's in Luke 15. He viewed his faithful relationship with his father as a drag. He focused only on his own hard work, not on his dad's love, nor on his brother's deprivation and misery. If we view Christian faithfulness like that we'll never understand grace.

Grace is God's to give. Grace is out of our control, and sometimes we wonder if God isn't out of control too. He's nice to some of the ugliest, meanest and least deserving people. We'd like to tell Him how to run His grace business. Forget about grace being fair — by our standards.

People who grumble at grace are the most miserable creatures alive. What is there in us that resents God not doing things our way? That resents Him for being too good to some people? I'll tell you what it is: envy. "Or are you envious because I am generous?" (v. 15b). And the story uncovers an even deeper evil. It's the devilish sense that man can earn his keep with God, the idiotic belief that we have earned it, and our upset that others may be *given* theirs. Those deceits lie at the root of all our distortions of grace. May God have patience with us until we realize that we haven't earned our salvation, that we can't, and that we need it *given* to us just as much as the least deserving sinner we can think of does.

There's an economics problem again with grace. That's no way to run a business! Paying full time wages for part time work? And if you want to really cause trouble let the full time people know that the part timers earn the same salary! First, the sea of God's forgiveness isn't about to run dry. Economics don't interest Him. Second, God lets the full time people know so they won't get any ideas that anybody (especially themselves) can earn eternal life. Hopefully, they (and we) can get beyond jealousy to rejoicing.

Grace is backwards. "So the last will be first, and the first will be last" (v. 16). This is just one more example of God throwing us a curve. "Has not God made foolish the wisdom of the world?"

(I Cor. 1:20b). Yes God, you sure have!

OTHER INSPIRED DEFINITIONS OF GRACE

John 1:14-17 — The Word became flesh and lived for a while among us. We have seen his glory, the glory of the one and only Son, who came from the Father, full of grace and truth. John testified concerning him. He cries out, saying, "This was he of whom I said, He who comes after me has surpassed me because he was before me." From the fullness of his grace we have all received one blessing after another. For the law was given through Moses; grace and truth came through Jesus Christ."

Jesus was "full of grace," i.e., He embodied the best of God's gifts to mankind. And there was sufficient favor in Him that each of us could receive "one blessing after another." This brief phrase portends all the spiritual blessings we receive in the Christian life. It corresponds to Paul's phrase "every spiritual blessing in Christ" with which he begins his letter to the Ephesians.

Acts 15:11 — "No! We believe it is through the grace of our Lord Jesus that we are saved, just as they are."

These were the final words in a discussion of the means of salvation, whether by keeping the Law of Moses, or by the gift of Jesus' sacrificial death. The loud "No!" was Peter's rebuttal to those who taught that salvation was God's payment to men who kept the Law of Moses.

Acts 18:27b — On arriving, he was a great help to those who by grace had believed.

In this passage (as well as the previous one) grace is seen as the vehicle of salvation. The whole redemptive work of God is so clothed in giving that you can't separate salvation itself (the gift) from the means of obtaining it. These Achaians are described as

49

people who had become believers because of God's graciousness. And wherein did that graciousness lie? In God providing His Son who was fully recommended to their intellect by His signs and wonders, the sublimity of His teachings, and by His substitutionary death.

Romans 3:21-5:2 — But now a righteousness from God, apart from law, has been made known, to which the Law and the Prophets testify. This righteousness from God comes through faith in Jesus Christ to all who believe. There is no difference, for all have sinned and fall short of the glory of God, and are justified freely by his grace through the redemption that came by Christ Jesus. God presented him as a sacrifice of atonement, through faith in his blood. He did this to demonstrate his justice, because in his forbearance he had left the sins committed beforehand unpunished — he did it to demonstrate his justice at the present time, so as to be just and the one who justifies the man who has faith in Jesus.

Where, then, is the boasting? It is excluded. On what principle? On that of observing the law? No, but on that of faith. For we maintain that a man is justified by faith apart from observing the law. Is God the God of Jews only? Is he not the God of Gentiles too? Yes, of Gentiles too. Since there is only one God, who will justify the circumcised by faith and the uncircumcised through that same faith. Do we, then, nullify the law by this faith? Not at all! Rather, we uphold the law.

What then shall we say that Abraham, our forefather, discovered in this matter? If, in fact, Abraham was justified by works, he had something to boast about — but not before God. What does the Scripture say? "Abraham believed God, and it was credited to him as righteousness."

Now when a man works, his wages are not credited to him as a gift, but as an obligation. However, to the man who does not work but trusts God who justifies the wicked, his faith is credited as righteousness. David says the same thing when he speaks of the blessedness of the man to whom God credits righteousness apart from works: "Blessed are they whose transgressions are forgiven, whose sins are covered. Blessed is the man whose sin the Lord will never count against him."

Is this blessedness only for the circumcision, or also for the uncircumcised? We have been saying that Abraham's faith was credited to him as righteousness. Under what circumstances was it credited? Was it after he was circumcised, or before? It was not after, but before! And he received the sign of circumcision, a seal of the righteousness that he had by faith while he was still uncircumcised. So then, he is the father of all who believe but have not been circumcised, in order that righteousness might be credited to them. And he is also the father of the circumcised who not only are circumcised but who also walk in the footsteps of the faith that our father Abraham had before he was circumcised.

It was not through law that Abraham and his offspring received the promise that he would be heir of the world, but through the righteousness that comes by faith. For if those who live by law are heirs, faith has no value and the promise is worthless, because law brings wrath. And where there is no law there is no transgression.

Therefore, the promise comes by faith, so that it may be by grace and may be guaranteed to all Abraham's offspring — not only to those who are of the law but also to those who are of the faith of Abraham. He is the father of us all. As it is written: "I have made you a father of many nations." He is our father in the sight of God, in whom he believed — the God who gives life to the dead and calls things that are not as though they were.

Against all hope, Abraham in hope believed and so became the father of many nations, just as it had been said to him, "So shall your offspring be." Without weakening in his faith, he faced the fact that his body was as good as dead — since he was about a hundred years old — and that Sarah's womb was also dead. Yet he did not waver through unbelief regarding the promise of God, but was strengthened in his faith and gave glory to God, being fully persuaded that God had power to do what he had promised. This is why "it was credited to him as righteousness." The words, "it was credited to him" were written not for him alone, but also for us, to whom God will credit righteousness — for us who believe in him who raised Jesus our Lord from the dead. He was delivered over to death for our sins and was raised to life for our justification.

Therefore, since we have been justified through faith, we have peace with God through our Lord Jesus Christ, through whom we have gained access by faith into this grace in which we now stand. And we rejoice in the hope of the glory of God.

After descending the pit of repulsion in Romans 1:18-3:20 and seeing ourselves wallowing in it, Paul now takes us up to a mountaintop of hope. Self-attained righteousness is beyond our reach. But God has come to our rescue offering complete righteousness to us if we will put our confidence in His Son Jesus, and the atonement He purchased for us on the cross. We can barely lift our heads, bowed down as we are by sin, but when we see a brilliant beacon of hope, we sneak a glance. We believe what we see: Jesus' blood pouring out for our sins. Now we discover that we can look fully into the face of Him who would have condemned us, but now justifies us. We hold our heads high, not because we deserve such treatment, but because we have been gifted by our Creator.

God's gracious justification of sinners is no new doctrine. Exhibit A is Abraham. Contrary to the perception of most Jews, he was not self-righteous, i.e. righteous of his own doing. For he was credited with righteousness before he had done any of the things Jews thought produced righteousness. Before he was circumcised — before he founded the nation of Israel — before there was a Mosaic Law to keep. He was declared righteous by God at the moment he chose to believe God. Abraham also shows us how to believe. Faith is inseparable from obedience. His obedience was his faith lived out, nothing more. It had no merit of its own. It was merely the outward evidence of his inward trust in God. No obedience, no faith, and vice versa.

Our justification by faith ends the warfare which we, in our sinful behavior, waged against God. Peace reigns. And we enjoy a special standing with God called "grace," or "giftedness." Because of this standing we live joyfully, with hope that one day we will share in God's eternal glory.

Romans 5:6-11 — You see, at just the right time, when we were still powerless, Christ died for the ungodly. Very rarely will anyone die for a righteous man, though for a good man someone might possibly dare to die. But God demonstrates his own love for us in this: While we were still sinners, Christ died for us.

52

Since we have now been justified by his blood, how much more shall we be saved from God's wrath through him! For if, when we were God's enemies, we were reconciled to him through the death of his Son, how much more, having been reconciled, shall we be saved through his life! Not only is this so, but we also rejoice in God through our Lord Jesus Christ, through whom we have now received reconciliation.

The incredibility of God's love and graciousness is highlighted in this passage by the downward spiral of the human condition. First, we are pictured as merely "powerless," viz., we had no defenses against sin; so we became "sinners" in that we joined the enemy himself; and finally, we became "God's enemies" by actually fighting against God. If this seems too harsh an assessment, you'll have to take that up with Paul.

Under these circumstances, and in the cases of those living since the cross before they (we) ever become so entrapped in sin, God gave us His Son to die in our place. This death reversed everything sin had done to us: it gave us power over sin; we became forgiven sinners; and we were returned to friendship with God. But God's gifts always have that little extra, the frosting on the cake. While we wait for eternal life, joy reigns! Our religion is not a harsh discipline which makes us long for heaven. In Paul's word picture I see us hugging God, dancing and singing with delight, while Jesus, the one who made it possible, joins the festivities!

Romans 5:12-21 — Therefore, just as sin entered the world through one man, and death through sin, and in this way death came to all men, because all sinned — for before the law was given, sin was in the world. But sin is not taken into account where there is no law. Nevertheless, death reigned from the time of Adam to the time of Moses, even over those who did not sin by breaking a command, as did Adam, who was a pattern of the one to come.

But the gift is not like the trespass. For if the many died by the trespass of the one man, how much more did God's grace and the gift that came by the grace of the one man, Jesus Christ, overflow to the many! Again, the gift of God is not like the result of the one man's sin: The judgment followed one sin and brought condemnation, but the gift followed many trespasses and brought justification. For if, by the trespass of the one man, death reigned through that one man, how much more will those who receive God's abundant provision of grace and of the gift of righteousness reign in life through the one man, Jesus Christ.

Consequently, just as the result of one trespass was condemnation for all men, so also the result of one act of righteousness was justification that brings life for all men. For just as through the disobedience of the one man the many were made sinners, so also through the obedience of the one man the many will be made righteous.

The law was added so that the trespass might increase. But where sin increased, grace increased all the more, so that, just as sin reigned in death, so also grace might reign through righteousness to bring eternal life through Jesus Christ our Lord.

Probably J.W. McGarvey's paraphrase and discussion of this passage is as clear as any commentator's.[5]

Here Paul illustrates the magnificence of God's gift by contrasting it with the sin of Adam, the act which ushered sin into the world. The curse of sin, which is physical death, is contrasted to the beauty of justification (being declared righteous), which was brought to the world by Jesus. Adam's sin condemned many (almost all must die); our own sins confirm that we are his offspring and deserve physical death; the gift of Jesus Christ brought the chance of eternal life to all. Our sins condemn us all to spiritual death; God's gift makes eternal spiritual life with God available to us all.

Between Adam and us the Law of Moses was added to magnify sin, and increase man's sense of futility. What was God up to? He wanted His creatures to respond all the more overwhelmingly to His marvelous gift.

Romans 6:23 — For the wages of sin is death, but the gift of God is eternal life in Christ Jesus our Lord.

54

This well-known verse requires little comment, except perhaps to put it in context. When we have died to sin by symbolically going into a tomb (baptism), our slavery to sin is ended, being replaced by willing slavery to Jesus. What is the result of this change of owners? Instead of receiving spiritual death (eternal separation from God) as payment for services rendered (to Satan), we receive eternal life (heaven) as an absolute gift, granted before we had offered God our first act of service. Civil law and civil reality validate the doctrinal truth of what Paul just said (Rom. 7:1-6).

Romans 11:5,6 — So too, at the present time there is a remnant chosen by grace. And if by grace, then it is no longer by works; if it were, grace would no longer be grace.

Whatever Jews who were Christians at the time Paul wrote this letter were such because they looked at God's beautiful gift and reached out to accept it as their own. Their reaching in no way qualified as work, for when you talk about justification, work and grace are antithetical.

I Corinthians 15:9,10 — For I am the least of the apostles and do not even deserve to be called an apostle, because I persecuted the church of God. But by the grace of God I am what I am, and his grace to me was not without effect. No, I worked harder than all of them — yet not I but the grace of God that was with me.

"The saving and transforming effect of this grace is graphically illustrated in the dynamic experience of every regenerate life, as it was in a very wonderful manner in the experience of the apostle Paul . . . . This verse indicates that Paul attributed not only his conversion to God's grace, but also all that he was able to do and achieve throughout the course of his life and ministry as an apostle. In other words, the grace of God is determinative of the whole pilgrimage of the Christian, from conversion to glorification."[6] Paul attributed his whole spiritual life to God's gifts, first conviction, then conversion, then Christian service. But he also knew that his own cooperation with grace made it all possible.

> *II Corinthians 5:17-6:3* — Therefore, if anyone is in Christ, he is a new creation; the old has gone, the new has come! All this is from God, who reconciled us to himself through Christ and gave us the ministry of reconciliation; that God was reconciling the world to himself in Christ, not counting men's sins against them. And he has committed to us the message of reconciliation. We are therefore Christ's ambassadors, as though God were making his appeal through us. We implore you on Christ's behalf: Be reconciled to God. God made him who had no sin to be sin for us, so that in him we might become the righteousness of God. As God's fellow workers we urge you not to receive God's grace in vain. For he says, "In the time of my favor I heard you, and in the day of salvation I helped you." I tell you, now is the time of God's favor, now is the day of salvation.

God took the initiative to put us in Christ, viz., in the condition of salvation. His act was unilateral, for the purpose of reconciling us to himself. But He wasn't through giving. He also gave us this gift to dispense among our fellows. And because we are possessors of the gift ourselves our appeal to others sounds like it is coming from God himself. But the offer is too generous to be human: "Someone died to pay for your sins, thus enabling God to credit you with righteousness."

Some commentators feel Paul begins a new subject in verse one of chapter six. But it seems to me to be adding urgency to the believer who is God's ambassador offering His gift. Because salvation is a gift the hearer may take it lightly. It may be wasted on some. And the offer will eventually be withdrawn. Old Testament Israel certainly received God's favor, but not forever. This dimension is what gives grace its inestimable value. Whatever God gives He can withdraw.

> *II Corinthians 8:9* — For you know the grace of our Lord Jesus Christ, that though he was rich, yet for your sakes he became poor, so that you through his poverty might become rich.

In II Corinthians 8 and 9 grace is used repeatedly in its non-soteriological sense, meaning basically generosity with material possessions. However, Paul reaches for the ultimate example of giving, Jesus (though His gift was not material), to spur the Corinthians to material generosity. This passage, perhaps better than any other in the New Testament, reveals the cost of the gift God gave: Jesus had to invest thirty-three years of His celestial glory and fellowship with the Father (Phil. 2:7,8) in order to come to earth as God's sacrificial lamb. That investment makes us rich spiritually and eternally.

Galatians 1:6,7a — I am astonished that you are so quickly deserting the one who called you by the grace of Christ and are turning to a different gospel — which is really no gospel at all.

The letter to Galatian congregations, perhaps the sternest of Paul's letters, was prompted by a full-scale effort by Judaizers to require all Christians to seek justification by the grace of God *plus* obedience to the Law of Moses. This is no gospel at all, says Paul. The good news had become bad news. The entire epistle is aimed at correcting this error.

As in Romans 11:5,6 grace here is pictured as the means of our reconciliation to God. God called us to himself using the gift of His Son to catch our attention. Paul says that was the way he was attracted: "But when God . . . called me by his grace . . . " (Gal. 1:15). When this shade of thought is coupled with Romans 5:2, "This grace in which we now stand," we realize that God wasn't pulling a theological version of the merchants' "bait and switch" skulduggery. He caught our attention with Calvary and then gave us its full value (forgiveness, reconciliation, and resurrection to eternal life)! Nothing less.

Galatians 3:18 — For if the inheritance depends on the law, then it no longer depends on a promise; but God in his grace gave it to Abraham through a promise.

Since this is but one sentence in the classic dispute between Paul and the Judaizers, perhaps a thorough study of the entire section (Gal. 3:1-5:12) is in order. That will be done in Chapter Five. For now let it be noted that grace is not just a New Testament phenomenon. This passage depicts God's disposition as being gratuitous when He promised Abraham that "all peoples on earth will be blessed through you" (Gen. 12:3b). Jesus was never intended as a Christmas present payoff for good Jews. (How's that for a mixed metaphor?) Jesus was a gift "to those who believe" (Gal. 3:22b), of whatever race.

Galatians 5:4 — You who are trying to be justified by law have been alienated from Christ; you have fallen away from grace.

As Paul comes to the climax of his arguments against the Judaizers, he sets the grace (free) way over against the law (pay by obedience) way. It was a nefarious plot for them to try to combine grace and law like this. This was bad news, he had already declared in Galatians 1:6-7. Salvation is either free or it's not. Salvation by law keeping was a fatal attraction of these Judaizers. It nullified grace.

Ephesians 1:3-8 — Praise be to the God and Father of our Lord Jesus Christ, who has blessed us in the heavenly realms with every spiritual blessing in Christ. For he chose us in him before the creation of the world to be holy and blameless in his sight. In love he predestined us to be adopted as his sons through Jesus Christ, in accordance with his pleasure and will — to the praise of his glorious grace, which he has freely given us in the One he loves. In him we have redemption through his blood, the forgiveness of sins, in accordance with the riches of God's grace that he lavished on us with all wisdom and understanding.

In two separate bursts of praise Paul holds up God's giving disposition as the cause of our good fortune as believers. Besides "every spiritual blessing" which we enjoy daily, there are the factors of our salvation which are highlighted in this paragraph: His choosing of us, His predestining our adoption, and His redeeming us through the blood of Jesus. Every one of these is a unilateral act issuing from the giving part of God's character. What more heart-warming characterizations of God could our wildest imagination create? There He sat, before speaking the worlds into existence, thinking about us! Thinking about what kind of love He can shower on fallen creatures that will catch our attention and elicit a loving response. Thinking about a kind of lifestyle we might enjoy ("holy and blameless in his sight"). Thinking about what kind of relationship He might endow us with ("adopted us as his sons"). And thinking about how expensive all this would be ("redemption through his blood"). All this coming from His giving heart! God doesn't give penuriously. He "lavishes."

> **Ephesians 2:4-9** — But because of his great love for us, God, who is rich in mercy, made us alive with Christ even when we were dead in transgressions — it is by grace you have been saved. And God raised us up with Christ and seated us with him in the heavenly realms in Christ Jesus, in order that in the coming ages he might show the incomparable riches of his grace, expressed in his kindness to us in Christ Jesus. For it is by grace you have been saved, through faith — and this is not from yourselves, it is the gift of God — not by works, so that no one can boast.

Here the gem of grace is turned to the same angle as in Romans 5:6-10. Conceived in love and mercy, the gift of new life with Christ is held out while we are "dead in transgressions," totally unhearing, unseeing, unfeeling. Paul makes this point so we won't mistake our faith response for something meriting this gift. So far as God is concerned, the gift, with our names on it, was given before we ever reached out to possess it. It was given *whether* or not we ever reached out to possess it. The only string (if it may be called that) attached to this gift is this: God wants to use us as testimonials to the "incomparable riches of his grace." "Just shine," is all God asks of us.

II Thessalonians 2:16,17 — May the Lord Jesus Christ himself and God our Father, who loved us and by his grace gave us eternal encouragement and good hope, encourage your hearts and strengthen you in every good deed and word.

What God has given us to date, viz., a salvation which provides us with "eternal encouragement and good hope," is a gift which never stops giving. It cheers and motivates the recipient to "every good deed and word." This passage expresses the ideal motivation for Christian works, a subject that is treated fully in Chapter Six.

I Timothy 1:12-16 — I thank Christ Jesus our Lord, who has given me strength, that he considered me faithful, appointing me to his service. Even though I was once a blasphemer and a persecutor and a violent man, I was shown mercy because I acted in ignorance and unbelief. The grace of our Lord was poured out on me abundantly, along with faith and love that are in Christ Jesus.

Here is a trustworthy saying that deserves full acceptance: Christ Jesus came into the world to save sinners — of whom I am the worst. But for that very reason I was shown mercy so that in me, the worst of sinners, Christ Jesus might display his unlimited patience as an example for those who would believe on him and receive eternal life.

"The gift is not like the trespass," Paul had told the Romans (5:15). And he knew so personally. His sins were so unseemly (blasphemer, persecutor, violent man)! Yet they didn't tax God's capacity to forgive. And as he had written to the Ephesians (2:4-9), all God asked of Paul was to go on display to demonstrate that there is no floor under God's forgiveness. No matter how much we have wasted our earthly lives, He still wants to give us eternal life. What an incredible thought!

Titus 2:11 — For the grace of God that brings salvation has appeared to all men.

The gift of Jesus Christ for our salvation was not (and is not) God's only gift to humanity. But it is surely the crowning one. The power of this gift is seen in verses 12-14: It teaches us to retain its benefits by denying eroding worldliness and waiting patiently for the eternal unfolding of our salvation. The scope of the gift attests to God's generosity: it was given to all men, the interested and the disinterested, the worthy and the unworthy, regardless of their response to it.

Titus 3:4-7 — But when the kindness and love of God our Savior appeared, he saved us, not because of righteous things we had done, but because of his mercy. He saved us through the washing of rebirth and renewal by the Holy Spirit, whom he poured out on us generously through Jesus Christ our Savior, so that, having been justified by this grace, we might become heirs having the hope of eternal life.

Our salvation arises solely out of God's disposition to mercy, His decision to give us more than we deserve (or is it less?). His agent is the Holy Spirit, who uses rebirth (John 3:3,5) and renewal as His methods. The Holy Spirit is also God's gift (Acts 2:38), as is heaven. So when all is said and done, God has said and done it all. Our righteousness is totally God's act.

Hebrews 2:9 — But we see Jesus, who was made a little lower than the angels, now crowned with glory and honor because he suffered death, so that by the grace of God he might taste death for everyone.

C.H. Dodd notes that the phrase "by the grace of God" "covers the divine motive, the mission of the Son, the very methods of suffering, and the wide object in mind."[7] The divine motive was love, the mission of the Son was service, the method of suffering was the righteous for the unrighteous (II Cor. 5:21), and the object was forgiveness within the parameters of God's absolute justice.

I Peter 1:10,11 — Concerning this salvation, the prophets who spoke of the grace that was to come to you, searched intently and with the greatest care, trying to find out the time and circumstances to which the Spirit of Christ in them was pointing when he predicted the sufferings of Christ and the glories that would follow.

The prophets who predicted the sufferings of Christ and the glories that were to obtain in them were actually searching for the details of God's gift. What was obscure to them is clear to us, namely, that Jesus' suffering and death were for our sins, and the glory was spiritual and eternal. Perhaps only Isaiah, in chapter 53, had a very clear view of this. That chapter is bathed in grace if any Old Testament passage is!

I John 4:9,10 — This is how God showed his love among us: He sent his one and only Son into the world that we might live through him. This is love: not that we loved God, but that he loved us and sent his Son as an atoning sacrifice for our sins.

John understood grace. God's act in sending Jesus to atone for (legally pay the penalty due) our sins was motivated by love. His act was not dependent upon nor motivated by our love, nor was it tied to our anticipated response. Grace is God's demonstration of unconditional love.

RECEIVING THE GIFT

If Bible writers (Paul in particular) were so painstaking in establishing God's grace as being the only viable solution to man's sin problems, and in their unanimous description of the solution as an unconditional gift, is it not reasonable to expect that the Bible will also contain explicit directions for receiving grace? Or is it just "out there," like ozone and nitrogen in our air, sustaining us invisibly?

"Gift" is a word of rather explicit meaning in itself. A gift may be totally free and already given in your behalf (such as a gift certificate at a department store), but until it is in your possession it is of absolutely no value to you or to others who might benefit secondarily. I John 2:2 says Jesus is the covering for the sins of the world, but no serious exegete would have John teaching that all sinners are now saved, forgiven and in possession of eternal life. That is obvious universalism. The gift is there, but it must be received to have value for you and me.

I have often illustrated this principle in public meetings by inviting someone from the audience (usually a teenager) to come to the front and receive a gift of five dollars. I hold out the bill while I teach the lesson.

"Do I owe you this? Is it for some job you did for me?"

They ususally answer in the negative. In case I really do owe it to them, I pay up and start over.

"Do you possess the five dollars I am holding out to you?"

"No, it's still in your hand," they will usually answer.

"You mean you can't spend it on a hamburger, fries and a soft drink?"

"Nope."

"But I'm giving it to you!" I insist.

My straight man will usually think "This is too good to be true," and answer something like, "It won't be true until I actually have it in my hand and know it's mine."

"Oh, I see." About here I actually place it in his hand, but I don't let go of it quite yet.

"You didn't earn it?" I ask.

"Nope."

"Not even by reaching out to get it?"

"No way. You sure can't call reaching out to get it work," he'll usually reply.

About then I release the bill to his hand. "It's yours, a gift from me. Just remember, it has value, but you didn't earn it. Likewise, salvation is a gift, the most valuable gift in the whole world, but we don't have it until we reach out in faith to receive it. Those people you read about in the Book of Acts were reaching out in faith when they turned from their sins and were immersed in water. They came up from their baptism rejoicing, not because they had worked hard enough to earn salvation, but because they had reached out and received the free gift."

God's remedy is received by faith. "But now a righteousness from God . . . has been made known . . . . This righteousness from God comes through faith in Jesus Christ to all who believe" (Rom. 3:21,22). "For it is by grace you have been saved, through faith . . . " (Eph. 2:8). "Righteousness by faith" is a recurring theme in Paul's writings (Rom. 1:17; 4:5,13; 10:6; Gal. 2:16; Phil. 3:9). Reread Romans 3:21-5:21 if you have any doubts.

THE NATURE OF SAVING FAITH

In describing saving faith the Bible parts ways with modern "believe only" theology. Believing is the way, says the Bible. But believing as depicted in Scripture is more than an intellectual transaction. Luther knew that faith was more than this. "If faith were only knowledge, then the devil would certainly be saved because he possesses the greatest knowledge of God and of all the works and wonders of God from the creation of the world. Accordingly faith must be understood otherwise than as knowledge. In part, however, it is assent."[8] The intellectual transaction is only the beginning. Can what comes out of that transaction be called anything other than faith? Not when both Testaments illustrate faith in terms of an intellectual transaction that fueled action.

All one need do to discover the meaning of saving faith is read Hebrews 11 and leave out the verbs of action that the writer employed to illustrate faith of Old Testament heroes. It makes a mockery of the chapter. And then we understand precisely what was troubling James when he asked, "What good is it, my brothers, if a man claims to have faith but has no deeds? Can such faith save him?" (James 2:14). And then he issues the challenge: "Show me your faith without deeds, and I will show you my faith by what I do" (v. 18b).

Saving faith is implicit trust in God. The kind Abram had when, at God's bidding, he left his homeland for a destination known only to God (Gen. 12:1-9). The kind Abraham and Sarah had when they had sexual relations for the purpose of producing a son even though they were much beyond the childbearing age (Gen. 18:1-15; Rom. 4:18-21). The kind Abraham had when he proceeded to offer that miraculously born son as a human sacrifice though to do so seemed to contravene the plans of God (Gen. 22:1-19). You cannot separate his deeds from his implicit trust, for they complement one another.

WHAT ABOUT WATER BAPTISM?

Following the death of Christ it is not surprising to see faith illustrated in this broader definition. When people in Acts 2:38 were told to "Repent and be baptized, every one of you in the name of Jesus Christ so that your sins may be forgiven," we feel no contradiction in theology. Neither are the words "Whoever believes and is baptized will be saved," from the lips of Jesus (Mark 16:16a) any contradiction to Paul's theology of salvation by grace through faith. Repentance and baptism are faith in the same sense that building an ark was for Noah, or leaving Ur of the Chaldees was for Abram. Are they necessary? Was the ark necessary for Noah? Were sexual relations necessary for Abram and Sarah?

Most evangelicals today are anxious to talk about grace and the mechanics of justification by it, but they prefer to confine the conversation to Romans and Galatians. But what are you going to do with the Acts of Apostles which illustrates the transaction in the lives of real people? Jews, Gentiles, pagans, and believers in God — all are represented in Luke's exciting book. The answer seems to be: Acts keeps talking about baptism, and they've already written it out of God's program.

To be as completely honest as I know how in the matter of baptism, more than a decade ago I produced and published a tract entitled, "You and Your Bible Answer Life's Most Important Question." It was *another* "plan of salvation" tract. (How many have well meaning Christian writers produced over the centuries to help the Bible answer the question "What must I do to be saved?) Most of them string together Bible passages to give the reader some kind of answer, and many of them contain a little prayer of commitment that goes something like this:

> Dear Father, I admit that I'm a sinner and cannot save myself. I trust in Jesus to forgive all my sins, and I receive Him as my personal savior.

Often a signature line follows. Mine was different. It contained six stories of conversion from the Book of Acts, photographed directly from the Bible, with no comment of my own. The reader was asked to read the stories and answer one simple question: What were these people told to do to be saved? Space was provided for answers. Then, at the conclusion, the reader was asked to write what he himself must do to be saved, based on what he just read. Tens of thousands of those went all over the world, and the only complaint I ever received was from a young Baptist seminary graduate who said I had "stacked" the verses in favor of baptism. I wonder what Luke did in the Book of Acts?

Repentance and baptism are those dimensions of faith in which the free gift is received. Nowhere in the New Testament are they depicted as meritorious works which purchase salvation for us. No wonder neither Paul nor Peter found it contradictory to speak of "obeying the gospel" in II Thessalonians 1:8 and I Peter 4:17. Martin Luther had no trouble seeing the place of water baptism in God's plan. Note the following quotations:

What is baptism? Baptism is not simply water, but it is the water comprehended in God's command, and connected with God's Word . . . . What benefits does baptism confer? It works forgiveness of sins, delivers from death and the devil, and gives everlasting salvation to all who believe this, as the words and promises of God declare. Which are those words and promises of God? Those which Christ, our Lord, says in the last chapter of Mark: "He that believeth and is baptized shall be saved; but he that believeth not shall be damned." How can water do such great things? It is not water indeed that does it, but the Word of God, which is in and with the water and faith which trusts this word of God in the water. For without the Word of God the water is simply water, and no baptism. But with the Word of God, it is a baptism, that is a gracious water of life and a washing of regeneration in the Holy Spirit; as St. Paul says, Titus 3:5-8.[9]

In this Holy Sacrament we must have regard to three things — the sign, the significance thereof, and the faith. The sign consists in this, that we are thrust into the water in the Name of the Father and of the Son and of the Holy Ghost; but we are not left there, for we are drawn out again . . . .

The significance of baptism is a blessed dying unto sin and resurrection in the grace of God, so that the old man, which is conceived and born in sin, is there drowned, and a new man, born in grace, comes forth and rises. Thus St. Paul, in Titus 3, calls baptism a "washing of regeneration," since in this washing man is born again and made new. As Christ also says, in John 3, "Except ye be born again of water and the Spirit of grace, ye shall not enter into the Kingdom of Heaven."

The sacrament, or sign, of baptism is quickly over, as we plainly see. But the thing it signifies, viz., the spiritual baptism, the drowning of sin, lasts so long as we live, and is completed only in death. Then it is that man is completely sunk in baptism, and that thing comes to pass which baptism signifies . . . .

In like manner the lifting up out of baptism is quickly done, but the thing it signifies, the spiritual birth, the increase of grace and righteousness, though it begins indeed in baptism, lasts until death, nay, even until the Last Day. Only then will that be finished which the lifting up out of baptism signifies. Then shall we arise from death, from sins and from all evil, pure in body and in soul, and then shall we live forever . . . .

Here, then, is the place to discuss the third thing in the sacra-

67

ment, i.e., faith, to wit, that a man should firmly believe all this; viz., that this sacrament not only signifies death and the resurrection at the Last Day, by which man is made new for an everlasting, sinless life; but also that it assuredly begins and effects this, and unites us with God, so that we have the will to slay sin, even till the time of our death, and to fight against it; on the other hand, that it is His will to be merciful to us, to deal graciously with us, and not to judge us with severity, because we are not sinless in this life until purified through death . . . .

This faith is of all things the most necessary, for it is the ground of all comfort. He who has not this faith must despair in his sins. For the sin which remains after baptism makes it impossible for any good works to be pure before God. For this reason we must hold boldly and fearlessly to our baptism, and hold it up against all sins and terrors of conscience, and humbly say, "I know full well that I have not a single work which is pure, but I am baptized, and through my baptism God, Who cannot lie, has bound Himself in a covenant with me, not to count my sin against me, but to slay it and blot it out.[10]

The first thing in baptism to be considered is the divine promise, which says: "He that believeth and is baptised shall be saved."This promise must be set far above all the glitter of works, vows, religious orders, and whatever man has added thereto; for on it all our salvation depends. But we must so consider it as to exercise our faith therein and in nowise doubt that we are saved when we are baptised. For unless this faith be present or be conferred in baptism, baptism will profit us nothing, nay, it becomes a hindrance to us, not only in the moment of its reception, but all the days of our life; for such unbelief accuses God's promise of being a lie, and this is the blackest of all sins . . . .[11]

Man baptises and does not baptise: he baptises, for he performs the work, immersing the person to be baptised; he does not baptise, for in that act he officiates not by his own authority, but in the stead of God. Hence, we ought to receive baptism at the hands of a man just as if Christ Himself, nay God Himself, were baptising us with His own hands. For it is not man's baptism, but Christ's and God's baptism, which we receive by the hand of a man . . . . Therefore beware of dividing baptism in such a way as to ascribe the outward part to man and the inward part to God. Ascribe both to God alone, and look upon the person administering it as the instrument in God's hands . . . .[12]

Baptism is called in the Greek language *baptismos*, in Latin *mersio*, which means to plunge something entirely into the water, so that the water closes over it . . . .

This usage is also demanded by the significance of baptism, for baptism signifies that the old man and the sinful birth of flesh and blood are to be wholly drowned by the grace of God.[13]

Tell me, why do you baptize a man when he has come to the age of reason? You answer: He hears God's Word and believes. I ask: How do you know that? You answer: He professes it with his mouth . . . .[14]

To view and use baptism aright we must let it become to us a source of strength and comfort when sin and conscience oppress us. Then you may say: It is a fact that I am baptized, but being baptized, I have the promise that I shall be saved and obtain eternal life for both soul and body. For this reason, two things take place in baptism: water is poured upon our bodies, which can perceive nothing but the water; and the Word is spoken to the soul, that the soul may have its share also. Now, as water and Word constitute one baptism, so shall both body and soul be saved and live forever: the soul through the Word, in which it believes; but the body because it is united with the soul and grasps baptism in such a manner as it may. Hence, no greater jewel can adorn our body or soul than baptism; for through it perfect holiness and salvation become accessible to us. Which are otherwise beyond the reach of man's life and energy.[15]

These lengthy quotations from Luther make it pretty obvious that he did not view water baptism as meritorious work, but as an expression of faith. Nor did he employ some of the current jargon that is designed to reduce baptism to a spiritual or ecclesiastical option.

Alexander Campbell held essentially the same view, as William J. Richardson wrote in an article in *Christian Standard*.

For Campbell, grace — not law — is the fundamental reality underlying God's relation to mankind. Hence, when describing the various institutions by which God had dealt with man from the beginning he used the phrase "covenants of grace."

"In the kingdom of heaven the antecedent blessings are the

69

constitution of grace, the King, and all he did, suffered and sustained for our redemption. These were finished before we came upon the stage of action. This is all favor, pure favor, sovereign favor: for there can be no favor that is not free and sovereign" (*Millennial Harbinger*, 1834, p. 425).

Hence there can be no conditions for the procurement of grace. "It cannot be merited, but must be received as a perfect gratuity. The conditions, then, are not the conditions of a *purchase* but of a *free* donation" (*Millennial Harbinger*, 1846, p. 312). "Let no man think that in the act of being born, either naturally or metaphorically, the child purchases, procures, or merits either life or its enjoyments" (*Christian System*, p. 233).

What then is the place of faith, repentence, baptism? They are not means of procurement (purchase) of grace but means of enjoyment of grace. Religion, said Campbell, consists of two departments: "the things that God has done for us, and the things we must do for ourselves . . . heaven, therefore, overtures; and man accepts, surrenders, and returns to God . . ." (*Christian System*, p. 20).

Thus while the blood of Jesus Christ is "the procuring cause of remission," faith is the "principle of enjoyment of remission," and baptism "the means divinely appointed for our actual enjoyment of this first and greatest of present blessings." But neither faith nor baptism procures remission. "The blood of Jesus through the favor of God procures; faith apprehends; and baptism takes hold of the boon of heaven, or is the means of our enjoyment" (*Millennial Harbinger*, 1832, p. 542).[16]

"Procurement," "enjoyment," — just word games, someone says. Not at all. These (and other explanations cited heretofore) are honest efforts of Bible students to understand how God has made grace available to us. How else shall we harmonize Paul's great treatise on grace (Romans) with his own testimony about his own baptism? Ananias told him to "Get up, be baptized and wash away your sins, calling on his name" (Acts 22:16). He did, and they were! Does Paul reverse himself in Romans? I think not.

And, can we put to rest once and for all any dream that we might have that there is any approach for us sinners to God except via His Son "who gave himself for our sins to rescue us from the present evil age, according to the will of our God and Father, to whom be glory for ever and ever. Amen" (Gal. 1:4-5)? I think so.

Endnotes

1. Hayden King, "The Imputed Righteousness of Christ," *Present Truth*, 2/73, p. 22.

2. Charles C. Ryrie, *The Grace of God*, Moody Press, 1963, pp. 20,24.

3. W.E. Vine, *An Expository Dictionary of New Testament Words*, Fleming H. Revell, Old Tappan, N.J., 1940, pp. 169-170.

4. Karl Barth, *The Epistle to the Romans*, Oxford University Press, N.Y., 1933, p. 31.

5. *The Standard Bible Commentary: Thessalonians, Corinthians, Galatians, and Romans*, Standard Publishing Co., 1916, pp. 333-341.

6. Philip E. Hughes, *But For the Grace of God*, Westminster Press, Philadelphia, 1964, pp. 9-10.

7. *The Bible and the Greeks*, Hodder and Stoughton, London, 1954, pp. 63-64.

8. *The Wisdom of Martin Luther*, Concordia Publishing House, St. Louis, 1973.

9. *Small Catechism, Lenker Edition, Vol. XXIV*, pp. 27ff.

10. *Treatise on Baptism, Works of Martin Luther, Vol. I*, pp. 56-63.

11. *The Babylonian Captivity of the Church, Works of Martin Luther, Vol. II*, p. 220.

12. Ibid., pp. 224f.

13. *Treatise on Baptism, Works of Martin Luther, Vol. I*, p. 56.

14. *Gospel Sermon, Third Sunday After Epiphany, Lenker Edition, Vol. XI*, No. 38.

15. *Large Catechism, Lenker Edition, Vol. XXI*, p. 165.

16. "Alexander Campbell: Grace and Obedience," *Christian Standard*, May 15, 1988, pp. 11-12.

3

GRACE AND "CREDITED" RIGHTEOUSNESS

In Paul's monumental work on grace, the Epistle to the Romans, the term "credited" righteousness is first introduced in 4:3. "What does the Scripture say? 'Abraham believed God, and it was credited to him as righteousness.' " He is quoting from Genesis 15:6, which is relatively early in the life of Abraham, while he was still called Abram, before circumcision, before the birth of Isaac, before the offering of Isaac, but after Abraham had trusted God by leaving Ur of the Chaldeans. That verse is in the midst of the covenant transaction into which he and God entered. His part of the "deal" was to accept as fact, and act upon as fact, God's promise regarding posterity and land. Upon making his decision to believe God, Abraham was "credited" with righteousness.

"Counted," "imputed," and "reckoned" are translations of the same Greek word *logizomai*, used in older translations. It means "to occupy oneself with reckonings or calculations; to

73

reckon or count; to reckon anything to a person, to put it to his account, either in his favour or what he must be answerable for."[1] Charles Hodges' fourth definition adds another dimension: "In strict connection with its primary meaning, it signifies to impute, to set to one's account; that is to number among the things belonging to a man, or chargeable upon him. It generally implies the accessory idea of 'treating one according to the nature of the thing imputed.'" The word obviously has its roots in mathematical or accounting terminology. "Credited," in the New International Version, is indeed a fortuitous rendering for us who live in the era of bank accounts, credit cards and income tax. That analogy will be pursued throughout this chapter, though the author is not unmindful of the limitations of all analogies.

Scripture itself explains the concept for us in some unusual ways, so that when we encounter it in the context of new covenant grace, it is not so difficult to understand.

Isaiah 53:6b — . . . and the Lord laid on him the iniquity of us all.

This reference is to Jesus, our sin-bearer. They were our sins, not His. Yet they were charged to him. Here the concept is illustrated negatively, as a debit, not a credit (for you with bookkeeping knowledge).

Acts 7:60b — Lord, do not hold this sin against them.

Though *logizomai* is not used here, the idea is conveyed.

Romans 4:17 — As it is written: "I have made you a father of many nations." He is our father in the sight of God, in whom he believed — the God who gives life to the dead and calls things that are not as though they were.

Here the concept is illustrated in time. At the moment Abraham had no son of promise. There's the debit. But God credited him with one right then because he trusted God. Since this was spoken of as an accomplished fact before Isaac was born (Gen. 17:5; 21:1-3), God was crediting Abraham with the title before it was legally and historically appropos.

> **Romans 9:8** — In other words, it is not the natural children who are God's children, but it is the children of the promise who are regarded as Abraham's offspring.

Logizomai is the word translated "regarded" here. And the context is grace. Abraham had two types of descendants: descendants of blood, and descendants of grace. The latter were not literally his offspring, but were counted, or credited as such by God's grace.

> **II Corinthians 5:19-21** — That God was reconciling the world to himself in Christ, not counting men's sins against them. And he has committed to us the message of reconciliation. We are therefore Christ's ambassadors, as though God were making his appeal through us. We implore you on Christ's behalf: Be reconciled to God. God made him who had no sin to be sin for us, so that in him we might become the righteousness of God.

This is full of business transaction terminology. "Not counting men's sins against them" — God needed to ignore our debit. But you can't just ignore debits and balance the books. So, "God made him who had no sin to be sin" — there's the debit; "so that in him we might become the righteousness of God" — there's the credit. The books are balanced!

> **II Timothy 4:16b** — May it not be held against them.

The Greek here is *logizomai*, and the passage clearly illustrates the concept.

> **Philemon 18** — If he has done you any wrong or owes you anything, charge it to me.

75

"Charge it" — how many times a day is that phrase spoken in the western world, do you think? "Charge Onesimus' debts to my account," Paul tells Philemon. Paul owed Philemon nothing, but he was willing to credit Onesimus' account with whatever it took to pay off his (Onesimus') debt and balance the books. Technically Onesimus owed the debt, but legally Paul had assumed it.

Moving from Biblical illustrations, Charles Hodge's explanation of "credited" righteousness is one of the best I've read: "It generally implies the accessory idea of 'treating one according to the nature of the thing imputed' (II Sam. 19:19; I Sam. 22:15; Psa. 32:2; II Cor. 6:19; II Tim. 4:16). Imputation is laying anything to one's charge, and treating him accordingly. It produces no change in the individual to whom the imputation is made; it simply alters his relation to the law. All those objections, therefore, to the doctrine expressed by this term, which are founded on the assumption that imputation alters the moral character of men; that it implies infusion of either sin or holiness, rest on a misconception of its nature. It is just as common and correct to speak of laying to a man's charge what does not belong to him, as what does. That a thing can be justly imputed to a person to whom it does not personally belong, is a matter of course. But that the word itself implies that the thing imputed must belong to the person concerned, is a singular misconception."[2]

"EXPLAIN YOURSELF, PAUL . . ."

"How can we be righteous, Paul, just because we have believed? Faith and justification seem to be worlds apart." That's not a silly question, because Paul seems to have anticipated it from those who first read Romans 1-3. Beginning in 4:1 he explains how God credits the believer with righteousness, while at the same time showing the quality of faith it requires. A careful look at this chapter should be helpful. (Once again, most good commentaries will provide deeper insights into word meanings and syntax here.)

> [1]What then shall we say that Abraham, our forefather, discovered in this matter?

Of righteousness through faith. J.W. McGarvey calls Abraham a "test case" put up by Paul to prove his point about justification by faith.

> [2]If, in fact, Abraham was justified by works, he had something to boast about — but not before God.

The consensus of rabbinical teaching was that Abraham was chosen by God to head the Jewish race *because* his deeds were so righteous. If so, his righteousness was his own, the result of his doing everything right.

> [3]What does the Scripture say? "Abraham believed God, and it was credited to him as righteousness."

But testifying against the rabbis was this statement of Scripture itself. As a matter of fact, Abraham was himself never intrinsically righteous. This is obvious because Scripture records his unrighteous deeds alongside his righteous ones. He had his debits. But overall his life was one of unquestioning faith, so God put righteousness into his life's account, balancing it for justification purposes.

> [4]Now when a man works, his wages are not credited to him as a gift, but as an obligation.

If you reduce the story of Abraham to one of wages paid for work done, salvation as God's gift is out of the picture. Credited righteousness is dead. But who wants to get into this kind of contract with God? The moment our works are less than perfect we will receive no wages (salvation).

> [5]However, to the man who does not work but trusts God who justifies the wicked, his faith is credited as righteousness.

It's not that Abraham did no good deeds. Of course he did, but he did not do them in order to earn God's favor. Believing got him that.

> [6]David says the same thing when he speaks of the blessedness of the man to whom God credits righteousness apart from works: [7]"Blessed are they whose transgressions are forgiven, whose sins are covered. [8]Blessed is the man whose sin the Lord will never count against him."

David concurs with this concept, though he wrote of it from the negative viewpoint (Psa. 32:1-2). Romans 4:1-8 announces very clearly that Abraham's righteousness did not come as wages paid for good deeds. There had to be another way.

Nor did it come through circumcision. That is the burden of Paul's argument in Romans 4:9-13. In this section Paul begins showing the broad scope of credited righteousness. A closer look at those verses will add to our assurance.

> [9]Is this blessedness only for the circumcised, or also for the uncircumcised? We have been saying that Abraham's faith was credited to him as righteousness. [10]Under what circumstances was it credited? Was it after he was circumcised, or before? It was not after, but before!

The removal of the foreskin of Jewish males was *prima facie* evidence of their covenant relationship with God. It proved they were God's special people. But it did not prove that they were righteous. And Abraham is proof of that because righteousness was credited to his account *before* he was circumcised. Fourteen years before! So circumcision didn't earn right standing with God for Abraham. Maybe there's hope for the uncircumcised (non-Jews).

[11]And he received the sign of circumcision, a seal of the righteousness that he had by faith while he was still uncircumcised. So then, he is the father of all who believe but have not been circumcised, in order that righteousness might be credited to them. [12]And he is also the father of the circumcised who not only are circumcised but who also walk in the footsteps of the faith that our father Abraham had before he was circumcised.

Circumcision didn't buy God's approval for Abraham. It was an evidence of his covenant relationship with God which was entered into by faith. Abraham then, became the father of a spiritual race, a people who walk in faith, circumcised or not. William Barclay says, "Paul has laid down the great principle that the way to God is not through membership of any nation, not through any ordinance which makes a mark upon a man's body; the only way to God is by the faith which takes God at His word, which makes everything dependent, not on man's achievement or record, but solely upon God's grace."[3] Credited righteousness is available to non-Jews!

[13]It was not through law that Abraham and his offspring received the promise that he would be heir of the world, but through the righteousness that comes by faith. [14]For if those who live by law are heirs, faith has no value and the promise is worthless, [15]because law brings wrath. And where there is no law there is no transgression.

Paul knew his Jewish readers wouldn't accept credited righteousness easily. So, another argument is in order: Abraham was not credited with righteousness because he was a keeper of law. They saw perfect law-keeping as the key to justification. And if anyone ever obeyed God's laws, surely Abraham did. Paul doesn't even address the fact that Abraham's obedience was imperfect. He just says God credits either by our faith or our law-keeping. As long as there is law, there will law-breaking. So it has to be by faith.

[16]Therefore, the promise comes by faith, so that it may be by grace and may be guaranteed to all Abraham's offspring — not only to those who are of the law but also to those who are of the faith of Abraham. He is the father of us all. [17]As it is written: "I have made you a father of many nations." He is our father in the sight of God, in whom he believed — the God who gives life to the dead and calls things that are not as though they were.

Yes, credited righteousness is for us all! Faith accesses God's unlimited bank account. The transaction is made once we demonstrate Abrahamic faith. And what kind of faith is that? Unequivocal confidence in and complete yieldedness to an outrageous God — One who defies His own laws of nature! (No wonder salvation by works has such wide appeal in the Christian religion today. It may be easier to achieve than Abrahamic faith!)

To show what complete abandonment of reason this faith required, Paul introduces one striking example from Abraham's life.

[18]Against all hope, Abraham in hope believed and so became the father of many nations, just as it had been said to him, "So shall your offspring be." [19]Without weakening in his faith, he faced the fact that his body was as good as dead — since he was about a hundred years old — and that Sarah's womb was also dead. [20]Yet he did not waver through unbelief regarding the promise of God, but was strengthened in his faith and gave glory to God, [21]being fully persuaded that God had power to do what he had promised.

Whew! Abraham took hope a step further. By adding unequivocal confidence and complete yieldedness to his hope, at age 100 he engaged in sexual intercourse with the woman who would seem to be the least likely to conceive in the whole country. He acknowledged that any results that came through his and Sarah's coitus was God's doing, not theirs. They were given a son, but that's not all. Abraham was credited with righteousness.

[22]This is why "it was credited to him as righteousness."

His quality of faith accessed God's giving spirit, and he was pronounced righteous, blameless, justified.

But where do we come in?

> [23]The words "it was credited to him" were written not for him alone, [24]but also for us, to whom God will credit righteousness — for us who believe in him who raised Jesus our Lord from the dead. [25]He was delivered over to death for our sins and raised to life for our justification.

We too can have justification on credit! We are asked to believe equally "unbelievable" things: that Jesus died a substitutionary death; that He came back to life in three days; and that that resurrection enabled God to legally discharge us from the sentence our sins deserved. Or to go back to the credited righteousness concept, if we can believe the unbelievable, and act on it like Abraham did, our faith will access the unlimited resources of God, and He will transfer enough to our account to clear our debits of sin.

Two other passages from Paul confirm that we have understood Romans 4 correctly. In I Corinthians 15:3 Paul states that the purpose of Jesus' death was "for our sins." Galatians 3:13 says He became "a curse for us." His was a substitutionary death. If He was sinless, yet died for our sins, then the benefit of His death was not for Himself but for us. However, that benefit had to be credited to our account some way. Our faith enables God to transfer the benefits of Jesus' death to our account. Credited righteousness is available to all who have Abraham-like faith. And may we never discount its quality!

Though Jesus said nothing about credited righteousness (apparently leaving that to Paul's written word), He used a related concept which corresponds perfectly. "For even the Son of Man did not come to be served, but to serve, and to give his life as a ransom for many" (Mark 10:45). Though the "ransom" concept puts us in a different setting, the transaction is identical. Ransom money is paid by someone else and the ransomed person in no way pays for or earns his freedom. It comes strictly from the generosity of someone else.

Peter acknowledged the concept in I Peter 3:18. "For Christ died for sins once for all, the righteous for the unrighteous, to bring you to God." Again, "the righteous for the unrighteous" accentuates the fact that the end result is not earned, but credited.

HOW "CREDITED" RIGHTEOUSNESS WORKS

Since it is a technical transaction that occurs here, perhaps a step-by-step explanation is in order.

1. God cannot legally justify sinners, any more than He allows us to (Deut. 16-17; 25:1-3).

2. We are all sinners.

3. So, God's first step was to accept Jesus' perfect life as a substitute sacrifice for man's sins.

4. He then credited that perfectly righteous sacrifice to the account of any sinner who would accept it by faith.

5. In exactly the same sense that Jesus "became sin" (by divine fiat), sinners "become righteous." If He was *really* a sinner, then we *really* are righteous. But of course He wasn't a sinner. Sin was only debited against His account. Righteousness is likewise credited to ours. Neither Jesus' nor our intrinsic value was affected by the transaction.

6. God's declaration that the repentant sinner is "not guilty" in no way removes the *fact* of his guilt, any more than declaring His righteous Son "guilty" establishes the *fact* of His guilt.

7. Credited righteousness gives the believer real power. Suppose the bank grants you a one million dollar line of credit. Does that make you a millionaire? Obviously not. But you would have the spending power of a millionaire, wouldn't you! (And if it were God who extended the credit, you wouldn't even have to pay it back.) It's somewhat like the power you feel behind the wheel of an automobile. You know the power isn't in you, but when used

by you it gets you where you want to go.

8. People who enjoy credited righteousness still sin. Abraham did, and so do we. But we are treated by God "as if" we were righteous, and therefore God gives us all the things that accrue to righteous people (gift of the Holy Spirit, sonship, guardian angels, repentance and forgiveness, etc.). We feel personally weak sometimes — because we are. But our faith in Jesus' justifying power rises and we are empowered. Call it "credit power" if you wish, or "as if" power, but with God behind it, it is very spendable.

9. This credited righteousness doesn't encourage loose living, but it gives us all the more reason to live obediently to the one who gave us this great gift. It is very spiritually ennobling to think of ourselves as "blessed . . . with every spiritual blessing in Christ" (Eph. 1:3).

10. Further, the absurdity of the fear that credited righteousness will be inimical to good works is seen in passages like II Corinthians 5:17 which alludes to both justification and sanctification. One is accomplished perfectly, outside us (justification), and the other is accomplished imperfectly, inside us and through us (sanctification). One is salvation, the other is the outgrowth of salvation. Why should they work against each other?

WHAT IS "INFUSED" RIGHTEOUSNESS?

This seems to be the proper place to discuss what appears to be an alternate way to explain credited righteousness, but is not. Infused righteousness is essentially a Roman Catholic view of credited righteousness. It says that righteousness is infused into a sinner's soul in the person of the Holy Spirit, thus making the person *actually* righteous. Sacramentalism, a related Roman Catholic doctrine, essentially teaches that the sacraments (baptism, communion, marriage, extreme unction, etc.) confer grace on the faithful, and thus make them actually righteous.

Much of Protestantism, even evangelicalism is moving into the error of infused righteousness. It may sound like a dispute over words, but it goes deeper than that. Infused righteousness makes salvation a matter of inner feelings. The focus of faith becomes internal, not historical.

Robert D. Brinsmead, editor of *The Christian Verdict*, through his writings over the past 15 years, has provided me with many excellent insights into Reformation theology, and specifically into the theology of grace. Mr. Brinsmead is an Australian sheep rancher, with a Seventh-day Adventist background. That means that whatever he writes about justification by faith through grace will be what he has learned from a combination of Scripture and Reformation theology, not from his Adventist training. I (and many of my colleagues in the Restoration Movement) have walked every step of the way with him from the hopelessness of justification by merit into the incredible thrill of justification by credit. I'm sorry to report that Mr. Brinsmead didn't stop there. His dislike for Adventism didn't end when he threw off their theology of grace. Today, and since 1984, he has moved away from Biblical authority for the Christian faith entirely, to where he now sees the Bible and the Christian religion as the enemies of the gospel of the resurrected Christ. However, believing his pilgrimage from a works to a grace theology to be a well studied and well explained one, I have made liberal use of his discoveries at this juncture in this volume.

Brinsmead expressed his vehement opposition to the concept of infused righteousness like this: "The New Testament message of justification by Christ's *imputed* righteousness means that we are accepted by a life lived and a work done outside of ourselves. The focus is not internal but external. It is Christ's experience that is of supreme importance to us. 'By His knowledge [His experience of bitter suffering and death] shall My righteous Servant justify many' (Isa. 53:11). 'We shall be saved by His life.' 'By the obedience of the One shall many be made righteous' (Rom.

5:10,19). All that is necessary for our acceptance and fellowship with God has been done. There is no need to chase after some elusive, mystical experience to give me status with God, with my fellows or with myself. Faith looks up and says, 'Mine are Christ's living, doing, and speaking, His suffering and dying; mine as much as if I had lived, done, spoken, and suffered, and died as He did.' *Luther's Works* (Muhlenberg Press: Philadelphia, 1957), Vol. XXXI, p. 297. Does this do away with Christian experience? Certainly not!"[4]

Following a supporting quotation from Luther, Brinsmead continues: "To learn that my acceptance with God is grounded on something entirely outside my own experience, brings the joy of sheer freedom. When faith grasps that my righteousness, security and real life are outside and above my own poor experience, I am liberated from all this internal groveling. Christ, my Representative, is accepted at the right hand of God; my Substitute is pleasing to God; His righteousness satisfies justice. By faith I am accepted, pleasing and righteous before God 'in the Beloved' (Eph. 1:6)."[5]

To get an idea of how serious a threat he considers this to be (and I concur), hear his warning: "It is not hard to demonstrate that Protestant revivalism, following in the tradition of Charles Finney, thinks very poorly of the great Reformation doctrine of justification. The inner experience of being saved or sanctified is overwhelmingly the center of almost all revivalism. It has become a kind of Protestant *gratia infusa*. Neither can anyone challenge the observation that Pentecostalism, neo-Pentecostalism and Campus Crusade are entirely devoted to a focus on internal experience. It is the old Roman Catholic theology of *gratia infusa* wrapped up in some evangelical trimmings."[6]

Salvation by experience does stand in opposition to salvation by credited righteousness. Brinsmead continues in the same context: "The apostles did not begin by proclaiming that their hearers could be saved by having Christ come into their hearts to produce an internal experience. Their focus was not an internal happening but an external happening. Christ lived, died and rose again for the sinner's justification. The apostles proclaimed an objective, historical reality." [op. cit., p. 26] He claims that the prostitution of Calvin's doctrine of the perseverance of the saints into today's "eternal security" error arises out of the same infused righteousness falsehood. "The doctrine of 'once-saved-always-saved' and a supreme emphasis on the new-birth experience generally go along together. What happens then is that people tend to look to their 'new birth' experience for assurance of eternal security. Instead of finding all their needed security by identifying themselves with the experience of Christ, they try to find their assurance through identifying with their own past experience of being 'saved.' This is one of the greatest single weaknesses of most evangelical Protestantism today." [op. cit., p. 28]. Passages like Acts 13:32-33,38-39 show the historical, external focus of justifying faith.

And if all this weren't frightening enough, try this on for size: "The absence of a central theology on justification by faith and the concentration on internal experience, are swiftly moving the Protestant movement into greater and greater harmony with Rome. Will the popular wave of revivalism succeed in turning the Protestant movement into 'an image to the beast'? In view of the prophecy of Revelation 13:13-14, we ought to give serious thought to where things are headed in the bond of union which is developing between Rome and the neo-evangelicals. The time has surely come for a 'new' Reformation which will restore the truth of the intercession of Christ's imputed righteousness to its rightful place."[7]

William Childs Robinson speaks to the issue from the standpoint of the Holy Spirit in his book, *The Reformation: A Rediscovery of Grace*. Though we offer a lengthy quote here, it is vital, worthy of your consideration.

Indeed, the enthusiasts so emphasized the sovereign freedom of the Spirit as to sever the connection between the mission of the

86

Spirit and the historical Christ. Their emphasis fell upon the sub-jective experience of the Spirit's mission of enabling the believer to appropriate the redemption wrought by Christ . . . God's objec-tive revelation of Himself is the work of Christ; God's subjective revelation that of the Spirit. The Spirit speaks not of Himself; He takes of the things of Christ and shows them to us, thus glorifying Him (John 16:13-24). In severing this connection, enthusiasm left itself with no objective criterion and exposed itself to the danger of unregulated spirituality. Instead of the saving knowledge of God revealed in Jesus Christ, it offered sundry varieties of religious experience. For, "where the Holy Spirit is sundered from Christ, sooner or later He is always transmuted in-to quite a different spirit, the spirit of religious man, and finally the human spirit in general." As Luther pointed out, the Holy Spirit is called witness, because He witnesses to Christ and to no other. The Apostles declare, "We preach not ourselves, but Christ Jesus the Lord" (II Cor. 4:5).

The true Holy Spirit comes from God, from the ascended Christ, and brings in His hand to shed abroad in our hearts the love of God revealed in the death of Christ for sinners. Conse-quently, it is not enough for a preacher to be a religious genius who fancies that by the recital of his own or some other's current experiences he can awaken the dormant possibilities of religion in the heart of the hearer. Nor is it sufficient to have a philosopher of religions presenting himself as an example of faith or as a possessor of human understanding, or even using the crucifixion of Jesus or the stoning of Stephen as a stimulus to bring an ex-istential decision to a student. While these may give the ap-pearance of devotion to Christ they do not locate the glory of salvation in His atoning work for us. Rather, the historical revela-tion of Christ is treated as the stimulus to a subjective spiritual ex-perience in the individual, not as itself the content of that ex-perience. The spiritualist individual experiences his conversion and the resultant spiritual glow rather than Jesus Christ and Him crucified, so that when he bears testimony, it is to speak of his newfound peace and happiness rather than to confess that Jesus is Lord.

Representatives of this school frequently declare that it is not the birth in Bethlehem but the re-birth in their hearts which counts, not the cross on Golgotha but their own dedication to live for eternity rather than time, not His bodily resurrection but their own faith in immortality. But true preaching from the Holy Spirit who came at Pentecost leads the hearer back through all his experiences to the Source of all true and proper experiences; that is, to Jesus Christ. It calls him to no other faith than faith in the Christ who was born in Bethlehem, who died for our sins on Calvary, who rose from the dead on the third day.[8]

All the above should not only help us see the inherent dangers of the doctrine of "infused righteousness," but it should serve also, by contrast, to make credited righteousness more clear in our minds. Mark my word, if we fail to take the distinction seriously, we will travel down the road to religious subjectivism. And in religious subjectivism there is no right and wrong. Whatever God is supposedly doing in one's heart cannot be denied — even if it is conflict with Scripture. And a phrase so innocuous sounding as "Receive Christ in your heart" (which is both non-Scriptural and anti-Scriptural) can be the first step down that road.

WHERE'S THE HOLY SPIRIT IN ALL THIS?

"Doesn't the Holy Spirit within us make us righteous?"someone asks. No, the saving "righteousness from God" (Rom. 3:21) and the work of the Holy Spirit in our hearts (Rom 5:5,17) are two separate gifts. The gift of righteousness, our initial salvation, is credited. True, the Holy Spirit may be said to move people to conviction and faith in the first place (John 16:8-11), but justification is the work of God through Jesus Christ. The gift of the Holy Spirit, God's continuing work in us, is imparted following our new birth (Acts 2:38; 5:32). The Holy Spirit does not make us acceptably righteous. He is given to us because we have been declared righteous.

His work within us is to stir us to righteous living, but none of the virtues of righteousness that He produces in us is sufficient to justify us. Fruits of the Holy Spirit are not the cause, but the result of our justification.

This work of the Spirit is called sanctification. Robert Brinsmead is in Robinson's corner on this one. "Certainly justification must be distinguished from sanctification. We must not transfer the property of one benefit to the other. But it is just as certain that they can never be separate. Union with Christ by saving faith results in justification as a judicial benefit, but it also results in sanctification as a moral benefit. One blessing cannot be enjoyed without the other. They are as related as light and heat. Where there is light, there will be heat."[9]

THE COLLAPSE OF THE "GOD'S PART VS. MAN'S PART" THEOLOGY

The popular presentation of salvation as being a cooperative effort of God and man is incongruous with Paul's presentation in Romans, no matter how neat a package it seems to be. Man's salvation is totally God's effort. With all due respect to whoever put together the first "God's Part — Man's Part" chart, and to those who have used it (myself included), it is a subtle effort to make sure faith, repentance, confession of faith, and baptism (acts done by converts in Acts) are not left out of the "plan of salvation," to make sure we know we have to do something. What we have to do to be credited with righteousness is believe (according to Rom. 4). Repentance, confession of faith and baptism are elements of obedient faith, in the tradition of Abraham and the other believers of Hebrews 11. This is obviously what Paul had in mind when he began Romans with the expression "the obedience that comes from faith" (Rom. 1:5). Melanchthon's famous quote says it clearly: "It is faith alone which saves, but the faith which saves is not alone." C.C. Crawford's chapter entitled, "Justification by Faith," in this *What the Bible Says About . . .* series, is an excellent elaboration on this. Let us who cling so tenaciously to baptism not do so to the point of jeopardizing our stand for credited righteousness. Whatever salvation we have is "God's Part." Period. Our faith is surely an effort, but it is our reception of the gift, not the *cause* of it.

REFORMATION AND POST-REFORMATION QUOTATIONS ON "CREDITED" RIGHTEOUSNESS

These are offered as elaboration on the points made in this chapter.

Martin Luther — "This then, is the amazing definition of Christian righteousness. It is the divine imputing or accounting for righteousness or unto righteousness because of faith in Christ or for Christ's sake. When the sophists hear this definition, they laugh, because they imagine righteousness to be a certain quality that is poured into the soul and then spread into all the parts of man . . . . Therefore this unspeakable gift excels all reason: God accounts and acknowledges him as righteous without any works who apprehends His Son by faith alone."[10]

John Bunyan — "I conclude then, our persons are justified, while we are sinners in ourselves. Our works, even the works of faith, are not otherwise accepted but as they come through Jesus Christ, even through his intercession and blood. So then, Christ doth justify both our person and works, not by way of approbation, as we stand in ourselves, or works before God, but by presenting of us to his Father by himself; washing what we are and have from guilt in his blood, and clothing us with his own performances."[11]

Bunyan — "Objection: But faith is said to be an act of obedience. Answer: And well it may; for it is the most submitting act that a man can do; it throweth out all our righteousness; it makes the soul poor in itself; it liveth upon God and Christ, as the almsman does upon his lord; it consenteth to the gospel, that it is true; it giveth God and Christ the glory of their mercy and merit; it loveth God for his mercy, and Jesus Christ for his service;

whatever good it doth, it still crieth, Hereby am I not justified; but he that justifieth me is the Lord. Well, but is there in truth such a thing as the obedience of faith? Then let Christians labour to understand it, and distinguish it aright; and to separate it from the law, and all man's righteousness; and remember, that it is a receiving of the righteousness of Christ, an accepting of the righteousness of Christ, and a trusting to these for life." [11]

Bunyan — "That this righteousness still resides in and with the person of Christ, even then when we stand before God thereby, is clear, for that we are said when justified to be justified 'in him.' — 'In the Lord shall all the seed of Israel be justified.' And again: 'Surely, shall one say, in the Lord I have righteousness,' &c. And again: 'For of him are ye in Christ Jesus, who is made unto us of God righteousness.' Isa. xiv. 24-25; I Cor. i. 30.

"Mark, the righteousness is still 'in him,' not 'in us'; even then when we are made partakers of the benefit of it, even as the wing and feathers still abide in the hen when the chickens are covered, kept, and warmed thereby . . . .

"It is absolutely necessary that this be known of us; for if the understanding be muddy as to this, it is impossible that such should be sound in the faith; also in temptation, that man will be at a loss that looketh for righteousness for justification in himself, when it is to be found nowhere but in Jesus Christ."[13]

Bunyan — ". . . if you do not put a difference between sanctification wrought by the man Christ without, and sanctification wrought by the Spirit of Christ within . . . you are not able to divide the word aright; but contrariwise, you corrupt the word of God, and cast stumbling-blocks before the people, and will certainly one day most deeply smart for your folly, except you repent."[14]

John Witherspoon, 18th century Protestant American clergyman — "On the contrary, the belief and acceptance of justification by the grace of God through the imputed righteousness of Christ makes men greater lovers of purity and holiness and fills them with a greater abhorrence of sin."[15]

H.A. *Ironside* published a book in 1912 entitled *Holiness: the False and the True*. In it he describes the ecstatic joy of his conversion, followed by his horror at striking a man in a fit of anger. The shock of his backsliding only a month after his conversion was exceeded only by the pain of an up-and-down Christian life thereafter. This kind of pain, says Ironside, was exacerbated by the teaching he was receiving which he described as follows: "Substantially, the teaching was this: When converted, God graciously forgives all sins committed up to the time one repents. But the believer is then placed in a lifelong probation, during which he may at any time forfeit his justification and peace with God if he falls into sin from which he does not at once repent. In order, therefore, to maintain himself in a saved condition, he needs a further work of grace called sanctification. This work has to do with sin the root, as justification had to do with sins the fruit.

"The steps leading up to this second blessing are, firstly, conviction as to the need of holiness (just as in the beginning there was conviction of the need of salvation); secondly, a full surrender to God, or the laying of every hope, prospect and possession on the altar of consecration; thirdly, to claim in faith the incoming of the Holy Spirit as a refining fire to burn out all inbred sin, thus destroying in toto every lust and passion, leaving the soul perfect in love and as pure as unfallen Adam. This wonderful blessing received, great watchfulness is required lest, as the serpent beguiled Eve, he deceive the sanctified soul, and thus introduce again the same kind of an evil principle which called for such drastic action before.

"Such was the teaching; and coupled with it were heartfelt testimonies of experiences so remarkable that I could not doubt their genuineness, nor that what others seemed to enjoy was likewise for me if I would fulfill the condition.

"One aged lady told how for forty years she had been kept from sin in thought, word, and deed, Her heart, she declared, was no longer 'deceitful above all things, and desperately wicked,' but was as holy as the courts of heaven, since the blood of Christ had washed away the last remains of inbred sin. Others spoke in a similar way, though their experiences were much briefer. Bad tempers had been rooted out when a full surrender was made. Evil propensities and unholy appetites had been instantly destroyed when holiness was claimed by faith. Eagerly I began to seek this precious boon of holiness in the flesh. Earnesty I prayed for this Adamic sinlessness, I asked God to reveal to me every unholy thing, that I might truly surrender all to Him. I gave up friends, pursuits, pleasures — everything I could think of that might hinder the incoming of the Holy Ghost and the consequent blessing. I was a veritable 'book-worm,' an intense love for literature possessing me from childhood; but in my ignorant desire I put away all books of pleasurable or instructive character, and promised God to read only the Bible and holiness writings if He would only give me 'the blessing.' I did not, however, obtain what I sought, though I prayed zealously for weeks."

Ironside describes his ultimate reception of the "second blessing" in an arroyo near Los Angeles on a Saturday evening. His spiritual "high" lasted several weeks before he fell, and he picked himself up time and time again before he began to have serious doubts about this holiness theology. He wrote: "And now I began to see what a string of derelicts this holiness teaching left in its train. I could count scores of persons who had gone into utter infidelity because of it."

He finally describes his own retreat into infidelity, at least isofar as the holiness teachings he had believed were concerned. But deliverance came at last. "Little by little, the light began to dawn. We (the author and an acquaintance) saw that we had been looking within for holiness, instead of without. We realized that the same grace that had saved us at first alone could carry us on. Dimly we apprehended that all for us must be in Christ, or we were without a ray of hope . . . . The great truth was getting a grip on me that holiness, perfect love, sanctification, and every other blessing, were mine *in Christ* from the moment I had believed, and mine forevermore, because all was of pure grace. I had been looking at the wrong — all was in another Man, and in that Man for me! But it took weeks to see this."[16]

G.C. Brewer — "Long ago I heard a preacher, whom I respected and loved, say: 'If there is any such a thing as imputed righteousness taught in the Bible, I have never seen it.' Along about the same time of life I heard another preacher, regarded by me as a great man, say this: 'You hear people talk of God's righteousness or Christ's righteousness being imputed to a man — of the righteousness of Christ covering a man like a garment, etc. This is all false doctrine. The Bible says, 'He that doeth righteousness is righteous, even as he is righteous' (I John 3:7); and David says, 'All thy commandments are righteousness.' So you see that a man who does the commandments of God is righteous — no one else is. You can have no righteousness except the righteousness that *you do*.'

"These statements impressed me, and after I began to preach I made the same statements and quoted the same Scriptures to prove them! May the Lord forgive us all and let his righteousness not only supply our lack of righteousness, but also our lack of understanding of his word.

"I learned the truth on this point by studying Paul. I found it without help when I began examining Romans — not to find something to offset what someone else teaches, but to see what Romans teaches. I know other men who have had the same experience that I have had in this respect."[17]

R.L. Kirkpatrick — "The great theological issue of the 16th century Reformation was not Luther's 'Justification by Faith' versus Rome's 'Justification by Works.' Justification by faith was and still is a Roman Catholic doctrine. But the difference between Luther and Rome was in the manner in which the sinner received the 'righteousness' of God which effected his salvation. Luther maintained that the sinner was justified by faith in the *act* of Jesus on the cross, and that God's righteousness was *imputed* on the basis of that faith. Rome taught that God's righteousness was a 'grace' to be received by *infusion* into the sinner's soul, and which changed the quality of the soul. Luther taught that the redemptive act was God's *work in Christ* on the cross for the benefit of mankind, whereas, Rome taught that God's redemptive act of the cross allowed the Holy Spirit to *work in mankind.*"[18]

R.L. Kirkpatrick — "If peace and unity are ever to become a reality in our time, or at any other time, it will have to come through the restoration of the doctrine of 'Justification by Faith,' which naturally includes the teaching of imputed righteousness. The only doctrine powerful enough to rally God's forces on earth to unite all believers in one body will have to be the teaching that removes the attention of mankind from himself and gives it to Jesus and his suffering on the cross — from man's own personal righteousness through good works to the work of Christ and his righteousness . . . .

"I believe that most brethren agree that perfect righteousness is a prerequisite for salvation. Now, if we could agree that man, having once sinned can never of himself possess true righteousness, then we should have no problem with the idea that the righteousness which saves is the righteousness which Christ shares (or imputes) to us, since the prerequisite is not found in us but in him. When these facts are realized, it seems now only a matter of thinking the subject through to its conclusion.

"It is immaterial whether we say that man is saved by the 'merit of Christ's righteousness,' or that man is saved by the 'imputation of Christ's perfect obedience to the sinner's account.' They both say the same thing. Jesus 'earned' true righteousness by his perfect obedience, and since perfect righteousness is a prerequisite for eternal life, and since it is not found in man, then there is no other way for sinners to be saved other than through the imputation of Christ's merited righteousness to the sinner's account."[19]

R.L. Kirkpatrick — "Our brethren (and especially our brethren) have fallen headlong into the abyss of subjectivism, moral renewal, goodness in the heart, as the means of justification. Few, if any, of our people would use the familiar 'Holiness' expression 'Open up your heart and let Jesus come in and save you,' but they will say, 'Obedience to God's commandments makes us righteous because it is God's righteousness that we do.' Or, 'We are saved by God's grace because His grace gave us commandments to obey.' The thought in each case is that an inward change in one's moral state takes place and that acceptance before God is on the basis of this moral change. The 'Holiness' idea is that Jesus comes into the heart in some mysterious or miraculous way to change its moral condition and their concept is actually more preferable to our own. They at least give Christ credit for the change. But our people have even rejected the indwelling Spirit who might conceivably bring about such a change. This means that our people live with the concept that they stand before God solely on the merit of their *doing* good works. This is the kind of thinking that belongs to the dark ages, and to which the Protestant family seems bent on returning."[20]

Albert Barnes — "It is not meant that the righteousness of Christ is transferred to them, so as to become personally theirs — for moral character cannot be transferred — nor that it is infused into them, making them personally meritorious — for then they could not be spoken of as ungodly; but that Christ died in their stead, to atone for their sins, and is regarded by God to have died; and that the results or benefits of his death are so reckoned or imputed to believers as to make it proper for God to regard and treat them as if they had themselves obeyed the law; that is, righteous in his sight."[21]

Charles Hodge — "To impute righteousness is the apostle's definition of the term justify. It is not making men inherently righteous, or morally pure, but it is regarding and treating them as just. This is done, not on the ground of personal character or works, but on the ground of the righteousness of Christ."[22]

SUMMARY

The following question and answer chart gets to the heart of the credited righteousness theology as presented by the Apostle Paul.

Christ	**Believer**
Q. Why did Jesus, who did no sin, receive the penalty for sin — death?	*Q. Why do believing sinners, who have done no righteousness, receive the reward of righteousness — eternal life?*
A. Because our sins were accounted to Him.	A. Because Christ's righteousness is accounted to us.
Q. Does this mean that He was actually sinful in Himself?	*Q. Does this mean that we are actually righteous in ourselves?*
A. No. He was treated as if He were actually sinful.	A. No. We are treated as if we were actually righteous in ourselves.
Q. Were the sins that were placed on Him real sins, or was this whole drama merely an act?	*Q. Is the righteousness that is placed upon us real righteousness, or is this transaction merely an act?*
A. The sins on Him were real. The weight of them caused Him great anguish and crushed out His life.	A. The righteousness placed upon us is real. It is "even the righteousness of God," bringing joy to us as we pass from death into life.
Q. When sin was imputed to Jesus, how did this affect His standing with God?	*Q. When righteousness is imputed to us, how does this affect our standing with God?*
A. It caused God to reject Him, to withdraw His presence from Him, for God cannot dwell with sinners.	A. It causes God to draw us into His presence, for He loves to have fellowship with the righteous.
Q. Would it have been necessary for Jesus to have some sin in Him to merit such utter rejection by God?	*Q. Would it be necessary for us to have some righteousness in us to merit such complete acceptance by God?*
A. No. It was sufficient that our	A. No. It is sufficient that the righ-

sins only be imputed to Him.

teousness of Christ only be imputed to us.

Q. Then, in the sight of God, was imputed sin equal to innate sin as far as Christ's standing with God was concerned?

A. Yes, and even more so, for the sins of the whole world were imputed to Him.

Q. Then, in the sight of God, is imputed righteousness equal to innate righteousness as far as our standing with God is concerned?

A. Yes, and even more so, for the righteousness of the Godhead is imputed to us.

Used by permission of Verdict Publishers, "The Imputed Righteousness of Christ," by Hayden King, *Present Truth*, Vol. 2, No. 1, p. 23.

Endnotes

1. Ethelbert W. Bullinger, *A Critical Lexicon & Concordance to the English and Greek New Testament*, Zondervan Publishing House, Grand Rapids, MI, 1975.

2. *A Commentary on Romans*, The Banner of Truth Trust, London, 1835/1972, p. 106.

3. *The Letter to the Romans, Translated and Interpreted by William Barclay*, The Westminster Press, Philadelphia, 1975, p. 64.

4. "Justification by Faith and the Current Religious Scene," *Present Truth*, 8/73, pp. 16,17.

5. Ibid., p. 18.

6. Ibid., pp. 25-26.

7. Ibid., p. 29.

8. William Childs Robinson, *The Reformation: A Rediscovery of Grace*, Wm. B. Eerdmans, Co., Grand Rapids, MI, 1962, pp. 171-173.

9. "Justification by Faith and the Current Religious Scene," *Present Truth*, 8/73, p. 27.

10. *What Luther Says*, Vol. 3, Compiled by Ewald M. Plass, Concordia Publishing House, St. Louis, 1959, pp. 1229-1230.

11. *The Complete Works of John Bunyan, Vol. I*, "Justification by an Imputed Righteousness," The National Foundation for Christian Education, Marshallton, DE, 1968, p. 404.

12. Ibid., p. 406.

13. Ibid., p. 383.

14. *The Riches of Bunyan*, The American Tract Society, New York, NY: 1850, p. 140.

15. William C. Robinson, "John Witherspoon on Justification," *Present*

Truth, Vol. 6, No. 2.

16. H.A. Ironside, *Holiness: the False and the True*, Loizeaux Brothers, Neptune, NJ, 1912, pp. 7-40.

17. *Gospel Advocate*, January 24, 1946.

18. "Balancing Law & Gospel," *Ensign*, Vol. IV, No. 9.

19. "Justification and Imputed Righteousness," *Ensign*, Vol. V, No. 12.

20. "Justification: The Legal and Moral Aspects," *Ensign*, Vol. X, No. 1.

21. *Notes on the New Testament, (Romans),*Baker Book House, Grand Rapids, MI, 1972, p. 103.

22. *A Commentary on Romans*, The Banner of Truth Trust, London, 1835/1972, p. 115.

4

SOLA

Four Latin slogans have come to characterize Reformation theology. Their origin seems to have been somewhat evolutionary, though they particularly epitomize Martin Luther's views of grace. They are: *sola gratia, sola Cristo, sola fide,* and *sola scriptura.* The phrases collectively express the basic elements of the Biblical doctrine of justification by faith, but the word *sola* expresses exclusivity in each case. *Sola* means "alone," or "only." Reformers wanted it clearly understood that justification was by grace alone, through Christ alone, by faith alone, and based on Scripture alone. These slogans were to stand in powerful defiance of Roman Catholic theology which essentially denies them.

Martin Luther felt especially the need to employ the word "alone" to set justification by faith in clear contradistinction to justification by meritorious works. He felt it so strongly that he inserted the word in his own German translation of the Bible at Romans 3:28. Such a practice is deserving of criticism to be sure and he has gotten his share over it. However, his defense is deserving of notice.

> In Romans iii, I know right well that the word *solum* was not in the Greek or Latin text . . . . It is a fact that these four letters *s-o-l-a* are not there . . . . At the same time . . . the sense of them is there and . . . the word belongs there if the translation is to be clear and strong. I wanted to speak German, not Latin nor Greek, since I had undertaken to speak German in the translation. But it is the nature of our German language that in speaking of two things, one of which is admitted and the other denied, we use the word 'only' along with the word 'not' or 'no.' So we say, 'The farmer brings *only* grain and no money;' 'No, I have no money now, but *only* grain;' 'I have *only* eaten and not drunk;' 'Did you *only* write it, and not read it over?' There are innumerable cases of this kind in daily use.
>
> In all these phrases it is the German usage, even though it is not the Latin or Greek usage, and it is the way of the German language to add the word 'only,' in order that the word 'not' or 'no' may be more complete and clearer. To be sure, I can also say, 'The farmer brings grain and no money,' but the words 'no money' do not sound as full and clear as if I were to say, 'The farmer brings *only* grain and no money.' Here the word 'only' helps the word 'no' so much that it becomes a complete, clear German phrase . . . .
>
> I was not only relying on the nature of the languages and following that when, in Romans iii, I inserted the word *solum*, 'only,' but the text itself and the sense of St. Paul demanded it and forced it upon me. He is dealing, in that passage, with the main point of Christian doctrine, viz., that we are justified by faith in Christ, without any works of the law, and he cuts away all works so completely, as even to say that the works of the law, though it is God's law and His Word, do not help us to righteousness. He cites Abraham as an example and says that he was justified so entirely without works, that even the highest work, which had then been newly commanded by God, before and above all other works, namely circumcision, did not help him to righteousness, but he was justified by faith, without circumcision and without any works at all. So he says, in Chapter iv, 'If Abraham was justified by works, he may glory, but not before God.' But when works are so completely cut away, the meaning of it must be that faith alone

justifies, and one who would speak plainly and clearly about this cutting away of all works, must say, 'Faith alone justifies us, and not works.' The matter itself, and not the nature of the language only, compels this translation . . . .

I am not the only one or the first to say that faith alone justifies. Ambrose said it before me, and Augustine and many others; and if a man is going to read St. Paul and understand him, he will have to say the same thing and can say nothing else. Paul's words are too strong; they endure no works, none at all; and if it is not a work, it must be faith alone. How could it be such a fine, improving inoffensive doctrine, if people were taught that they might become righteous by works, beside faith? That would be as much as to say that it was not Christ's death alone that takes away our sins, but that our works, too, did something toward it; and it would be a fine honoring of Christ's death to say that our works helped it and could do that which He does, and that we were good and strong like Him. This is of the devil, who cannot leave the blood of Christ without abuse![1]

It is not hard to see the strain through which Luther put that passage, is it? The argument sounds not too different than that summoned by Jehovah's Witness officials to defend their rendering of "a god" in John 1:1. However, Luther was coming from genuine agony of soul during this period, not a desire to protect a religious empire. Here's how he described his restlessness:

I greatly longed to understand Paul's Epistle to the Romans and nothing stood in the way but that one expression, 'the justice of God,' because I took it to mean that justice whereby God is just and deals justly in punishing the unjust. My situation was that, although an impeccable monk, I stood before God as a sinner troubled in conscience, and I had not confidence that my merit would assuage him. Therefore I did not love a just and angry God, but rather hated and murmured against him. Yet I clung to the dear Paul and had a great yearning to know what he meant.

Night and day I pondered until I saw the connection between the justice of God and the statement that "the just shall live by his faith." Then I grasped that the justice of God is that righteousness by which through grace and sheer mercy God justifies us through faith. Thereupon I felt myself to be reborn and to have gone through open doors into paradise. The whole of Scripture took on a new meaning, and whereas before the "justice of God" had filled me with hate, now it became to me inexpressibly sweet in greater love. This passage of Paul became to me a gate to heaven . . . ."[2]

The "pendulum effect" in Biblical interpretation is certainly present in those two quotations from Luther and it is lamentable. But since we are all reactionary to some degree in our handling of Scripture, surely we can at least understand it in Luther.

More important than examining history, these four phrases do have their roots in Scripture. They are not rooted merely in some Biblical collage of unrelated passages (a practice in which we indulge ourselves occasionally, sometimes called "proof-texting," that festering sore on our hermeneutics). All four phrases appear at the very point in Romans where Paul takes off the wrappers on God's marvelous gift of justification by grace.

"ALONE" IN ROMANS 3:21-26

[21]But now a righteousness from God, apart from law, has been made known, to which the Law and the Prophets testify. [22]This righteousness from God comes through faith in Jesus Christ to all who believe. There is no difference, [23]for all have sinned and fall short of the glory of God, [24]and are justified freely by his grace through the redemption that came by Christ Jesus. [25]God presented him as a sacrifice of atonement, through faith in his blood. He did this to demonstrate his justice, because in his forbearance he had left the sins committed beforehand unpunished — [26]he did it to demonstrate his justice at the present time, so as to be just and the one who justifies the man who has faith in Jesus (Rom. 3:21-26).

Though we might deny Luther the right to insert "only" in verse 28, we can comfortably affirm that salvation is by

GRACE ALONE.

We are "justified freely by his grace" (v. 24a). Salvation, the restoration of our standing and fellowship with God, is either God's gift or God's payment of wages for work we have done. Either He gave it or we earned it. Paul says it is grace alone in Romans 4:1-8. "So too, at the present time there is a remnant chosen by grace. And if by grace, then it is no longer by works; if it were, grace would no longer be grace" (Rom. 11:5-6).

Prevailing scholarship in Luther's day described justification by grace as the act of God infusing qualities into man which made him acceptable to God. But Luther couldn't find these in himself no matter how godly he tried to be. From his studies of Romans he came to understand that grace was God's decision to accept the unacceptable, to love the unlovely (on the basis of their faith, of course).

Fred P. Thompson Jr. puts Alexander Campbell solidly behind Luther on this point. "Alexander Campbell was a true son of the Reformation at this point. He never mistook the response of man to the overtures of God as purely autonomous action. The 'Christian System,' as he termed it, is a system of grace, not law. Law works by human effort. Grace works by divine gifts. Thus Campbell spoke of the 'means' of grace, every one of which has been determined by God himself. He states emphatically that, *the means of each and every Grace promised and vouchsafed to man are a portion of that Grace itself* (*Millennial Harbinger*, 1859, p. 132). In the same context Campbell refers to the grace of faith, the grace of repentance, the grace of confession, and the grace of baptism. None of these gifts of God may correctly be regarded as law."[3]

Any theology that construes salvation as some sort of cooperative effort between God and man is false. Whatever man does in reference to his salvation may be seen as responsive, not causal. Jesus, God's gift, is the sole cause. Our own description of the reception process (Chapter Two), Luke's descriptions of conversions in Acts of Apostles, and James' description of saving faith in his own chapter two do not negate this conclusion. (Further discussion of these issues will be given later, under Sola Fide.)

Edward Fudge said it well: "At this point we have but two choices. Either God saves us because we deserve it (debt), or He saves us although we do not deserve it (grace). There is no middle ground. It is finally a matter of grace or merit. There can be no compromise."[4]

If I seem to be "beating a dead horse" on this issue, please recognize that we in the Restoration are accused of doing the same thing when we get on the subject of baptism. If we are not guilty in the latter case, let me plead not guilty in this case. Without a doubt the undergirding strength of the first eight chapters of Romans is grace. Though our discovery may not be as profound as Luther's was, still give us our rejoicing!

CHRIST ALONE

Our relationship to Christ is restored *"through the redemption that came by Christ Jesus"* (v. 24b). On its face, hardly anyone who claims to be a Christian would deny this. But the deeper issue (discussed in more depth in Chapter Three) is the fact that our salvation was accomplished *outside* us, by the death of Christ. This is what the writer is saying in Hebrews 13:9-13 in comparing the death of Jesus to the Old Testament sin offering: "And so Jesus also suffered outside the city gate to make the people holy through his own blood. Let us, then, go to him outside the camp . . ." (Cf. Rom. 5:9; Gal. 1:4; 2:20).

On this point Luther laid a great burden on us all. "What we are concerned about is that we may recognize and accept this forgiveness . . . . The sun continues to shine and to radiate light even though I close my eyes. Just so this mercy seat or forgiveness of sin stands forevermore even though I fall."[5]

FAITH ALONE

"This righteousness from God comes through faith in Jesus

Christ to all who believe" (v. 22). As previously noted, faith has always been the means to a restored relationship with God (Rom. 4:3). But despite the centuries of trying to gain God's favor by law-keeping, and failing, the Jews were hardly ready to give up and trust Christ. And neither are we.

No matter how much lip service we give to salvation by grace through faith (Eph. 2:8), we struggle to please God sufficiently by our pious hearts and virtuous deeds. We offer those (as though they were *our* fruits), when what He wants is our absolute trust and yieldedness. Salvation is not by faith *plus* works (Rom. 4:4-5), nor by dead faith (James 2:20), but by "faith expressing itself through love" (Gal. 5:6b).

If it is only by faith, then the critical issue becomes: What exactly is faith? Several Old Testament illustrations are used in Paul's writings to leave no doubt in any mind that faith is an intellectual decision, based on some evidence, that finds expression in loving obedience to God. Melanchthon is supposed to have said: "It is faith alone which saves, but the faith which saves isn't alone." If this strikes a blow at our pride, so be it.

The reception process described in Chapter Two, which has us reaching out to receive forgiveness and justification, is merely the completion of the transaction, else we are saved without our compliance, perhaps even against our will. That process requires faith, turning against sin, and dying to sin. It is illustrated in life situations in Acts of Apostles (believing, repenting, accepting immersion) so we cannot miss it. To further reinforce that these acts (if they may be called that) are not meritorious in the sense of purchasing or earning our salvation, Fred P. Thompson Jr. comments: "Faith is His gift. Not in any Calvinistic predestinarian sense, but as the divinely ordained response to the preaching of the Word. Persons come to faith when they hear the Word of God. Back of the preaching, back of the Word is the gracious God whose providence initiated the entire series of acts which bring about reconciliation. Repentance is His gift. Baptism is His gift. (Perhaps if we spoke of baptism more often in this way we

107

would encounter less resistance from our denominational friends. Much preaching of baptism comes perilously close to being law.) The Holy Spirit is His gift. A godly life is certainly the gift of grace.

"Does this mean that we have no responsibility for our own decision? Does grace make human action irrelevant? By no means. Nothing God does exempts us from authentic personal response. It is *my* decision to confess Christ, to repent, to receive baptism, that is crucial for my destiny. Nevertheless, I would have no power to take the first step had God not preceded my action by His matchless grace."[6]

But what do you do with James 2:24 which says, "You see that a person is justified by what he does and not by faith alone"? No wonder Luther called the book of James "an epistle of straw" in the preface to his New Testament translation of 1522. He even offered his doctor's beret to anyone who would reconcile Paul and James on the subject of faith and works. But Luther can keep his beret. He did some of his own reconciling. " 'Faith,' he wrote, 'is a living, restless thing. It cannot be inoperative. We are not saved by works; but if there be no works, there must be something amiss with faith.' "[7] J.E. Sagebeer comes from a different angle: "By works, Paul means works of law; James means by works, works of faith."[8]

Paul says that justification comes only as a gift received by faith; James says it comes by works, not by faith. What is the answer?

1. It is clear that both are discussing the same concept, justifying faith. They both use Abraham to illustrate it.

2. In James 2:14 James is doing exactly what Paul did in Romans 4 — defining and illustrating the kind of faith which justifies. They agree perfectly that it is not a dead faith, but one that expresses itself in deeds.

3. Some might argue that James is talking about faith that operates in the Christian life, not justifying faith. But 2:24 makes it clear that it is justifying faith. "You see that a person is justified by what he does not by faith alone." Whether it is the kind that

brings us to initial justification or faith that operates in the Christian life seems to be a moot point. Is there any difference? Is the faith of Ephesians 2:8 any different from what goes into the works of verse 10? We would be hardpressed to demonstrate that in Scripture. Both require deeds to be valid.

4. Thus, Paul's and James' statements might be harmonized like this: We see that justification only comes by faith, but only by a faith that works. No works with your faith = no faith; no faith = no justification at any time in your quest for God.

THE SCRIPTURES ALONE

There should be more consensus on this one than any of the four, but perhaps it is only the appearance of consensus. *"But now a righteousness from God, apart from law, has been made known, to which the Law and the Prophets testify"* (v. 21). If our salvation is accomplished outside us (which assures an objective, not subjective relationship), then the word of that salvation is outside us (for the same reason). Salvation is an objective transaction, rooted only in the Word.

Surely one of Satan's cleverest coups has been to internalize salvation to the point that the Bible becomes excess baggage. People talk about their "salvation experience," and it is usually just that: first, an experience, and secondly, their own custom-made one. Usually people are reluctant to lay their own "salvation experience" alongside the experiences that Inspiration has put in the Bible, in the Book of Acts in particular (because it alone chronicles conversions after the blood of Christ was shed). It is because they don't compare at all. They have operated on feelings, not on the Word. I once read a rather detailed description of one of these subjective, emotions-only conversions. The writer described the burning in the pit of his stomach, the goose-bumps, the fever, etc., and then God gloriously came into his heart and saved him, he said. But I had already diagnosed his case as

109

stomach flu. An antibiotic and bed rest would have cured it within a few hours.

If people don't need God's Word to find out what salvation is and how to receive it, then they won't need it to find out how saved people are to live. No wonder there's such loose living among professing Christians!

No, people who haven't heard the Word cannot be saved. Romans 10:17 says they can't. "Consequently, faith comes from hearing the message, and the message is heard through the word of Christ." Only on Judgment Day will the extent of this fraud be revealed.

Surely we owe a great deal to the Pre-reformers and to Luther and his band of Reformers who are responsible for these statements of Christian faith. Kostlin calls Luther "the first great, clear preacher of the righteousness of faith sent to the Christian church since the days of the apostle Paul."[9] "He is one of the few great prophets of the Christian church, and his greatness is overwhelming . . ." wrote Paul Tillich.[10]

Endnotes

1. Hugh T. Kerr, ed., *A Compend of Luther's Theology*, The Westminster Press, Philadelphia, 1943, pp. 110-112.

2. Roland H. Bainton, *Here I Stand*, Abingdon, Nashville, 1950, p. 65.

3. "By Grace Alone," *Envoy*, Emmanuel School of Religion, May, 1979.

4. *Four Gospel Slogans*, 1978.

5. Ewald M. Plass, ed., *What Luther Says*, Vol. II, pp. 705-706.

6. "By Grace Alone," *Envoy*, Emmanuel School of Religion, May, 1979.

7. Roland H. Bainton, *Here I Stand*, Abingdon, Nashville, 1950, p. 331.

8. Augustus H. Strong, *Systematic Theology*, Judson Press, Valley Forge, PA, 1907, p. 852.

9. Julius Kostlin, *The Theology of Luther*, pp. 77-78.

10. Carl E. Braaten, ed., *A History of Christian Thought*, Simon & Schuster, New York, NY, 1967, p. 227.

5

GRACE AND LAW

Hardly anybody would argue that the impact of the religion of Jesus Christ is on the decline as it nears the end of its second millennium. Competing ideologies are gathering a larger share of the market of world attention. The TV moguls would tell us that our ratings are down. Materialism, secularism, communism, and even Islam are stealing our audience. On a closer, more personal level, the movement to unite the denominations and restore the first century church has nearly ground to a halt. One of our own sociologists/strategists even predicted our demise as a movement unless some radical changes occur.

With the risk of sounding simplistic tatooed on my forehead, let me humbly suggest that renewal in the Restoration Movement, yea in all of Christianity should begin with a restudying of the issue of grace and law. Historically, nothing has numbed parts of the body of Christ any more totally than two fundamental errors surrounding grace and law. They are:

111

Grace without law and
Law without grace.

Neither error is quite as simple as the wording used above, but for now they make two tidy titles.

Having laid a solid foundation from Scripture in earlier chapters regarding the absolute adequacy of grace, we need now to completely understand where law comes into both justification and sanctification. When it is given its rightful place in God's scheme grace shines all the more brightly and so do we. Christians really become the "light of the world," and "a city set on a hill" (Matt. 5:14). When Paul asked, "What shall we say, then? Shall we go on sinning so that grace may increase?" (Rom. 6:1), he asked the question, the answer to which will determine the vitality of the Christian faith. Surely nobody would say yes to Paul, at least not to his face. But the fact of the matter is that many Christians live lives that say yes. And then some who answer no resoundingly become so scrupulous about not breaking God's laws that they make law-keeping their hope of salvation. So you have antinomianism (living without the law) and legalism (seeking salvation through law-keeping) trying to pass themselves off as butter when they're margarine. They may look like like butter; taste like butter; smell like butter; but no self-respecting cow would claim them. Neither will God claim these abuses of grace. And for reasons they often aren't even aware of, large segments of humanity won't buy the product either.

In keeping with the wisdom of the ages and sages, let us appeal first to Scripture to understand the relationship of law to grace. We begin with Him of whom cousin John said, "For the law was given through Moses; grace and truth came through Jesus Christ" (John 1:17). And then we consult the one who said, "By the grace of God I am who I am" (I Cor. 15:10).

JESUS: LAW-KEEPER OR LAW-BREAKER?

Jesus' view of the Law of Moses and His relationship to it are

112

most interesting. Behaviorally, He evidenced a radically different attitude than other religious luminaries of the day. Consider a few examples:

In Matthew 12:1-8 He allowed His disciples to break the law by picking grain on the Sabbath, and took their side against their critics. His rationale? Strict adherence to law is never to be preferred over mercy and consideration of the human condition.

In Mark 7:1-23 He allowed His disciples to ignore laws of ceremonial washing and answered the Pharisees' protests with teaching that put righteousness on the basis of having a right relationship with God, not on the basis of compliance with external codes.

He healed on the Sabbath several times, each time by design, apparently hoping for, and receiving, the castigation of teachers of the law. He used those altercations as forums for explaining His radical views about the law.

In Matthew 23, just before He was silenced by His enemies, He verbally scourged the teachers and Pharisees for acts which seemed so law-abiding and which enhanced their standing with the common people. Jesus pulled their rug of self-righteousness right out from under them and left them standing on the dirty floor of their evil hearts. They were law-abiding all right, but they lacked a heart for the law.

Thus, the guardians of the law were surprised when they heard Jesus say and watched Him do the following:

—"Do not think that I have come to abolish the Law or the Prophets; I have not come to abolish them but to fulfill them. I tell you the truth, until heaven and earth disappear, not the smallest letter, not the least stroke of a pen, will by any means disappear from the Law until everything is accomplished" (Matt. 5:17-18).

—Begin His ministry in the synagogue in Nazareth by reading from Isaiah.

—Send a cleansed leper to the priest to have his healing validated legally (Luke 5:14).

—Observe the Passover with His disciples at His final meeting with them before His arrest and crucifixion (Luke 22:7ff).

So, it is not surprising to read that He came both to "establish" (Matt. 5:17; Rom. 3:31) and to "abolish (Eph. 2:15; Col. 2:14; Gal. 3:9-24) the law. Can we not see that the law was established, i.e., given its rightful place in God's system, by being abolished and fulfilled? How about illustrating it like this?

> A father has a little son whom he wants to become considerate of others. He imposes upon his child arbitrary rules he is expected to perform (e.g., lights out at 8 p.m., ask permission to leave the yard, eat all vegetables before dessert, etc.). When his son reaches maturity, however, the father tells him that he is old enough to live by the principle of considering others and is no longer bound by childhood regulations. The son is now old enough to put out the lights and do many other things at his own discretion. We may ask, has the father abolished the law or not? With regard to its real spirit and intent, his law has not changed. But with regard to its form, it has changed. So it was with the law of God. God's ideals for man were not changed by the coming of Christ. But the Mosaic form of the law, adapted to the needs of a community in its spiritual minority, was replaced by a form suited to the age of the gospel.[1]

CHRIST, OUR NEW LAW

And what is this new form? It is not a new set of laws given by Christ, a kind of "Christian code," but Christ himself. In his Sermon on the Mount He repeatedly positioned himself and His words alongside the Law of Moses, but superior to it. The law said so-and-so, ". . . but I tell you . . . ." The following passages illustrate that He himself as well as New Testament writers saw Him as God new law:

> *John 8:12* — "I am the light of the world. Whoever follows me will never walk in darkness, but will have the light of life."
> *John 10:10* — "I have come that they might have life, and have it to the full."

John 10:28 — "I give them eternal life, and they shall never perish."

John 14:6 — "I am the way — and the truth and the life. No one comes to the Father except through me."

Acts 3:22, the words of Peter — "For Moses said, 'The Lord your God will raise up for you a prophet like me from among your own people; you must listen to everything he tells you. Anyone who does not listen to him will be completely cut off from among his people . . . .' "

I Corinthians 1:23-24 — But we preach Christ crucified . . . Christ the power of God and the wisdom of God.

Colossians 3:11 — Here there is no Greek or Jew, circumcised or uncircumcised, barbarian, Scythian, slave or free, but Christ is all, and is in all.

I John 2:7 — Whoever claims to live in him must walk as Jesus did.

What do these passages say collectively? Following, listening, and walking — these are all expressions of the same truth, that Jesus is our new law. And then these passages lead us to many others which clearly show that His attitudes, behavior, and ethics in His relationships are designed to be the source for ours. Here are a few. Notice how His life becomes the basis for Christian living.

John 13:34 — "A new commandment I give you: Love one another. As I have loved you, so you must love one another."

The only thing new about this commandment was the quality of love: "As I have loved you." Jesus set himself up as the new law on loving.

Romans 12:1 — Therefore, I urge you, brothers, in view of God's mercy, to offer yourselves as living sacrifices, holy and pleasing to God — which is your spiritual act of worship.

The expression "in view of God's mercy" refers specifically to Jesus' sacrifice on the cross. That act of His is to animate our

Christian lives.

> *I Corinthians 6:19-20* — Do you not know that your body is a temple of the Holy Spirit, who is in you, whom you have received from God? You are not your own; you were bought with a price. Therefore glorify God with your body.

The price was Jesus' death. Again this act is seen as the guiding principle of Christian behavior.

> *I John 4:9-11* — This is how God showed his love among us: He sent his one and only Son into the world that we might live through him. This is love; not that we loved God, but that he loved us and sent his Son as an atoning sacrifice for our sins. Dear friends, since God so loved us, we also ought to love one another.

Our law on love is God and His Son's demonstration of love on Calvary.

> *Ephesians 5:25* — Husbands, love your wives, just as Christ loved the church and gave himself up for her.

There's a law to live by, husbands: Jesus' love and sacrifice for the church.

> *Colossians 3:1,5* — Since, then, you have been raised with Christ, set your hearts on things above, where Christ is seated at the right hand of God. Put to death, therefore, whatever belongs to your earthly nature . . . .

Paul urged us to conquer evil using the power that raised Jesus from the dead.

> *Colossians 3:13* — Bear with each other and forgive whatever grievances you may have against one another. Forgive as the Lord forgave you.

Jesus is our rule of forgiveness.

116

Romans 15:7 — Accept one another, then, just as Christ accepted you, in order to bring praise to God.

Jesus' attitude and conduct become our law in this vital area of human relations.

I Timothy 1:9-11 — We also know that the law is made not for good men, but for lawbreakers and rebels, the ungodly and the sinful, the unholy and irreligious; for those who kill their fathers or mothers, for murderers, for adulterers and perverts, for slave traders and liars and perjurers — and for whatever else is contrary to the sound doctrine that conforms to the glorious gospel of the blessed God, which he entrusted to me.

Bad conduct is not measured only in relation to the law, but by the "glorious gospel of the blessed God," which is the good news about Jesus' life, death and resurrection on our behalf.

Such an ethical system may seem unorthodox, or awkward, but it is the new covenant system. While human nature yearns for some expression of God's requirements for our behavior in a tightly codified form, we're really not given that in the new covenant. The old already proved that we're incapable of measuring up to it anyhow. So we're given a Man, a perfect man, to be our law. If you remember, this is Charles M. Sheldon's thesis in his Christian classic work *In His Steps*. His characters found that trying to answer every ethical dilemma with the question "What would Jesus do?" was a very demanding, but exciting and authentic adventure in Christian living.

Oh how the quest for orthodoxy haunts us! Could it be that we've taken a wrong turn in this quest? Paul began his letter to the Ephesians by using the expression "in Christ" ten times in the first thirteen verses. Obviously their security rested in being "in Christ" more than in being right about everything. Can't we reverse our emphasis?   Now we appeal to the experiential expert on law and grace.

117

"PAUL, I'VE GOT QUESTIONS ABOUT LAW"

The apostle Paul knew that people who had lived all their lives seeking justification by law would see it as a security blanket and would not shed it easily. Or if they did, they might become dangerously antinomian. So he discussed the issue of law and grace in several of his epistles, and when these discussions are collated, a marvelous harmony emerges. Grace and law are perfectly compatible; both the legalist and the antinomian are convinced. Following are questions about the relationship of law and grace answered from Paul's epistles.

Q. *Is everyone under law?*

A. Yes, according to Romans 2:12-16. "All who sin apart from the law will also perish apart from the law, and all who sin under the law will be judged by the law. For it is not those who hear the law who are righteous in God's sight, but it is those who obey the law who will be declared righteous. (Indeed, when Gentiles, who do not have the law, do by nature things required by the law, they are a law for themselves, even though they do not have the law, since they show that the requirements of the law are written on their hearts, their consciences also bearing witness, and their thoughts now accusing, now even defending them.) This will take place on the day when God will judge men's secrets through Jesus Christ, as my gospel declares." Jews received codified laws of God in the form of "The Law" (Matt. 7:12; Luke 10:26; John 1:17, et al.). They were amenable to it, and would be judged by it (v. 12).

Gentiles (all non-Jewish people) "are a law for themselves," that is, they have the same basic requirements contained in the Law of Moses, but "written in their hearts."

Behavior, with reference to both forms of law, was God's judging point. Jews had correct behavior spelled out; Gentiles had the intuition to learn God's laws and consciences to validate or invalidate their behavior (v. 13,15).

Q. *Could a person be justified (declared righteous) by law-*

118

keeping?

A. *Technically*, yes, according to Romans 2:13b and Philippians 3:9, which say, "But it is those who obey the law who will be declared righteous," and "Not having a righteousness of my own that comes from the law." Presumably, the same was true of Gentiles who kept the "law . . . written on their hearts" (Rom. 2:15,26). But Galatians 2:16 states the *reality* of it: "Know that no man is justified by observing the law."

Q. *If so technically, how?*

A. Here's where reality strikes. A person could only be declared righteous by the law if he kept it *perfectly*. Obedience must be complete, without any failures. Quoting from the Old Testament Paul writes, " 'Cursed is everyone who does not continue to do everything written in the Book of the Law' " (Gal. 3:10b). Galatians 5:3 states, "Again I declare to every man who lets himself be circumcised that he is obligated to obey the whole law." Implied in seeking justification by law-keeping was total, perfect compliance.

Q. *Did anyone ever attain perfect obedience to law?*   A. For sure, Israel didn't. "But Israel, who pursued a law of righteousness, has not attained it" (Rom. 9:31). Neither did Gentiles. "We have already made the charge that Jews and Gentiles alike are all under sin" (Rom. 3:9b). Paul's familiar conclusion settles it once for all: "For all have sinned and fall short of the glory of God" (Rom. 3:23). Law and sin are inseparable. For this reason Paul states unequivocally throughout his letters that "Clearly no one is justified before God by the law" (Gal. 3:11a. See also Gal. 2:1,16; 3:21, et al.).

Christians who advocated justification by keeping the Law of Moses didn't make it either. Speaking of such Christians, Paul wrote: "Not even those who are circumcised obey the law . . . ." (Gal. 6:13a). That was why their heresy was so patently ridiculous. They advocated something they knew was impossible.

The most graphic illustrations of people's failure to obey law perfectly are found right in Romans. Gentiles' failure to live up to their God-given moral intuition resulted in the ugly specter of godlessness, debauchery and perversion described in chapter 1:18-32. Jews became arrogant and judgmental toward these Gentile law-breakers, all the while indulging in discreet (and some not so discreet) forms of law-breaking. "Now you, if you call yourself a Jew; if you rely on the law and brag about your relationship to God; if you know his will and approve of what is superior because you are instructed by the law; if you are convinced that you are a guide for the blind, a light for those who are in the dark, an instructor of the foolish, teacher of infants, because you have in the law the embodiment of knowledge and truth — you, then, who teach others, do you not teach yourself? You who abhor idols, do you rob temples? You who brag about the law, do you dishonor God by breaking the law? As it is written: 'God's name is blasphemed among the Gentiles because of you' " (Rom. 2:16-24).

Only Jesus kept it perfectly. No charge of law-breaking was ever substantiated against Him. In that sense, it could be said that He fulfilled it (Matt. 5:17), and met God's requirements of justice. "Can any of you prove me guilty of sin?" He challenged His enemies (John 8:46a). Many passages proclaim His sinlessness.

"The law made nothing perfect," the writer of Hebrews states (Heb. 7:19a). That settles it.

Q. *What was one prominent failure of people who thought they could be justified by law-keeping?*

A. Elevating some laws over others, and thinking that in so doing, God overlooked the laws they considered less important. An example: Circumcision, since it was an outward sign of a law-keeper and a tremendous source of Jewish pride, became more important to them than moral laws which non-Jews often kept as a matter of habit. All sorts of incredible mythology surrounded circumcision, such as the story that should a Jew be condemned to hell a special angel waited at the gates to *uncircumcise* him before he went in. But Paul wrote, "Circumcision has value if you observe the law, but if you break the law, you have become as

though you had not been circumcised. If those who are not circumcised keep the law's requirements, will they not be regarded
as though they were circumcised? The one who is not circumcised physically and yet obeys the law will condemn you who, even
though you have the written code and circumcision, are a
lawbreaker" (Rom. 2:25-27).

Justification by law-keeping promoted religious snobbery
("They want you to be circumcised that they may boast about
your flesh," Gal. 6:13b), and was despised by the Almighty. Paul
spoke of the confidence in the flesh that accrued from his circumcision and Jewishness, and he quickly reduced it to "loss" in
Philippians 3:4-7. God did not consider physical circumcision important at all (Rom. 2:29; 3:27). Religious snobbery was a trait
Jesus had tried to paint ugly with his parable of the Pharisee and
the tax collector in Luke 18:9-14. In it He has the admitted
scoundrel going home "justified before God" and not the self-
righteous, rigid lawkeeper who suffered from a case of "terminal
arrogance." Later He gave these same Pharisees a long (and
painful) lecture on their bad habit of elevating some of God's laws
over others (Matt. 23). Not only did they make wrong choices
about what was important and what was not, the idea that you
can do that was wrong.

Q. *Was there any advantage to having the Mosaic law and all
that went with it?*

A. Paul said yes in Romans 3:1-2. "What advantage, then, is
there in being a Jew, or of what value is there in circumcision?
Much in every way! First of all, they have been entrusted with the
very words of God." The Law of Moses was "the very words of
God." Those who received it knew exactly what God expected.
No guesswork. Speaking of his countrymen, the Jews, he said,
"Theirs is the adoption as sons; theirs the divine glory, the
covenants, the receiving of the law, the temple worship and the
promises. Theirs are the patriarchs, and from them is traced the
human ancestry of Christ, who is God over all, forever praised!
Amen" (Rom. 9:4-5). Count them — eight distinct advantages

the Jews had, and one was the Law of Moses.

Q. *Does "law" in scripture always refer to the Law of Moses?*

A. No. In Romans 3:21 ("But now a righteousness from God, apart from law, has been made known, to which the Law and the Prophets testify.") both forms of law are included: the written and the law of the heart. In most New Testament passages the context will usually dictate the kind of law which is meant. However, in discussions of justification it doesn't matter, for no one can keep any code of laws fully and thereby be declared righteous. Laws and sins are inseparable; sins and righteousness are incompatible.

Q. *"Do we, then, nullify the law by this faith?" (Rom. 3:31a).*

A. The question is: if righteousness is found in believing, not in law-keeping, then isn't the law a waste of time? "Not at all! Rather we uphold the law" (v. 31b). Faith and law seem antagonistic or at least incongruous. But no, says Paul. And he produces the case of Abraham (Rom. 4), who illustrates that faith has always worked with law, but has always ranked above it. No Mosaic code was in force when Abraham lived, therefore his justification couldn't have come through law-keeping. In fact, Abraham wasn't even perfect in keeping the simple, personal laws God gave him. All his spiritual benefits came by faith: "It was not through law that Abraham and his offspring received the promise that he would be heir of the world, but through the righteousness that comes by faith" (Rom. 4:13). Genesis 15:6 had said the same thing centuries before Paul wrote it. If Abraham's justification had to come by law-keeping, he had none. And neither have we.

Commenting on Romans 3:31 J.W. McGarvey says, "It (law) was given to show that no man could attain salvation by self-righteousness, and we establish it by showing that it accomplished the end for which it was framed. We have shown that it was of no service to justify men; but of great service to convict them of sin, and thus lead them to Christ for justification."[2] Don DeWelt summarizes Paul's question and answer thus: "Is it now of no use? No, God forbid. Shall we, simply because the law has been proven valueless in securing justification, believe that it does not serve some other good purpose? 'No, not at all,' says Paul. 'I preach and teach the real value of the law which is to point out right and wrong, thus I establish the law's true purpose.' Moses E. Lard has said, 'Law may be wholly useless for one purpose and yet indispensable for others.' "[3]

Q. *Then what purpose did the Law have?*

A. Several, actually. First, it is clear from Old Testament books which tell of the giving and administration of the Law of Moses that its obvious purpose was to govern a people. Jews, who were the recipients of these God-given statutes, would be the actors on God's stage. The play bill would read: God & His People. The story line would be based on verses like Deuteronomy 30:15-16. "See, I have set before you today life and prosperity, and death and destruction. For I command you today to love the Lord your God, to walk in his ways, and to keep his commands, decrees and laws; then you will live and increase, and the Lord your God will bless you in the land you are entering to possess." And the grand climax of the drama would be the birth of the Messiah into this civilized, godly society. We know it didn't work out exactly like that (God was developing counterplots). Whatever may be said negatively about Israel, when it followed God's laws even reasonably well, it was a civilized, godly society, fit to give birth to cosmic royalty. Paul recognized this obvious purpose of the law: "If you know his will and approve of what is superior because you are instructed by the law" (Rom. 2:18). Though spoken satirically, it was nevertheless true. The law informed people exactly what God's will was. "Thou shalt nots" and "thou shalts" give clear direction for living. But they also set in motion something else.

Secondly, as Paul looks at the Law of Moses in the larger context of God's scheme of grace, he sees another, loftier purpose: to wrench from mankind any hope of justification through law-keeping, and having done this to point to Jesus Christ as our only hope for justification. Theologians call this "the second use of the law." Luther saw God grinding down Old Testament Jews with laws so that they might give up on attaining righteousness by law-keeping and be ready to hear about righteousness as God's gift. Many passages in Paul's letters treat this purpose:

Romans 3:19 — Now we know that whatever the law says, it says to those who are under the law, so that every mouth may be silenced and the whole world held accountable to God.

There's accountability. Once told "thou shalt" or "thou shalt not," man was held to answer for his deviations therefrom.

Romans 5:13-14 — For before the law was given, sin was in the world. But sin is not taken into account when there is no law. Nevertheless, death reigned from the time of Adam to the time of Moses, even over those who did not sin by breaking a command, as did Moses, who was a pattern of the one to come.

Law took any vagaries out of right and wrong. Sin had always been around, because God spoke His will from the Garden of Eden forward. But law defined it. To illustrate: you might sense it is improper to park on a narrow thoroughfare where no other vehicles are parked, but all it takes is a NO PARKING sign to convince you that it is wrong. I Timothy 1:9-10 puts into words what we sense: "Laws are only troublesome to lawbreakers." Laws hardly exist, or we hardly know they exist unless we break them. Then they break us. Romans 7:7-8,12,14 and 16 make this same point.

Romans 4:15 — Because law brings wrath. And where there is no law there is no transgression.

The condition previously described sets up wrath, or conflict between the lawgiver and the subject. "The power of sin is the law," I Corinthians 15:56 says. "The power or poisonous strength of sin is found in the curse which the law pronounces upon the sinner," says J.W. McGarvey.[4]

Galatians 3:19-25 — What, then, was the purpose of the law? It was added because of transgressions until the Seed to whom the promise referred had come. The law was put into effect through angels by a mediator. A mediator, however, does not represent just one part; but God is one. Is the law, therefore, opposed to the promises of God? Absolutely not! For if a law had been given that could impart life, then righteousness would certainly have come by the law. But the Scripture declares that the whole world is a prisoner of sin, so that what was promised, being given through faith in Jesus Christ, might be given to those who believe. Before this faith came, we were held prisoners by the law, locked up until faith sould be revealed. So the law was put in charge to lead us to Christ that we might be justified by faith. Now that faith has come, we are no longer under the supervision of the law.

This is the grand passage on the "second use of the law." Once we all stand condemned as law-breakers, unable to be justified by law-keeping, we're ready for some other answer. The law couldn't impart life to us, but it could make us so convicted of sin and fearing punishment that we would be ready to hear about justification by faith in Jesus. It was indeed our "schoolmaster," as some older translations render in verse 24.

Hebrews 10:1-10,28 — The law is only a shadow of the good things that are coming — not the realities themselves. For this reason it can never, by the same sacrifices repeated endlessly year after year, make perfect those who draw near to worship. If it could, would they not have stopped being offered? For the worshippers would have been cleansed once for all, and would no longer have felt guilty for their sins. But those sacrifices are an annual reminder of sins, because it is impossible for the blood of bulls and goats to take away sins. Therefore, when Christ came into the world, he said: "Sacrifice and offering you did not desire, but a body you prepared for me; with burnt offerings and sin offerings you were not pleased. Then I said, Here am I — it is written about me in the scroll — I have come to do your will, God." First he said, "Sacrifices and offerings, burnt offerings, and sin offerings you did not desire, nor were you pleased with them" (although the law required them to be made). Then he said, "Here I am, I have come to do your will." He sets aside the first to establish the

125

second. And by that will, we have been made holy through the sacrifice of the body of Jesus Christ once for all. Anyone who rejected the law of Moses died without mercy on the testimony of two or three witnesses.

The whole Jewish legal system, including ceremonial laws, served to teach about the Christian system by employing shadows, of which the Christian system was the reality. Consequently, an honest Jew was a prime candidate for justification by faith and a transfer from the Jewish to the Christian system.

Galatians 2:19 — sums up this "second use of the law" perfectly: For through the law I died to the law so that I might live for God.

"After trying to find justification through perfect law-keeping, and seeing myself a dead duck, I gave up on it, and found my justification through the perfect work of Christ," Paul is saying.

Q. *Are Christians still under the Law in any sense?*

A. Romans 6:14 and Galatians 3:25 both say no. "For sin shall not be your master, because you are not under law, but under grace." "Now that faith has come, we are no longer under the supervision of the law." Neither of these verses means to suggest that Christians are antinomian, not bound by any law, able to live as they please.

The sixth chapter of Romans answers the hypothetical question: "Shouldn't we sin all the more so God's grace in forgiving us will shine all the more brilliantly? Especially since we are not under law anyway?" Paul's answer appeals to the symbolism of our baptismal death. "What shall we say then? Shall we go on sinning so that grace may increase? By no means! We died to sin; how can we live in it any longer? Or don't you know that all of us who were baptized into Christ Jesus were baptized into his death?" (vv. 1-3). Further on he urges us to learn to think of ourselves as "dead to sin but alive to God in Christ Jesus" (v. 11). Throughout the chapter he speaks openly about sin and its danger to the Christian. In chapter seven he describes the constant warfare Christians wage against sin. And the existence of sin demands law.

The Galatians 3:25 context is justification by faith, not law, and in that sense, law no longer has the same relationship to us it once had. We were under it until it delivered us safely to faith in Christ. Now its involvement in our justification is finished.

F.L. Lemley calls it "legal grace," this concept that Christians must make passing grades in order to achieve and hold their standing in God's kingdom. "Legal grace," he explains, "extends grace only to those who keep the law perfectly." To show how impossible this is he writes, "According to this 'law' one must remember, confess, repent and pray for each individual sin, or else one unforgiven sin on our record in the judgment will condemn us to hell. Ask the ones indoctrinated in this 'law' what they would do if they knew they had only five more minutes to live and you will likely get the answer, 'I would pray to be sure all my sins were forgiven.' " He concludes his thoughts by saying,"May God deliver us from this doctrine of 'legal grace' which forever keeps us in doubt of our salvation, not knowing if we are saved or lost until the judgment. Let's quit frustrating the grace of God (Gal. 2:21) and see the glory of salvation to the uttermost. God has declared us 'Not Guilty!' (Rom. 8:33)."[5] And I might add, we *are* guilty, but have been credited with righteousness, enabling God to declare us "Not Guilty."

An unforgettable experience early in my ministry put the first glitch in my own system of legalism. While calling house to house in Tulsa, Oklahoma, I met a man who engaged me in a discussion of my probationary view of Christian living. (He believed in eternal security, I in eternal insecurity.) I defended it rather well (I thought), expressing my conviction that one must be completely right in his beliefs and conduct if he expects to go to heaven. Then he shorted my circuit with the following scenerio:

Suppose you had come into Christ and lived an exemplary Christian life from youth to old age. Now at age 80 you're standing on a street corner, preparing to cross, when a sudden gust of wind blows up the skirt of a pretty young lass standing near you. You turn to glance, step off the curb, in front of an oncoming car, and are killed by the impact. Would you go to heaven?

Now that I'm getting closer to that age, I can appreciate that his story is not wholly hypothetical. I can also appreciate better the fact that none of us can orchestrate the time and means of our death. Plus, I also understand and appreciate grace much more than I did then. But, at the time, I was forced by my probationary views, to consign the poor devil (or angel become a devil in an instant) to hell where he belonged.

That story haunted me for years. I didn't know if I wanted to serve a God like that. Finally, I reexamined Scripture and found that He "longs to be gracious" (Isa. 30:18), and that He has made an "abundant provision of grace and of the gift of righteousness" (Rom. 5:17). I found that mercy toward us sinners is perhaps more His disposition than is punishment: "As a father has compassion on his children, so the Lord has compassion on those who fear him; for he knows how we are formed, he remembers that we are dust" (Psa. 103:13-14).

What we are talking about here is sometimes labeled "Galatianism," the concept that it takes the gospel of grace *plus* something else to get us to heaven. For the Galatians it was plus circumcision, observance of the law, and observing Jewish holidays. Paul called this a "different gospel — which is really no gospel at all" (Gal. 1:6b-7a). The gospel of legalism just has different elements: grace *plus* proper worship, *plus* proper church organization, *plus* proper holiness, *plus* proper performance, *plus* whatever else we choose to add. Don't misunderstand, there is proper worship, proper obedience, proper church organization, etc., but none of these obtain our justification. How long will it take us to see this truth and drop all these *pluses* from the gospel we preach?

Q. *"Shall we sin because we are not under the law but under grace?" (Rom. 6:15a).*

A. "By no means!" (v. 15b). As stated above, the very existence of sin implies law (Rom. 4:15 also). While we no longer seek justification by the failed method called law-keeping, we seek to obey God's will as demonstrated in His Son as a love lifestyle since we are now new creatures, freed from sin's power (Rom. 6:7). Obedience to God becomes a whole new ballgame, played for entirely different purposes, Chapter Six discusses those.

After ridding the gospel of its law-based accessories, and issuing a proclamation of freedom to the Galatians, Paul warned: "But do not use your freedom to indulge the sinful nature; rather serve one another in love" (Gal. 5:13b). That very verse contains two commands, or laws. Are we to ignore them?

Q. *What does Paul mean about the law having "authority over a man only as long as he lives"? (Rom. 7:1).*

A. The first six verses of Romans 7 are an argument proving that Christians are no longer under law. He uses a common illustration from widowhood. His application is as follows: Once a husband (the old person seeking justification by law-keeping) dies, the wife (the new person, a Christian) is no longer legally bound to him, but may marry another (Christ) and live with him. And life with the new husband is radically different from the old: "We serve in a new way of the Spirit, not in the old way of the written code" (v. 6).

Q. *What was wrong with the law?*

A. Nothing. "So then, the law is holy, and the commandment is holy, righteous and good" (Rom. 7:12). The problem lay with humans. "For what the law was powerless to do in that it was weakened by our sinful nature, God did by sending his own Son in the likeness of sinful man to be a sin offering . . . because the sinful mind is hostile to God. It does not submit to God's law, nor can it do so" (Rom. 8:3,7). The holy, righteous and good law would make us perfect except for our sinful nature.

Critics of the law abound. Robert D. Brinsmead, in an article entitled, "Jesus and the Law," finds seven inadequacies in the Law of Moses. They are: "1. The unwritten code was an inadequate vehicle to communicate the will of God . . . . 2. The law stimulates that which it forbids . . . . 3. The law is an inadequate agent for the conviction of sin. Instead of convicting people of sin, it readily becomes a vehicle of self-congratulation and self-satisfaction . . . . 4. The law too easily lends itself to ethical distortions . . . . 5. The law tends to become too impersonal . . . . 6. The law is a middle wall of partition (Eph. 2:14-15). While the law kept the Jew separate, it caused hostility between Jew and Gentile . . . . 7. Subjection to the law is a form of slavery. It is here that Paul's criticism of the law is sharpest."[6]

His arguments have merit in all seven cases. However, they aren't arguments setting Paul against himself in Romans 7:12. Surely it is not hair-splitting to see them as "inadequacies," as Brinsmead does, but to stop short of calling them proofs that the law is unholy, unrighteous and evil.

Hebrews 7:18-19 appears to contradict the point being made here: "The former regulation is set aside because it was weak and useless (for the law made nothing perfect), and a better hope is introduced, by which we draw near to God." How can the "weak and useless" of this passage harmonize with "holy, righteous and good" of Romans 7:12? The words used by the Hebrews writer have to be seen as words of *comparison*, not contrast. The law was "weak and useless" in comparison to the gospel. The law was "holy, righteous and good" in itself, but in comparison to the gospel it finished a poor second.

One has to seek to justify a bias against the Law of Moses in particular, and law in general, to come away from an inductive study of the subject convinced that God made a mistake in lawgiving which He repaired in the covenant of grace. That hardly seems compatible with the Almighty's character.

Q. *Paul spoke of "another law" at work in himself in Romans 7:23. What was that?*

130

A. Here, in verses 21 and 25, and in 8:2, "law" might be understood as "principle," or "dynamic," the more generic use of the Greek word *nomos*. Abbott-Smith assigns the following meaning to *nomos* in these verses: "of a force or influence impelling to action"[7] Specifically, it was the condition he had been describing in earlier verses in chapter seven, i.e., "When I want to do good, evil is right there with me" (v. 21b). It was his basic fallen nature which struggled against his spiritual nature and often delivered him over to the law of sin, as a law-breaker. His conclusion about the whole matter is in Romans 7:25b. "So then, I, of myself, in my mind am a slave to God's law, but in my sinful nature a slave to the law of sin." For certain it doesn't refer to a new set of laws by which he would be judged now that the old Law of Moses had been fulfilled.

Q. *What is "the law of the spirit of life" in Romans 8:2?*

A. Based on Abbott-Smith's (and other reputable lexicographers') definition, it refers to the "force or influence impelling" him to action in the Christian life, namely the Holy Spirit. And since the Holy Spirit now uses Scripture to "force or influence" Christians to godly living, in that very generic sense the epistles may be seen as containing law. Law in the influencing sense, not in the justifying or condemning sense.

Q. *How had Jews of Paul's time generally failed in the area of law and grace?*

A. "What then shall we say? That Gentiles, who did not pursue righteousness, have obtained it, a righteousness that is by faith; but Israel, who pursued a law of righteousness, has not attained it. Why not? Because they pursued it not by faith but as if it were by works" (Rom. 9:30-32a). Their failure had been in seeking justification by law-keeping and not by faith in Jesus.

Q. *Explain how "Christ is the end of the law" (Rom. 10:4) if He said He didn't come to destroy the law.*

A. Jesus is the end of man's search for justification. Righteousness is now available to everyone who believes in Him. He "fulfilled" the law in the sense of providing what it could not

— legal justification. In no way can that be construed as destroying the law.

Q. *How can love be the fulfillment of the law when love is a new covenant concept?*

A. At issue here is Romans 13:8-10: "Let no debt remain outstanding, except the continuing debt to love one another, for he who loves his fellow man has fulfilled the law. The commandments, 'Do not commit adultery,' 'Do not murder,' 'Do not steal,' 'Do not covet,' and whatever other commandment there may be, are summed up in this one rule: 'Love your neighbor as yourself.' Love does no harm to its neighbor. Therefore love is the fulfillment of the law." Love is far more than a new covenant concept. It underlies all divine law. It is the generic behind all specifics. Since Jesus Christ is God's love in bodily form, He fulfills the law, as He Himself stated in Matthew 5:17.

Q. *Paul says in I Corinthians 9:20 that he is not under law. How do you harmonize that with his obvious law-keeping described in the Acts of the Apostles?*

A. All the references to Paul's Sabbath/synagogue preaching experiences can be understood as evangelistic strategy. He went where Jews, supposedly the people most prepared to accept Christ, would be found. His circumcision of Timothy was preacher strategy, as was his non-circumcision of Titus (Acts 16:3; Gal. 2:3). Other references to Jewish religious observance (Acts 21:20-26, etc.) find explanation in the fact that Paul was a Jew. Yet he understood that keeping a vow or a holiday had nothing to do with justification by law-keeping. He was not under law for justification purposes. Law meant everything to him at one time, but now it had nothing to do with justification. He clearly disassociated himself from any merit of righteousness one might seek in such activities: "Therefore do not let anyone judge you by what you eat or drink, or with regard to a religious festival, a New Moon celebration or a Sabbath day. These are a shadow of the things that were to come; the reality, however, is found in Christ" (Col. 2:16-17).

Furthermore, let it be said that to believe that Jews who became Christians instantaneously dropped their Old Testament beliefs and practices is a very Pollyanna view. Obviously it didn't work that way (Gal. 4:10). We get very disturbed about the former Catholic who still displays his crucifix. Paul wouldn't. His concern seemed not to be so much with the carryover of beliefs and practices in themselves as with the inevitablitiy that some would seek justification in them. One of those carryovers was circumcision. The Jerusalem council (Acts 15) didn't find anything wrong with Christians being circumcised. But they found a lot wrong with requiring circumcision for salvation.

Q. *How serious is it to seek justification by law-keeping? Isn't it just another way to heaven?*

A. "I do not set aside the grace of God, for if righteousness could be gained through the law, Christ died for nothing" (Gal. 2:21). If that were true for first century Christians trying to be justified by God's laws given at Sinai, is it any less true of Christians in the twentieth century trying to be justified by law-keeping? Are New Testament regulations, even ones given by our Lord, any more sacred? Does the fact that Christ gave them instead of Moses somehow change us so we can keep them? Do better laws make better people? If one could not be justified by the Law of Moses, can he be justified by the Law of Christ? We're back to an earlier answer: No man can ever be justified by keeping laws, because he can never keep them perfectly. At issue is not by whom, to whom, or when laws were given, but whether law-keeping itself can ever achieve justification for sinners. Justification is by faith, not by law-keeping *of any sort.*

Justification by law-keeping denies the presence and work of the Holy Spirit, God's agent in our sanctification, according to Galatians 3:5. "Does God give you his Spirit and work miracles among you because you observe the law, or because you believe what you heard?" A powerful rhetorical question!

Then too, passages like Galatians 5:18; 3:24-25; Romans 6:14; and 10:4 seem to have a generic application when they

133

declare that no man will ever be justified by law-keeping. Cannot that be seen as a universal axiom, applying to any and all people and any and all law? I believe so.

Yes, it's serious. Paul's solemn declaration in Galatians 5:4 applies to any and all law, not just the Decalogue and the 600-plus other regulations that made up the Mosaic Law. "You who are trying to be justified by law have been alienated from Christ; you have fallen away from grace." Galatians 3:21 affirms that "if a law had been given that could impart life, then righteousness would certainly have come by law." Law does not now nor has it ever imparted life. Can Scripture be any more plain?

Q. *What is the "law of Christ" in Galatians 6:2 and I Corinthians 9:21? Is it connected with James' "perfect law" in James 1:25 and 2:12?*

A. The law of Christ was to love (Luke 10:27; Matt. 22:36-40; John 15:12). All God's dealings with humanity are summed up in the commands to love God and our neighbors. If Jesus had intended that we make of all the New Testament a mini-law book (as compared to the Old), He surely would have said so. At the very least He would not have answered their questions in the above passages so generally.

Some would like to view the new law of Christ (love) as a new and improved version of the Mosaic Law. Where's the improvement? Or are we to believe that it is the people to whom they are given who are new and improved? The truth is, there was nothing wrong with the old law (God was its author), and the basic nature of man hasn't changed under this new law (we are still unable to keep law perfectly). The old law couldn't justify and neither could a new one.

So, God chose to provide justification freely, unconditionally, and then to give His creatures "a force or influence impelling them to action" called love. This "law of love" would draw them to their Creator and to the rest of creation better than any Ten Commandments ever could.

Maybe the best feature of this rule of love is the fact that it was played out before us in living color. "My command is this: Love each other as I have loved you" (John 15:12). His life is the force impelling us to right living. Robert D. Brinsmead, in his piece entitled, "The Superiority of the Law of Christ," takes us powerfully to Christ himself as our new covenant law.

> While Judaism made the written code its food and drink, Christian faith cannot do this. Said Paul, "For to me, to live is Christ" (Phil. 1:21). "Christ . . . is your life" (Col. 3:4). "I have been crucified with Christ and I no longer live, but Christ lives in me. The life I live in the body, I live by faith in the Son of God, who loved me and gave himself for me" (Gal. 2:20). If rules, laws, principles, programs, denominational policies or even theology take the place of devotion to the living Christ, we have mistaken the way of Judaism for the way of Christianity.
>
> In Judaism an elaborate tradition provided casuistic rules for all the concrete situations of life. Thus, a law-abiding Jew could always know how he had to act. The New Testament believer, however, does not have an elaborate code or blueprint to tell him how to act in every situation. In Christ, however, he has the supreme revelation of God's will for mankind. While the Jew found his pattern for living by following the Torah, the Christian finds his pattern for living by following Christ. Jesus declared, "I am the light of the world. Whoever follows me will never walk in darkness, but will have the light of life" (John 8:12).[8]

As to the distinctions between the two laws, the writer to the Hebrews twice quotes Jeremiah 31:31-34, and it is to that same passage Paul alludes in his letter to the Corinthians.

> *Hebrews 8:8-13* — But God found fault with the people and said: "The time is coming, declares the Lord, when I will make a new covenant with the house of Israel and with the house of Judah. It will not be like the covenant I made with their forefathers when I took them by the hand to lead them out of Egypt, because they did not remain faithful to my covenant, and I turned away from them, declares the Lord. This is the covenant I will make with the house of Israel after that time, declares the Lord. I will put

135

my laws in their minds and write them on their hearts. I will be their God, and they will be my people. No longer will a man teach his neighbor, or a man his brother, saying, Know the Lord, because they will all know me, from the least of them to the greatest. For I will forgive their wickedness and I will remember their sins no more." By calling this covenant "new," he made the first one obsolete; and what is obsolete and aging will soon disappear.

Hebrews 10:15-17 — The Holy Spirit also testifies to us about this. First he says: "This is the covenant I will make with them after that time, says the Lord. I will put my laws in their hearts, and I will write them on their minds." Then he adds: "Their sins and lawless acts I will remember no more."

I Corinthians 3:3 — You show that you are a letter from Christ, the result of our ministry, written not with ink but with the Spirit of the living God, not on tablets of stone but on tablets of human hearts.

These passages don't imply that there are no written instructions from God in the new covenant. There obviously are. Neither do they imply that the ones that are written are inconsequential to Christians. The verses following the Hebrews 10 passage quoted above are clearly instructional. There are the famous "lettuce" verses (22-25) that we generally view as commandments. "So do not throw away our confidence . . . . " (v. 35a) — that sounds like a command too. But grace is no longer grace if we try to make each new covenant command justificatory.

Q. *What is the 'good' use of the law Paul alludes to in I Timothy 1:8?*

A. "We know that the law is good if a man uses it properly," he said. The context holds the answer. Verses 3-7 describe some teachers who used the law to promote controversy. The good use is to reveal our sinfulness and helplessness, and to deliver us to the One who has the solution to both problems. The "second use of law" says that the function of law is to convict us of our sins. Verses 9 and 10 describe that process: "We also know that law is made not for good men but for lawbreakers and rebels, the ungodly and sinful, the unholy and irreligious . . . and for whatever else is contrary to the sound doctrine." As long as those and similar sins attach themselves to Christians, law performs the good service of convicting them.

Romans 7:6 seems to be a description of the transition from the first to the second use of law. "But now, by dying to what once bound us, we have been released from the law so that we serve in the new way of the Spirit, and not in the old way of the written code." "The new way of the Spirit" — this refers to the Holy Spirit guiding Christians to loving, obedient living. And what does He use if not the Word which contains the example and teachings of Jesus and His inspired apostles?

Leroy Garrett seems to be addressing this same good use of the law in answering the question, "Is the church under law?"

> We are to rejoice in God's grace through Christ, which delivers us from the bondage of the law, and yet we are to be law-abiding believers . . . . We are not under law in that law-keeping saves us, but we do have laws that the Spirit of God helps us to obey . . . . We are not, then, under law as Israel was, shut up to a system that saves only through personal righteousness . . . . But we do have law or laws (which would include some application of the Old Covenant Scriptures) that we are to keep . . . . The big difference is God's grace given through Jesus, which helps us to fulfill the law in our own lives. The Holy Spirit is our helper, so that, "directed by the Spirit, the law may find fulfillment in us."[9]

Garrett goes on to make his point that the church is under law only in the sense that we seek to be law-abiding and obedient to the One who graciously gives eternal life.

IRRESPONSIBLE GRACE: GRACE WITHOUT LAW

Against the beauty of grace and law as they cooperate to bring us into right standing with God, abuses of God's marvelous plan stand out hideously. Grace without law, grace without respon-sibility, "cheap grace" as Dietrich Bonhoeffer called it, is truly repulsive. Many reform theologians, anxious to put plenty of distance between justification by credit and justification by merit, have moved much of Protestantism to an almost antinomian (against law) position. Their thinking seems to be: Since law-keeping won't secure salvation, and the best way to keep people from thinking it will is to get it out of the picture; let's scrap all law. They regard law as the enemy of grace. The results have been sad. A large percentage of professing disciples live undisciplined, uncommitted lives, and the faith of Jesus Christ has suffered enormously because of it. Virtually every moral standard in the United States is in jeopardy of falling because Christians stand for nothing and fall for anything.

Reform theology had so gutted Christianity in Bonhoeffer's time (pre-World War II) that he saw German Christianity impo-tent against the Third Reich's godless philosophy. He inveighed against the theology of his own Lutheran denomination, a theology in which one was so comfortable in grace that he felt no need to obey God's commands. He was right. And the rest is history. A holocaust, while most Protestant and Catholic ec-clesiastics smoothed their surplices.

All forms of religious subjectivism are antinomian. Evangelical and fundamentalist denominations abound in this error. Accord-ing to the view of subjectivists salvation is first received in one's heart, and from there heart feelings predominate over Biblical facts. If salvation is not seen as an objective act, accomplished outside us solely by the work of our Savior, then the whole Chris-tian life is based in feelings. "If it feels good, do it" becomes the motto of the very people who would most vociferously deny that same philosophy to the unregenerate sinner. Subjectivism opens the door to dialogue with the devil on just about any subject: abortion on demand, euthanasia, legalization of life destroying behavior such as drug abuse and prostitution, pornography, gambling, homosexuality, etc. All these "feel OK" under some circumstances. And there is some prelate who will approve every one of these behaviors in spite of the condemnations written in the Word. Even the very spiritual Pentecostals and charismatics are not safe from this trap. They have been known to prostitute the Holy Spirit into condoning (and even inspiring) unspiritual, unChristian behavior.

Is it possible to overstate the evil of irresponsible grace? Protestantism is an ineffective force for morality in the world today essentially because the instructions, commands, and laws of God have been drained of their power. The Ten Commandments have become the Ten Suggestions. The Sermon on the Mount has become nothing more than beautiful prose. Instructions to the church contained in the epistles are viewed by most denominations as ideals. The people of God have become virtually indistinguishable from the people of Satan. Twilight has replaced light and darkness (I Pet. 2:9). And, if a teacher, preacher, or writer hoists one of God's commands into prominent view, and dares suggest that we should be obeying it (even out of the motivation of love), he may be called a legalist (usually by someone who doesn't even know what one is). And no religious professional would want that label!

"See to it that no one misses the grace of God" is how the writer to the Hebrews begins a lengthy section which warns of the danger of irresponsible grace. A careful look at the whole section in Hebrews 12 may save us and our people from the disaster that lies at the end of taking grace for granted.

> [15]See to it that no one misses the grace of God and that no bitter root grows up to cause trouble and defile many.

If this is written to Christians, and it is, then Christians face the danger of missing the grace of God which provided their salvation. What a horrible possibility! How could something so valuable as eternal life be missed?

> [16]See that no one is sexually immoral, or is godless like Esau, who

139

for a single meal sold his inheritance rights as the oldest son. [17]Afterward, as you know, when he wanted to inherit this blessing, he was rejected. He could bring about no change of mind, though he sought the blessing with tears.

Grace can be thrown away, just like Esau threw away an earthly inheritance. Perhaps at the time he sold it to Jacob he thought it was really irrevocable, that in the end it would be his anyway. He thought his father was as casual about the inheritance as he was. Isaac was very generous, but not foolish. So Esau's foolish thought followed by an irresponsible deed cost him the gift.

> [18]You have not come to a mountain that can be touched and that is burning with fire; to darkness, gloom and storm; [19]to a trumpet blast or to such a voice speaking words, so that those who heard it begged that no further word be spoken to them, [20]because they could not bear what was commanded: "If even an animal touches the mountain, it must be stoned." [21]The sight was so terrifying that Moses said, "I am trembling with fear."
> [22]But you have come to Mount Zion, to the heavenly Jerusalem, the city of the living God. You have come to thousands upon thousands of angels in joyful assembly. [23]to the church of the firstborn, whose names are written in heaven. You have come to God, the judge of all men, to the spirits of righteous men made perfect, [24]to Jesus the mediator of a new covenant, and to the sprinkled blood that speaks a better word than the blood of Abel.

The magnitude of the possible loss faced by the Jewish Christians to whom this book was written is seen in the contrast between the way God's two great covenants were given and received. The covenant that came to the Jews through Moses was accompanied by very frightening phenomena: a mountain on fire, awesome trumpet blasts, and portentous warnings. Even Moses was terrified. But the new covenant God has given us, the covenant of love and grace, is altogether the opposite. Here the writer sketches a word picture of the final end of this covenant. The scene is heaven. Gathered are joyful angels and redeemed Christians, enjoying the heavenly Jerusalem. And it's all made possible by the gift of Jesus' blood. To throw away grace is unthinkable!

> [25]See to it that you do not refuse him who speaks. If they did not escape when they refused him who warned them on earth, how much less will we, if we turn away from him who warns us from heaven? [26]At that time his voice shook the earth, but now he has promised, "Once more I will shake not only the earth but also the heavens." [27]The words "once more" indicate the removing of what can be shaken — that is, created things — so that what cannot be shaken may remain.

The third "see to it" in this passage is the toughest one yet. Now he introduces punishment into God's grace. As Sovereign He has the right to deal harshly with those who despise His gift. Eventually God's voice is going to shake His entire universe to pieces (a slightly different view from Peter's in II Peter 3). All that will be left is what God's grace has provided.

> [28]Therefore, since we are receiving a kingdom that cannot be shaken, let us be thankful, and so worship God acceptably with reverence and awe, [29]for our "God is a consuming fire."

God's grace has provided us an eternal kingdom, or reign of God. We ought to receive and hold that grace tenaciously. After all, God only wants our worship in return. And worship is no more than what such an awesome God deserves.

IRREPRESSIBLE LAW: LAW WITHOUT GRACE

But let's address the abuse of grace which most often afflicts the heirs of the Restoration Movement. Like irresponsible grace, irrepressible law takes several forms. Grace is talked about, but it takes a poor second place to law. Roman Catholicism talks a lot about grace. But it teaches that the grace to perform perfect righteousness is infused into us, thereby enabling us to achieve right standing with God by performing religious duty (the sacraments). This is called sacramentalism, and it is not supported in Scripture. It's just a form of seeking justification by good deeds.

And then there's the doctrine of salvation by synergism. It says that if we keep God's laws the best we can God will make up the difference between our best and His minimum requirement with grace. That's a nice theory (one I espoused myself early on), but without foundation in Scripture. (For me it represented a transition from works-oriented salvation to grace. In that sense it wasn't all bad.) We are either saved by grace or we're not. If our law-keeping becomes partial payment for salvation, then it's not totally a gift. And Paul should have told us.

People who don't understand the place of law in God's system of justification may become legalists. Because justification is a legal concept they seek to arrive at and maintain right standing with God by law-keeping. Having your Christian life fully prescribed for you by some authority (theologian, preacher, pastor, teacher, or book), and feeling justified in it, is really very convenient and secure. Entire religious systems which function well, and give all sorts of signs of God's good pleasure with them, attest to the power of this system.

But God's amazing grace is never quiet. It wiggles its way into the heart of the staunchest legalist. Try as they might, the Pharisees couldn't get Jesus out of their minds. He disturbed their theology. But He wouldn't go away. Neither a cross nor a tomb could put grace away. So it isn't surprising that the legalist's tidy system of salvation by law-keeping may become unbearable; he may begin a reexamination of this theology and opt for grace. It's a good bet. Not over 4-1.

The concept of justification by law-keeping is wholly a human concept, doomed to failure. It was never God's idea. The Old Testament does not teach it. It teaches law, but not justification by law-keeping, else God (who knows we can't keep law perfectly) and Satan (whose job it is to keep us breaking law) are complicitous in our condemnation. May it never be! Men have always been declared righteous only because of their faith.

Legalism is sometimes called Galatianism (because it is the main issue of that epistle) or Phariseeism (because they were nearly perfect practitioners of it in Jesus' day). Oh what an ugly name it is!

"Legalist" is a label propagandists sometimes paste on people to divert attention from unpleasant truth. Just about any time you begin a sentence with "But the Bible says . . . . " you may be called a legalist. What a travesty when people have to disregard Scripture and live undisciplined, ungodly lives just to prove that they aren't legalists.

Even defining the term legalism is difficult. Rather than give you my definition, let me describe my personal entanglement with it. It probably began with the following passage: "For I tell you that unless your righteousness surpasses that of the Pharisees and the teachers of the law, you will certainly not enter the kingdom of God" (Matt. 5:20). That became my personal Christian *raison d'etre*. I had to be more righteous than the Pharisees were. From Matthew 5:20 I graduated to Matthew 23 and learned more precisely how extensive their righteousness really was. Awesome! But I could do it, I thought. So I set out to keep every spoken command, line up with every approved precedent, extrapolate every inference and principle I could from the Bible and live by them. What a merry-to-round! No, I felt like God had me on a treadmill and kept turning up the speed. I was a card-carrying, flag-waving legalist. I *honestly* (as opposed to arrogantly) saw how much better than others I was.

And then I discovered that legalism gives you a handy (and holy) way of manipulating people. I learned it in practice before I learned it from Scripture. Too bad, because Galatians 6:12-14 rips the robes of righteousness right off it and exposes it for what it is. "Those who want to make a good impression outwardly are trying to compel you to be circumcised. The only reason they do this is to avoid being persecuted for the cross of Christ. Not even

143

those who are circumcised obey the law, yet they want you to be circumcised that they may boast about your flesh. May I never boast except in the cross of our Lord Jesus Christ, through which the world has been crucified to me, and I to the world." Legalists sink their nails into people who have little or no security in Jesus, people who "have to be right about everything," people who find their own standing with God is enhanced when they are (humbly) better than other people, or conformists who don't want to think for themselves. I finally realized that my own motivation wasn't too much different from these Galatian legalists. I was most secure in a fellowship of religious rubber stamps. Diversity made me uncomfortable. By now I didn't want to read any more about myself from Galatians 6:12-14! Had I, I would have discovered that I had joined the Ancient and Loyal Order of Camel Swallowers (Matt. 23:24), those who keep easy laws, but ignore the hard ones.

Obviously, others have come to the same conclusion.

It (legalism) stems from the elemental fact that no one in the flesh can keep law perfectly. Therefore no flesh can be justified by law. One who thinks we are still under a written code must find something he can do without too much effort, and judge his faithfulness to God by attendance upon that. He is not greatly concerned about concentrating upon justice, mercy and honesty.

I shall never forget that once when I went to a southern state I visited the home of brother who was an elder in a little congregation back in the piney-woods. I went to invite him to my tent meeting but he could not come because the brethren with whom I was working used individual cups in the Lord's Supper. For two solid hours I listened to him as he argued for "the faithful church" with was "true to the Book" on what he referred to as "the cups question." One year later when I returned to the area he was in prison for moonshining. He was operating a still and the Feds had him under observation at the very time he was talking so earnestly to me. Bootlegging was not bad if you had only one cup on Sunday . . . . Not every case of camel-swallowing is as obvious as this. Some brethren have been engaged in the art for so long that they "pop camels" like others do pills.[10]

144

There is no Biblical definition of legalism, per se. But it's there! I know a legalist when I see one. Daniel P. Fuller seems to have researched the subject well and offers the following insights on Galatians 3:10:

> All exegetes, including Calvin, would agree that the "works of the law" . . . means living legalistically, that is seeking by means of what one does to *earn* favor with God.

Speaking of Swedish exegete Ragnar Bring's discussion of the same passage, Fuller continues:

> As he expounds Galatians 3:10 the argument runs, cursed is everyone who transgresses the law by trying to conform to its legalistic endeavors, for Deuteronomy 27:26 invokes a curse upon those guilty of such monstrous crimes as incest, bestiality, sodomy, bribery, murder for hire, and so on. On this line of interpretation the legalistic frame of mind, which seeks to earn God's favor, would be in a category with these heinous crimes, since it involves trying to bribe God to impart blessing on the basis of good works that one does.

If we have missed the point, Fuller adds:

> Instead of signifying adherence to the law, Paul used this term ("the works of the law") to represent the ultimate transgression of the law, the legalism which presumes that the Lord, who is not "served by human hands, as though he needed anything" (Acts 17:25), can nevertheless be bribed and obligated to bestow blessings by the way men distinguish themselves.[11]

Perhaps understanding legalism is more painful than it is difficult. Isn't it simply the elevating of law-keeping to the place that we make it our means of justification? Is that too difficult? It is the baggage that goes with it that is complicated. It makes law more important than Jesus' work on the cross; it reduces the sacrifice of Christ to an event in history, though no legalist would admit it; it's an attempt to codify the entire Christian lifestyle, and make right

Christian lifestyle the determining factor in one's standing with God; it makes the Christian life a legal contract rather than a loving relationship (John 3:16). Legalism has nothing to do with the "letter vs. spirit of the law" issue (II Cor. 3:6). In that passage Paul is contrasting the covenants, not telling us that we will be free from legalism if we keep both the letter and spirit of the law. Claiming justification because we keep both the letter and the spirit of the law is still legalism.

There are clear warnings in Scripture against a legalistic use of the law, as it was defined above:

> *Romans 3:20,28* — Therefore no one will be declared righteous in his sight by observing the law; rather through the law we become conscious of sin. For we maintain that a man is justified by faith apart from observing the law.

Any other use of law than that described in verse 20 is a misuse.

> *Romans 10:1-4* — Brother, my heart's desire and prayer to God for the Israelites is that they may be saved. For I can testify about them that they are zealous for God, but their zeal is not based on knowledge. Since they did not know the righteousness that comes from God and sought to establish their own, they did not submit to God's righteousness. Christ is the end of the law so that there may be righteousness for everyone who believes.

Jews in general were first-class legalists. There are only two ways to be saved: by perfect adherence to law, or by accepting God's gift of righteousness. In ignorant zeal they opted for the first way, not realizing its impossibility. If you can't keep law perfectly, you have to manipulate it until you at least feel righteous. That's legalism. It leaves Jesus standing in the cold with his offer of "righteousness for everyone who believes."

> *Galatians 5:2-4* — Mark my words! I, Paul, tell you that if you let yourselves be circumcised, Christ will be of no value to you at all. Again I declare to every man who lets himself be circumcised that

he is obligated to obey the whole law. You who are trying to be justified by law have been alienated from Christ; you have fallen away from grace.

It was either circumcision (and obedience to the whole law) or Christ. No matter how you present it, legalism is seeking justification by perfect obedience to law. Whole church systems may be built on it, but Paul castigates it as apostasy.

Philippians 3:8-9 — What is more, I consider everything a loss compared to the surpassing greatness of knowing Christ Jesus my Lord, for whose sake I have lost all things. I consider them rubbish, that I may gain Christ and be found in him, not having a righteousness of my own that comes from the law, but that which is through faith in Christ — the righteousness that comes from God and is by faith.

Righteousness that comes from law is an illusion, kept alive by a constant juggling of laws to keep ourselves fooled into thinking we are doing all right. The Pharisee of Luke 18 was confident of his own righteousness, but mostly because he had lived up to his scheme of law-keeping better than the publican had. But what if his scheme wasn't God's scheme? It wasn't and he lost out. Paul had been one of those Pharisees and learned the lesson of legalism.

From Galatians 2:16-3:5 writer Michael Hall points out some of the rank errors of legalism. His observations are worthy of note:

Legalism is stupid because it violates the justification by faith principle. "We . . . know that a man is not justified by observing the law, but by faith in Jesus Christ" (Gal. 2:15-16) . . . .

Legalism is stupid because it violates our "death to law." "For through the law I died to law — to live for God. I have been crucified . . ." (Gal. 2:19-20a, NEB) . . . .

Legalism is stupid because it nullifies the cross of grace. "I will not nullify the grace of God; if righteousness comes by law, then Christ died for nothing" (Gal. 2:21, NEB) . . . .

147

Legalism is stupid because it undermines the gift of the Holy Spirit. "Did you receive the Spirit by observing the law, or by believing what you heard?" (Gal. 3:2) . . . .

Legalism is stupid finally in Paul's exposition, because it nullifies our suffering for the good news. "Have you suffered so many things in vain?" (Gal. 3:4, KJV) . . . .[12]

As you may have guessed, I see the Pharisees of the New Testament era as consummate legalists — textbook examples. Rebecca Manley Pippert has one of the most interesting discussions of the Pharisees in contemporary literature. They were not all bad, or not all that bad, she says. That's what makes legalism so insidious. Some of the finest Christians I know are self-righteous legalists. (Sorry 'bout that, folks.) But even after her "fair" treatment of them, they are hardly role models. Actually, they are role models — of the ugliness of legalism. But worst of all, when you compare her almost flattering description of the Pharisees with Jesus' views of true righteousness, they come off miserable beggars.

The Pharisees have received a lot of bad press. But we must not forget that they were a lay movement who cared deeply about God. They probably had more in common with Jesus than any other theological school of his time, yet they were his severest critics. Louis Finkelstein says they were people who were drawn from the tradesmen of the town, not like the Sadducees who were descendants of the patrician landowners. They were popular and held in esteem by the people at large.

The derivation of their name is uncertain, although F.F. Bruce suggests, "It is . . . likely that they were called Pharisees in the sense of separatists because of their strict avoidance of everything which might convey ceremonial impurity to them." The Pharisees were devoted to maintaining the Levitical laws of purity concerning ritual, food and the Sabbath. They were scrupulous about tithing the produce of the soil (Luke 18:12; Matt. 23:23) as well as evangelizing faithfully. They believed that by studying and obeying the law and the Tradition of the Elders they could strictly avoid ceremonial impurity.

Give me a church full of them! They sound like they would raise the commitment level of most churches about 50%. Pippert continues:

> They shared many of Jesus' beliefs. "They took seriously the biblical doctrine of God's government of the universe and overruling of the actions of men for the furtherance of his own purpose," writes Bruce. "And . . . there was no difference between them with regard to the limits of holy writ, it was on their interpretation that they disagreed." They also shared a belief in the resurrection of the body and the existence of angels.
>
> The Pharisees fanatically studied the law, and in so doing they built up a body of traditional interpretation and application. Eventually their tradition became as sacrosanct as the law itself. They were traditionalists even more than literalists . . . .
>
> Why did the Pharisees build up an elaborate ceremonial code? There are no conclusive answers to that question. W.D. Davies argues that the Pharisees built up their Tradition of the Elders out of a deep desire to make the Mosaic Law applicable to life . . . . But Moses received the law over a thousand years before. The present conditions Israel faced were widely different, and that made relevant application of the law difficult . . . . Davies states that out of the Pharisees' attempt to bring the whole of life under control of the law they adopted the even more complex code of purification and separation. By examining and expounding the law, they sought to find the right conduct and to prescribe it for every circumstance in life . . . . Their preoccupation was in not breaking their laws; no small task, as their laws were ever increasing.
>
> They had laws concerning whether one should praise a bride extravagantly (which this writer thinks is a marvelous idea!) and laws on how to greet a bereaved person. There were laws for preventive medicine, such as the law that said no woman could look in the mirror on the Sabbath. The rabbis feared she might discover a gray hair and yank it out, thus performing work.
>
> What was the result of their exclusive emphasis on obeying the ceremonial laws of purity and their seeming neglect of the moral law — what Jesus called "weightier matters of the law, justice and mercy and faith" (Matt. 23:23)? It fed and eagerly encouraged the already existing social hierarchy. Their fervor for ceremonial purity led to an apartheid response to almost anyone who was not a

part of their exclusive sect. There was strict separation from Gentiles, from Samaritans and even an aloofness from fellow Jews who did not have the time or leisure to study the law as they did.[13]

Pick them out — those sterling qualities of the Pharisees: they cared deeply about God; they believed in studying and obeying; they were great tithers; they tried to make the law fit contemporary situations; they tried to bring all their disciples into a conformed lifestyle; in short, they tried to present a united front to the world. But the world saw it for what it was: a front. That's all legalism can accomplish, and it doesn't do that very well. And what drove them to it? The feeling that they had to obey the law perfectly to be saved.

A word of caution here. Biblical legalism has to do only with justification. It teaches that our eternal salvation is predicated on perfect (or in the case of synergistic legalism, almost perfect) adherence to the commands, laws, and rules of Scripture. Adherence to commands, laws, and rules of Scripture arising out of our justification by grace, motivated by love, is not legalism, though it is often so labeled. More on that in the next section.

In a recent conversation with a Palestinian Moslem, it was driven home to me as never before, the fact that all religions except Christianity make salvation (or whatever they may call it) the reward for law-keeping and good works. My friend told me that he expects to stand before Allah on the day of judgment and have his good deeds weighed against his evil ones. But never fear, because each good deed would be multiplied by ten so he would have enough to earn eternal life. As I listened, and thought of Romans 3:10-23, I thanked God for "a righteousness from God, apart from law."

God save us from legalism!

LAW AND GRACE: THE PERFECT MARRIAGE

Paul really throws us a curve in Romans when, after he has

made his iron-clad case for justification by grace through faith, and having shown baptism to be the watershed in the process, he immediately launches into commands for Christian living: "Therefore do not let sin reign in your mortal body so that you obey its evil desires. Do not offer the parts of your body to sin, as instruments of wickedness . . ." (Rom. 6:12-13a). Those sure sound like commandments, or rules, or law to me! Paul, I thought we were through with law!

What are you going to do with the four gospels, Acts of the Apostles, twenty-one epistles, and the Revelation, which contain hundreds of commands, or rules for Christian living? What you're going to do with them is reckon with them. Figure out what they're there for. It becomes immediately obvious that they're not there to ignore, or to treat as good advice or godly ideals. Of course, you're going to use them for their intended purpose: to translate Christians' appreciation for salvation into appropriate and loving responses to God and man. For sure, they're not there to justify us, for the same reason we've said several times now: justification is by grace, not works.

Commands, rules, laws just won't go away. We shouldn't be surprised at that really. Our very existence is wrapped up in divine fiat, divine command, "And God said, Let there be . . . ." From Eden to eternity God speaks and creation trembles (Nahum 1:5). We speak of the laws of nature, gravity, the harvest, etc. Sometimes God's laws have been spoken, sometimes written, and sometimes unspoken (Rom. 2:12-16). Even after explaining the good news about justification by grace in the first six chapters of Romans Paul acknowledged that he was "a slave to God's law" (Rom. 7:25b).

For many people grace and law are seen to be on opposite ends of some religious continuum. Nothing could be further from Biblical truth. To God they are complementary. Paul openly espoused grace as God's only means of justifying men, but he gave law its proper place too. Without law, grace gets cheap. Without grace, law gets repressive. He knew God's extraordinary gift would never be appreciated without law. His treatises on law and grace in Romans and Galatians, as well as brief mentions in other epistles may be seen as elaboration on Jesus' somewhat puzzling statement in Matthew 5:17, "Do not think that I have come to abolish the Law or the Prophets; I have not come to abolish but to fulfill them."

Our task at this juncture is to see how New Testament writers (particularly Paul) viewed the marriage. We already know how they viewed law and grace singularly, but we need to know how they cooperate for our justification. Once again, Paul, we have questions.

Q. *Are there not many new covenant commands, or laws? Or are they just suggestions?*

A. Commands, rules, laws, ordinances — call them whatever you want, they're there. And they're on both sides of our justification, before we are saved and after.

Luke 14:26-27 — If anyone comes to me and does not hate his father and mother, his wife and children, his brothers and sisters — yes, even his own life — he cannot be my disciple. And anyone who does not carry his cross and follow me cannot be my disciple.

Luke 17:3-4 — So watch yourselves. If your brother sins, rebuke him, and if he repents, forgive him. If he sins against you seven times in a day, and seven times comes back to you and says, "I repent," forgive him.

I Thessalonians 5:16-18 — Be joyful always; pray continually; give thanks in all circumstances, for this is God's will for you in Christ Jesus.

II Timothy 2:15 — Do your best to present yourself to God as one approved, a workman who does not need to be ashamed and who correctly handles the word of truth.

James 5:16 — Therefore confess your sins to each other and pray for each other so that you may be healed.

I Peter 1:13-15 — Therefore, prepare your minds for action; be self-controlled; set your hope on the grace to be given you when Jesus Christ is revealed. As obedient children, do not conform to the evil desires you had when you lived in ignorance. But just as he who called you is holy, so be holy in all you do; for it is written: "Be holy, because I am holy."

The form of new covenant commands might be different, we would grant for argument's sake, but they're still commands. They are bathed in love and thus elicit obedience on that basis, if possible. But, need we be reminded that love itself is commanded (John 13:34; 15:12)?

But let's not make commands harsher than they need be. Law is only law when we break it: "We know also that law is made not for good men but for law-breakers and rebels . . ." (I Tim. 1:9-11). You probably don't even own a copy of the Vehicle Code for the state in which you live. The only time those laws concern you very much is when you've been pinched. Yet they continue to function as silent sentries in a civilized society.

Q. *What are you going to do with these and hundreds of others worded similarly? Does grace mean that they don't matter? Since God has "done His thing" called grace, can we "do our own thing" and call it Christian living?*

A. No. We cannot live by our own rules and call ourselves His disciples. But there is a curious paradox here that may trouble the less than careful Bible student. On the one hand are several verses which say we are freed from law (Gal. 3:24-25; 5:18; Rom. 6:14-15; 10:4; I Cor. 6:12; 10:23), and on the other ones which say we are under law (Rom. 2:13; I Cor. 7:21; 14:34; Gal. 6:2; Heb. 8:10; James 1:25; 2:12). Hebrews 9:27 and Acts 17:21 tell us that we will all be judged, and who could imagine a judgment without laws? This seems like a clear contradiction, doesn't it? Many ministers and teachers among us are so uncertain on this paradox that they preach both sides of it, hopefully far enough apart that the audience won't notice the seeming contradiction.

I'm happy to say it is only a paradox! Here's what these verses mean in combination:

—*We are freed from trying to be justified by law.* The first group of Scriptures are in a justification setting. This means that I labor under no illusion of being able to keep law perfectly enough to be saved, or declared righteous. That's what the first half of Romans announces to us. "For what the law was powerless to do in that it was weakened by the sinful nature, God did by sending his own Son in the likeness of sinful man to be a sin offering. And so he condemned sin in sinful man, in order that the righteous requirements of the law might be fully met in us, who do not live according to the sinful nature but according to the Spirit" (Rom. 8:3-4). There is nothing inherently wrong with law. The problem is our "sinful nature." So God furnished righteousness for us, in the person of His Son. We may receive that gift by faith.

—*We enjoy our standing in Him by grace through faith.* Once again faith looms large. "Therefore, since we have been justified through faith, we have peace with God through our Lord Jesus Christ, through whom we have gained access by faith into this grace in which we now stand" (Rom. 5:1-2). If there's any uncertainty about our final justification it rests with our faith, not God's faithfulness: "If we are faithless, he will remain faithful, for he cannot disown himself" (II Tim. 2:13).

—*The faith that was our response to God's gift initially continues to operate in the Christian life.* We went to Romans 4 to define the nature and quality of the faith that is an acceptable response to God's grace in Chapter Two. There we defined it as "an intellectual response that fuels action." That definition still holds this side of our baptism. Faith, repentance and baptism are commands, or laws, which are the responses God seeks to His proffered gift of salvation. Likewise, He has given commands on this side of baptism which are the responses He seeks to His received gift of salvation.

—*Now God's Holy Spirit lives in us to aid us in keeping God's laws.* That's what Paul was alluding to in the last phrase of Romans 8:4: "who do not live according to the sinful nature but according to the Spirit." J.B. Phillips describes the cooperative effort of Son and Spirit like this: "So that we are able to meet the

Law's requirements, so long as we are living no longer by the dictates of our sinful nature, but in obedience to the promptings of the Spirit."[14] Hebrews 8:10-11 appears to be referring to this cooperative work by which people with sinful natures can learn to keep God's laws: "This is the covenant I will make with the house of Israel after that time, declares the Lord. I will put my laws in their minds and write them on their hearts. I will be their God, and they will be my people. No longer will a man teach his neighbor, or a man his brother, saying, 'know the Lord,' because they will all know me, from the least of them to the greatest."

This process is called sanctification by theologians. It is separate and distinct in Scripture from justification. Justification makes us legally right; in sactification God's Holy Spirit moves us toward being actually right. We will never reach actual righteousness, but we don't need to because God has already given it to us.

Q. *Won't people who don't believe they have to obey God's commands perfectly live ungodly lives?*

A. Yes they sure will! *Unless* they are taught carefully about grace and law — and love. Law was a schoolmaster, but love is a taskmaster. A far greater taskmaster than fear. The best quality human performance, the most scrupulous obedience comes from love. People's transition from law-motivated obedience to love-motivated obedience isn't instantaneous. Elders, preachers and teachers must take Paul's exhortation to Timothy personally: "correct, rebuke and encourage — with great patience and careful instruction" (II Tim. 2:2b). Often people who are released from law-without-grace salvation turn into illegals, even spiritual scofflaws. Paul knew about it. "You, my brothers, were called to be free. But do not use your freedom to indulge the sinful nature; rather serve one another in love" (Gal. 5:13). Freedom is scary, but not dangerous when it is God who has set us free and we understand the nature of that freedom.

Q. *How is this approach any different from legalism?*

A. Christians are still amenable to New Covenant demands

155

from God. But the pressure is off! The Jew living under Moses' Law worried that he might slip up and lose his standing with God. The Christian knows that he already has slipped up. But he also knows that his unconditional trust in the work of Jesus on the cross has obtained perfect righteousness for him — from the very moment he responded to Him. The pressure is off! He continues trusting. God has joined him in the person of the Holy Spirit to aid him in learning obedience. The pressure is off! He operates from love, not fear. He tries harder than ever, probably achieves better than ever, but never reaches perfect obedience. God is no longer his enemy, his accuser, but his Justifier, and Jesus is his Defense Attorney.

Martin Luther had more confidence in the power of love than many of us can imagine. He is supposed to have told his people to "Love God and sin as you please." Try your faith out on that one!

A perfect example of coming from love in the Christian life is found in Philemon. Paul writes his brother, "Therefore, although in Christ I could be bold and order you to do what you ought to do, yet I appeal to you on the basis of love" (v. 8-9a). Philemon's slave Onesimus had stolen money and run away from him. But Onesimus had been saved when he met Paul in Rome (v. 10). Philemon had every right under the law to have Onesimus killed. But he was under a higher law to forgive. Paul could have ordered him to obey that law, but he chose instead to appeal to a higher motivation in Philemon than the fear of disobeying God's law.

Q. *Won't this teaching tear up our churches?*

A. It depends on how legalistic they have been. If your people have been taught that their standing with God is dependent on how complete their obedience is, watch out. When I first began endorsing justification by grace among legalistic brethren, preachers and elders would often voice their concern that their people were turning into lawbreakers. They were trying out all the sins they had previously condemned. I tried to assure them that

156

this was just "new wine," and their people would sober up soon and when they did they'd be better disciples than ever. "No, grace isn't license," I assured them. "You don't have to cut all the command passages out of the New Testament. You don't have to quit preaching obedience. You just preach and teach it the way the Bible does, and trust God for good results." I was right too.

Q. *Is the church under law? Yes or no.*

A. How about yes *and* no? Yes, in that God's laws are always there (even in the new covenant), and relevant, and they achieve the lifestyle He wishes for His children. He even assists our obedience to law through the Helper He has given us. No, in that we are discharged from the law's demand of perfect obedience for salvation and are reliant instead upon the grace of God. So in this sense we are not under law but under grace.

Q. *Can we still say salvation is "a gift of God"?*

A. Since God gave us the *evidence* of the gospel (contained in His Word), and God gave us the ability to *examine* that evidence for credibility or incredibility (the human mind), and since He provided the *elements* of the gospel (sacrificial death, burial and resurrection of His only Son), and since He *enables* Christians (through the Holy Spirit who moves us to keep God's commands/laws), salvation can be unequivocally said to be "the gift of God" from beginning to end.

Q. *What happens when a Christian disobeys one of God's commands?*

A. He is sinning. He needs to repent of it and seek forgiveness. The oft misapplied passage in I John 1:9 applies here: "If we confess our sins, he is faithful and just and will forgive us our sins and purify us from all unrighteousness." That verse is set in a discussion of the Christian walk, which John says is beset by sin (vv. 8,10). Simon the Sorcerer's experience in Acts 8:9-24 confirms this answer.

Q. *But what if he just keeps on sinning?*

A. Hebrews 10:26-27 says something about that. Doesn't it? "If we deliberately keep on sinning after we have received the knowledge of the truth, no sacrifice for sins is left, but only a fearful expectation of judgment and of raging fire that will consume the enemies of God." That's strong language! When sinning becomes one's *lifestyle* God's wonderful gift of righteousness is lost. "No one who lives in him keeps on sinning. No one who continues to sin has either seen him or known him. No one who is born of God will continue to sin, because God's seed remains in him; he cannot go on sinning, because he has been born of God" (I John 3:6,9). The key idea for us moderns is the word *lifestyle*.

Q. *Let's be specific — what if I disobey I Thessalonians 5:17?*

A. It says, "Pray continually." If you don't your prayer life and relationship with God will be poor. You are sinning. If not praying becomes your lifestyle, you'll be lost. Grace notwithstanding. God offered you eternal life through a relationship with Him. You spurned it. There are many ways to fall from grace. But, all is not lost. You can have that relationship restored when you repent and seek forgiveness.

Q. *Are you saying that grace is worthless without obedience to commands?*

A. Yes. God's gift of justification is received by believing. Disobedient people are fundamentally disbelievers. The history of ancient Israel was ubelief. Behind every complaint, rebellion and disobedience was unbelief. This is why there are warnings like these in the Bible: "See to it that no one misses the grace of God and that no bitter root grows up to cause trouble and defile many. See that no one is sexually immoral, or is godless like Esau . . . . See to it that you do not refuse him who speaks. If they did not escape when they refused him who warned them on earth, how much less will we, if we turn away from him who warns us from heaven? Therefore, since we are receiving a kingdom that cannot be shaken, let us be thankful, and so worship God acceptably with reverence and awe, for our God is a consuming fire" (Heb. 12:15-16,25-29). Similar exhortations to "continue in the grace of God" are found in Acts 11:21-23; 13:43; II Cor. 6:1; Heb. 10:26-31; and Hebrews 12:14-15.

Q. *One sin won't condemn a Christian, will it?*

A. No, else we pass in and out of grace moment by moment. (By the way, that's not what the song by the same name is about.) Paul didn't say, "What shall we say, then? Shall we sin once . . .?" (Rom. 6:1). He spoke of going on in sin, making sin the lifestyle. Lifestyle is the issue.

Q. *Don't you make God soft on people?*

A. I hope not, because He isn't. But He is merciful, and that's what grace is all about. "Speak and act as those who are going to be judged by the law that gives freedom, because judgment without mercy will be shown to anyone who has not been merciful. Mercy triumphs over judgment!" (James 2:12-13). I want to be merciful, to obtain mercy, and to watch it triumph over judgment.

Q. *In a brief paragraph how would you describe these new covenant laws?*

A. They are God's will for people whose salvation is secured by their faith in Jesus Christ. "If you love me, you will obey what I command" (John 14:15). They enable us to give form to our faith and love for God. They come in the form of commands, precedents and principles, either from the mouth and life of Jesus or from His inspired apostles. They are not "casuistic rules for all the concrete situations of life" to use Brinsmead's description of the Torah. We will not be saved because we have kept every one perfectly, nor because we have kept most of them perfectly, nor because we have kept the ones we decide are most important perfectly, nor will we be damned if we've missed one. If we are saved at all it will be because God gave salvation to us.

Endnotes

1. Robert Brinsmead, "The Law of Moses — Abolished or Established by Jesus?", *The Christian Verdict*, 10/81, pp. 12-13.
2. *The Standard Bible Commentary: Thessalonians, Corinthians, Galatians and Romans*, The Standard Publishing Co., Cincinnati, 1916, p. 324.

3. *Romans Realized*, College Press, Joplin, MO, 1959, p. 59.

4. Ibid., p. 159.

5. *Legal Grace*, Integrity, 12/75.

6. *The Christian Verdict*, 10/81, pp. 8-11.

7. G. Abbott-Smith, *A Manual Greek Lexicon to the New Testament*, T. & T. Clark, Edinburgh, 1954.

8. *The Christian Verdict*, 10/81, pp. 22-24.

9. "Is the Church Under Law?" *Restoration Review*, 3/74.

10. W. Carl Ketcherside, "Swallowing Camels," *The Ensign Fair*, 1/78, p. 8.

11. *The Westminster Theological Journal*, Westminster Theological Seminary, Philadelphia, PA, Fall/1975, pp. 31-33,36-37.

12. "The Stupidity of Legalism," *Ensign*, 6/79, p.9.

13. Rebecca Manley Pippert, *Out of the Saltshaker*, InterVarsity Press, Downers Grove, IL, 1979, pp. 66-69.

14. Translated by J.B. Phillips, *The New Testament in Modern English*, Macmillan, NY, NY, 1957.

6

GRACE AND DEEDS

I have chosen to use the word "deeds" in this chapter instead of the more familiar "works" for the following reasons:

1. It is a correct rendition of the Greek words *ergon, praxis, poiesis,* and cognates used in most New Testament passages.

2. "Works" has so much prejudice against it in the minds of many modern evangelicals and other heirs of the Reformation. It has almost a Roman Catholic ring to it in the minds of many. Grace vs. Works is seen as the great matchup for the Christian Fight of the Centuries. (You know, "And now in this corner, weighing . . . .") It's really not quite that way in the Word, as we shall see.

3. "Deeds" are simply "things done" and in most people's minds the term is spared the prejudice mentioned above. In modern Christian thought we seem unable to separate works from the concept of merit. Two specific examples will suffice. *Webster's Seventh New Collegiate Dictionary* gives the following

161

under definition nine: "pl. performance of moral or religious acts (salvation by works)" [p. 1029]. James Inglis' *A Topical Dictionary of Bible Texts* has this entry: "WORKS, Insufficiency of, to Salvation." Following it is the entry: "WORKS, Good. See Obedience" [pp. 501-502]. Almost every Reformation theology book will have similar entries in its index. We seem unable, with the great reformers breathing down our necks, to use the word "works" any way but negatively.

So, deeds it shall be. This chapter will be much shorter than the previous one because deeds are generally human responses to divine commands. Everything said about commandment-keeping may also be said about deeds in general. But there are a few things left unsaid, so we shall try to say them this trip. Following will be my best effort at letting New Testament Scripture define itself in the various uses of the Greek words translated "work," "works," "deeds," etc. in the grace passages. I find three basic usages: deeds done to earn salvation; deeds done to receive the free gift of salvation; deeds done in loving response to the gift we have received. Each one will be introduced with a descriptive phrase, such as the following.

I DO, YOU PAY

Surely it has been amply demonstrated by now that deeds performed with the view of earning justification are deeds wasted. Salvation is not payment for services rendered. However, this was the view of the Jews ("Teacher, what good thing must I do to get eternal life?" Matt. 19:16b). It is the view of Roman Catholicism. And it is the view of many modern Christians. Even among those who talk the most about grace, and love to quote Ephesians 2:8-9, still people's standing with God tends to get measured on the basis of performance. Perhaps even more so in American life where people's very standing in society is measured by performance. Seldom during the get-acquainted ritual do we ask "What are you?" More often it is "What do you *do?*" In the church are we worried that people won't perform for the Lord unless they are paid? Are we hopelessly addicted to salvation by works?

Chapter Two in this work attempted to put to rest the notion that man is justified by works. In that chapter and the next we attempted further to harmonize the statements made mostly by Paul to the effect that salvation is a gift with the fact that sinners in New Testament times did something (or things) to receive the gift. If the reader is still uncomfortable with that harmony he or she should reread those chapters before proceeding to the next material.

I BELIEVE, I DO

The salutations which preface Paul's letters may sometimes seem like fluff, or mere social formality, but I doubt if they are. For sure his salutation to the Romans has one phrase in it that is pregnant with meaning. In Romans 1:5b he describes his ministry as being

. . . to call people from among the Gentiles to the obedience that comes from faith.

"Obedience that comes from faith" — what does that mean? It means that faith is not real unless obedience issues from it. Real faith results in deeds. If one's faith is in God, then one does what God prescribes. What Paul wrote in the succeeding chapters of Romans harmonizes with and illustrates this salutatory statement. In brief, he wrote the following:

We are all hopelessly lost, hopelessly unable to obey the laws of God or perform the works of God perfectly. We can never be legally righteous.

A new way to achieve righteousness has been provided by God. The new way is by faith in His Son, Jesus Christ.

But faith is not simply intellectual agreement with God. Rather than define faith etymologically, he illustrated it with the case of Abraham. Abraham had intellectual agreement with God, and it was so strong that he did what God commanded him to do. He did God's bidding immediately. There was no time lapse between God's promise and the obedience that came from Abraham's faith. Without his obedience God's promises would have lacked fulfillment. His faith would have been an illusion. No better than the faith demons had (James 2:19). But he illustrated the "obedience that comes from faith" perfectly. We might even say that his obedience was his faith (and vice versa). Upon his first act of faith he was credited with righteousness.

Further illustrations of this "obedience that comes from faith" are found in the case histories of conversion in Acts. They are recorded in Acts 2, 8, 9, 10, 16, 19, 22, 24, and 26. What these people did in the process of their conversions was either (a) to earn their salvation, or (b) to receive their salvation. If (a) is shown in Romans not to be a valid theology of justification, and nothing in Acts indicates otherwise, then (b) must be the case.

Lest some still worry that God (or their friends) might misconstrue their feeling of conviction, their deeds of repentance, confession of faith, and baptism as their attempt at earning their salvation, consider for a moment that what might appear to be self-aggrandizing deeds are actually passive in nature. For example, water baptism is sometimes disparaged as a deed people do in order to earn eternal life. But baptism is not something you do so much as it is something done *to* you. Conviction of sin is likewise something done to us by God's Spirit. Repentance may be something we do, but even it is described as something God gives us (Acts 5:31; 11:18, et al.). So, rather than arguing and splitting hairs, rather than setting the Scripture against itself, why can't we accept that deeds leading up to our justification are the "obedience that comes from faith"? And why can't we, like

Abraham (and other Old Testament Hall of Famers, Heb. 11), perform the deeds necessary for the reception of our gift of forgiveness, fellowship with God, and eternal life with thankfulness for our opportunity? Surely it's possible that people can be convicted of sin, repent and be baptized without feeling they have worked their way from darkness to light!

I LOVE, I DO

Now come all the deeds that Christians perform once they have found "this righteousness from God" (Rom. 3:21-22). What is the motivation for Christian deeds? What is their nature? Who prescribes them? Are we saved by them? Can we be saved without them? Is there a catalog of them somewhere?

Chapter six is the place in Romans where Paul begins to discuss the life of the Christian. Baptism is where new life begins. It is the dividing line between darkness and light, damnation and salvation. From baptism we arose to a new kind of life; we were freed from sin. Deeds of a different sort are expected to characterize our lives. Reread Romans 6 to feel the impact of baptism, and the kind of deeds it prescribes.

Chapter twelve is where Paul begins spelling out the behavior (deeds) of the newly justified sinner. In it he discusses such deeds as: sacrificing one's body to God; using gifts (talents) for God; practicing brotherly love and service; responding to wrongs done to you with practical service even to your enemies. Chapter thirteen speaks of submission to human government and moral behavior in an immoral world. And so go the epistles of Paul — many prescriptions for Christian deeds.

Likewise, Peter, John, Jude, and James give rules for Christian deeds, prescriptions for Christian performance. Many of these are in the form of principles which generically communicate God's plan for His people. In Acts are contained illustrations or examples of acceptable Christian living.

Rather than examining each one of these individually (which the reader can easily do with a concordance), can't we stipulate that there is a body of exemplified and commanded deeds for Christians contained in the New Covenant Scriptures? I believe we can. Now, three very crucial questions arise about them:

> 1. *Are new covenant commands, examples and principles pertaining to Christian thinking and behavior laws in the same sense the Mosaic covenant was?*
> 2. *Are we saved by performing these deeds?*
> 3. *Can we be saved without performing them?*

Consider first, that performing the deeds prescribed by New Covenant commands, examples and principles is no more justifying than keeping the Law of Moses was. And for the same reason: no one performs perfectly.

Second, we have the same hermeneutics problems with New Covenant commands, examples and principles the Jews had with the Law of Moses. We can't agree on which commands are binding. We can't agree on which examples are binding. Or which portions of the example are. And principles . . . wow, we really go wild here! One man's sensible principle is another man's nonsense. One man's necessary inference is totally unnecessary to another. So, we are left with an insoluble dilemma: Which deeds are necessary to be saved and which are not?

This is an enormous problem, with a simple solution. We have argued and divided from our brothers (and in many instances considered them damned) over individual communion cups, divorce and remarriage, support of missions, women using cosmetics and jewelry, eating in the meeting house, and even the name that should adorn the meeting house. Books have been written purporting to expound "sound doctrine" on each of these issues, and settle all arguments. All they did was inspire more. The fire that has heated our stoves comes from a deep-seated conviction that we have to perform perfectly in these areas or be lost. We have made every Bible verse a heaven-or-hell matter. We must be right! One hundred percent right. Right up to the end. But is being right the same as being righteous?

As a participant in five Unity Forums held during the 1980's involving the heirs of the Restoration Movement one thing has become very clear to me: We will never be united until we understand and enjoy justification by grace through faith. The underlying problem isn't instrumental music, or church organization. As important as basic communication is, it's not the cure-all either. Unless we come to the table secure in our own justification by faith, without perfect obedience, we'll eventually be tossing food across the table at one another, or off our chairs, down on the floor scrapping. Being right has become more important than being united. Once we become convinced that our being right with God depends on our faith, not on our orthodoxy, we'll blend together like the family we are.

No, we are not going to be saved by our perfect performance. Chapter Five looked at the laws behind good deeds (whether they be Mosaic or Christian) and found them to be incapable of justifying. If we make passages which declare the inablitiy of law to justify apply only to the Law of Moses, I believe we make a grave error. Law of any sort will never justify. Period. If it won't, then how will good deeds, their results, justify? There is simply not perfection there, and perfection in law-keeping is God's minimum requirement. Does this release us from trying? Of course not. Read on.

But we can't be saved without Christian deeds either. Our adherence to New Covenant commands, examples and principles arises out of our love for God. If real faith issued in obedience in our initial coming to Christ, then surely real love of the God of grace will issue in obedience too. "If you love me, you will obey what I command" (John 14:15). So then, disobedient, "out of duty" Christians will not be damned because their obedience wasn't perfect, but because they failed to love Jesus.

167

NOW CHRISTIAN LIVING GETS EXCITING!

The Family of God, newsletter from the Garnett Church of Christ, Tulsa, Oklahoma, had a marvelous little story told by Marvin Phillips, its minister, in the May, 1988, issue.

LET'S GET EVEN WITH GOD!

He approached me at the Soul Winning Workshop. Just a little fellow. He must have been about ten years old. He walked among the thousands of people passing out cards. Just little, "calling card" sized things. He was giving them to everyone who would take one. It read:

JUST GO AHEAD — GET EVEN WITH GOD
LOVE HIM BACK!
After all, He started it!

Now God gets blamed for a lot of the world's ills. "Where was God when I needed Him?" "Why me?" Many of us want to pull into God's Drive In, flash our lights, honk our horns, and expect Him to rush out to our car. We want service, and we want it now!

But when you think about it, "Every good and perfect gift is from above" (James 1:17). "He sends His sun and rain on the evil and good alike" (Matt. 5:45). And, "At just the right time, when we were still powerless, Christ died for the ungodly" (Rom. 5:6).

It is the "love of Christ that compels us" (II Cor. 5:14). To borrow the words of the beautiful song "O Sacred Head,"

What language would I borrow,
To thank Thee dearest friend,
For this Thy dying sorrow,
Thy pity without end?
O make me thine forever;
And should I fainting be,
Lord, let me never, never
Outlive my love to Thee.

Go ahead! Get even with God! *Love Him back!*

The Christian life is incredibly dull for many disciples. Duty, regimen, ritual, habit, obligation, performance — these end up spelling b-o-r-i-n-g. What's the problem? The motivation is wrong. Let me illustrate.

People do what they do in the Christian faith from three basic motivations: God is gonna git ya; God is gonna bless ya; or God loves ya. All three are legitimate, Biblical motivations, but the third is far superior. In fact, it might be called the motivation of grace.

God is to be feared, and fear is an acceptable motive for obedience. "And the Lord God commanded the man, saying, 'From any tree of the garden you may eat freely; but from the tree of the knowledge of good and evil you shall not eat, for in the day that you eat from it you shall surely die' " (Gen. 2:16-17). "For we know him who said, 'It is mine to avenge; I will repay,' and again, 'The Lord will judge his people.' It is a dreadful thing to fall into the hands of the living God" (Heb. 10:30-31). Obedience from fear is very Biblical.

The juxtaposition of Hebrews 10:30-31 to Hebrews 10:25 ("Let us not give up meeting together . . .") is not lost on most preachers. We would like to scare people into better church attendance. It can work all right, but fear doesn't produce the purest form of obedience. After God gave Ananias and Sapphira "early retirement" the Bible says that "Great fear seized the whole church and all who heard about these events" (Acts 5:11). But He didn't continue to zap wayward Christians like that. I think I know why. Fear doesn't produce quality obedience.

Sometimes fear doesn't work at all. God intended to strike fear into Cain's overheated head with His warning in Genesis 4:6-7. But Cain moved recklessly against Abel anyway. God issued stern warnings to ancient Israel, but she ignored many of them. The prophets stand as testimony to the relative ineffectiveness of fear as a motivation to right living.

In the New Testament there is a subtle, gradual move away from the use of fear to motivate us to good deeds. Other motivations rooted in love begin to surface. Here are just a few:

—*Good deeds as evidence of ownership* — "For we are

169

God's workmanship" (Eph. 2:10a). He made us, in His own image. Doing good is His nature. So should it be ours. See also Romans 6:16-18.

—*Good deeds as evidence of design* — We are "created in Christ Jesus to do good works, which God prepared in advance for us to do" (Eph. 2:10). Good deeds are what we're made for.

—*Good deeds as an investment* — "Let us not become weary in doing good, for at the proper time we will reap a harvest if we do not give up" (Gal. 6:9). "And everyone who has left houses or brothers or sisters or father or mother or children or fields for my sake will receive a hundred times as much and will inherit eternal life" (Matt. 19:29). See also Ephesians 6:7-8 and Philippians 4:9. It is the blessing motivation. Hundreds of promised benefits await the obedient. But spiritual self-interest and self-preservation still aren't the purest motives for serving Jesus.

—*Good deeds as a demonstration of faith* — "What good is it, my brothers, if a man claims to have faith but has no deeds? Can faith save him? Suppose a brother or sister is without clothes and daily food. If one of you says to him, 'Go, I wish you well; keep warm and well fed,' but does nothing about his physical needs, what good is it? In the same way, faith by itself, if it is not accompanied by action, is dead" (James 2:14-17).

—*Good deeds as a proof of salvation* — "We know that we have come to know him if we obey his commands. The man who says, 'I know him,' but does not do what he commands is a liar, and the truth is not in him. But if anyone obeys his word, God's love is truly made complete in him. This is how we know we are in him: Whoever claims to live in him must walk as Jesus did" (I John 2:3-6).

—*Good deeds as evidence of the value we place on our salvation* — "As a prisoner for the Lord, then, I urge you to live a life worthy of the calling you have received" (Eph. 4:1). See also Philippians 1:27. The value we place on our salvation will determine our Christian performance.

—*Good deeds as glorification of God* — "Live such good

lives among the pagans that, though they accuse you of doing wrong, they may see your good deeds and glorify God on the day he visits us" (I Peter 2:12). This is surely a high motive for Christian service.

LOVE, THE PUREST MOTIVE OF ALL

God loves ya, love Him back! Now that's the purest motivation of grace. Serve Him, not because you have to, not because you're afraid not to, not just because it pays off handsomely, but because you love Him. "The only thing that counts is faith expressing itself through love," Paul declared in Galatians 5:6. "Serve one another in love" (v. 13b). "And I pray that you, being rooted and established in love, may have power . . ." (Eph. 3:17b-18a). There are scores of New Testament verses that urge obedience to God, and service to the body from the motivation of love. John explained how it works in I John 4:16-18. "And so we know and rely on the love God has for us. God is love. Whoever lives in love lives in God, and God in him. Love is made complete among us so that we will have confidence on the day of judgment, because in this world we are like him. There is no fear in love. But perfect love drives out fear, because fear has to do with punishment. The man who fears is not made perfect in love."

A brief visit to I Peter will illustrate how beautifully and naturally love motivates disciples of Christ to good deeds.

I Peter 1:17-2:3 — Since you call on a Father who judges each man's work impartially, live your lives as strangers here in reverent fear. For you know that it was not with perishable things such as silver or gold that you were redeemed from the empty way of life handed down to you from your forefathers, but with the precious blood of Christ, a lamb without blemish or defect. He was chosen before the creation of the world, but was revealed in these last times for your sake. Through him you believe in God,

171

who raised him from the dead and glorified him, and so your faith and hope are in God.

Now that you have purified yourselves by obeying the truth so that you have sincere love for your brothers, love one another deeply, from the heart. For you have been born again, not of perishable seed, but of imperishable, through the living and enduring word of God. For, "All men are like grass, and all their glory is like the flowers of the field; the grass withers and the flowers fall, but the word of the Lord stands forever." And this is the word that was preached to you.

Therefore, rid yourselves of all malice and all deceit, hypocrisy, envy, and slander of every kind. Like newborn babies, crave pure spiritual milk, so that by it you may grow up in your salvation, now that you have tasted that the Lord is good.

Notice how Peter begins with "reverent fear" as a motivator of good behavior and moves immediately to what is a more sublime motivator, namely the price that was paid for our redemption. What emotion does this evoke? Obviously, love. And if that price is fully appreciated the love it evokes will not only be vertical, but also horizontal: "Now that you have purified yourselves by obeying the truth so that you have sincere love for your brothers, love one another deeply, from the heart." And love for God will produce a lifestyle of love, a life which thrives on the "pure spiritual milk" of the Word and weans us from the poisons which were killing us (malice, deceit, envy and slander). Graciously God informs and reminds us of the value of His gift, directs us in appropriate demonstrations of love, and then stands back to enjoy.

JUDGMENT BY GOOD DEEDS

Someone is sure to unsettle us with these observations: "I thought we were saved by grace, God's gift. But both Jesus and Paul tell us that we'll be judged on the basis of privilege and deeds. Are we saved by works after all?" What do those (and other) passages mean? Let's review them.

Matthew 12:36-37 — But I tell you that men will have to give account on the day of judgment for every careless word they have spoken. For by your words you will be acquitted, and by your words you will be condemned.

I Corinthians 3:12-15 — If any man builds on this foundation using gold, silver, costly stones, wood, hay or straw, his work will be shown for what it is, because the Day will bring it to light. It will be revealed with fire, and the fire will test the quality of each man's work. If what he has built survives, he will receive his reward. If it is burned up, he will suffer loss; he himself will be saved, but only as one escaping through the flames.

II Corinthians 11:15b — Their end will be what their actions deserve.

I Peter 1:17 — Since you call on a Father who judges each man's work impartially, live your lives as strangers here in reverent fear.

Revelation 2:23b — Then all the churches will know that I am he who searches hearts and minds, and I will repay each of you according to your deeds.

I have grouped these together because they all say approximately the same thing: We will be judged according to the deeds we perform. We could take the easy way out with these and say they refer not to judgment for heaven or hell, but judgment for rewards. The I Corinthians passage may indeed be talking about that. But what do you do with "acquitted" or "condemned" in Matthew 12? And the Revelation passage is in a setting of immorality and idolatry, sins that surely do more than just diminish rewards.

And then you have well known parables like The Faithful and Wise Manager (Luke 12:35-48), The Tenants (Matt. 21:33-44), and The Ten Virgins, The Talents, and The Sheep and the Goats (Matt. 25). Boy, they sure do sound like our deeds will figure into judgment.

Once again we're faced with the hermeneutical dilemma of "either - or" or "both - and". Is it justification by faith or by deeds? Or can it be justification by faith *and* deeds? Let's go for a solution. If our standing with God is sealed by faith in the substitutionary death of His Son, and we now have a new Master, and He issues orders for our behavior, and we ignore, discount, rebel against, or by some other means disobey them and fail to produce acceptable works, we will be found to be willful sinners (Heb. 10:26) at worst or careless lovers at best. If that becomes our lifestyle, we have cheapened grace by considering it unworthy of our attention and affection. We have "insulted the Spirit of grace." That whole passage in Hebrews deserves thoughtful consideration.

> *Hebrews 10:26-31* — If we deliberately keep on sinning after we have received the knowledge of the truth, no sacrifice for sins is left, but only a fearful expectation of judgment and of raging fire that will consume the enemies of God. Anyone who rejected the law of Moses died without mercy on the testimony of two or three witnesses. How much more severely do you think a man deserves to be punished who has trampled the Son of God under foot, who has treated as an unholy thing the blood of the covenant that sanctified him, and who has insulted the Spirit of grace? For we know him who said, "It is mine to avenge; I will repay," and again, "The Lord will judge his people." It is a dreadful thing to fall into the hands of the living God.

There are some strong words there: "fearful expectation of judgment," "raging fire," "how much more severely . . . punished," "dreadful thing," etc. But the deeds of the apostate Christian are pretty ugly too: "deliberately keep on sinning," "enemies of God," "trampled the Son of God under foot," "treated as an unholy thing the blood of the covenant," "insulted the Spirit of grace."

Likewise, the deeds described in those earlier passages were pretty ugly too:

—Blasphemy against the Holy Spirit (Matt. 12);

—Being false apostles and deceitful workers (II Cor. 11);

—Immorality and idolatry (Rev. 2);

—Disregard of our Master's instructions (Parable of the Unwise Manager, Luke 12);

174

—Outright rejection of Jesus (Parable of the Tenants, Matt. 21);

—Disrespect for the Bridegroom (Parable of the Virgins, Matt. 25);

—Misfeasance as stewards (Parable of the Sheep and Goats, Matt. 25);

—Sins of omission (Parables of the Sheep and Goats, Matt. 25).

Do I need to point out that these are not everyday sins of conscientious Christians, disciples "caught in sin"? These passages depict Christians who have "insulted the Spirit of grace."

So, we may conclude that God doesn't have a big set of scales in the sky on which he weighs our good deeds against our bad. Nor does he weigh grace on one side and our good deeds on the other. The most we could ever say about our good deeds is that they illuminate the beauty of God's grace. Conversely, an evil, rebellious lifestyle cheapens grace to the point that we throw it away and face an angry God in judgment with our sins counted against us, and without any hope of acquittal.

A view of a Christian standing before God following death is found in the New Testament. James Montgomery Boice writes about the death of Stephen: "There is a beautiful picture in the book of Acts of how the Christian can stand before God. It is a picture of how the one who has believed in Christ will find him — miracle of miracles — not as judge but redeemer. The picture comes to us from the account of the death of Stephen, a common person who had preached in Jerusalem with such power that the authorities hated him and had him stoned to death. Before he died, however, God granted him a vision of the heavenly Christ. He saw Jesus, not seated on the throne of judgment at the right hand of God, but rather standing at God's side to welcome him to glory. His testimony was 'Behold, I see the heavens opened, and the Son of man standing at the right hand of God' (Acts 7:56). As he died he repeated his Lord's own statements: 'Lord Jesus, receive my spirit' (v. 59) and 'Lord, do not hold this sin against them' (v. 60).[1]

What a better life to live and judgment to await when we have loved and obeyed!

EXTRAORDINARILY EXCITING!

Just a fleeting glance at three passages which illustrate grace-motivated obedience will excite us to a whole new Christian mindset and lifestyle.

II Corinthians 5:14 — For Christ's love compels us, because we are convinced that one died for all, and therefore all died.

What a way to live! Under the compulsion of love. Convinced that we are undoubtedly blessed with "everything we need for life and godliness through our knowledge of him who called us by his own glory and goodness" (II Pet. 1:3), we are pulled along as if by some magnetic force. We ride the rising thermals of divine energy with hardly a calorie of our own energy burned. Even the most menial task we are called to perform in Jesus' name becomes more important than being president; we attack it with exuberance; we come away exhilarated, not exhausted (Psa. 103:1-5). We're happy to be doorkeepers at the house of God.

Ephesians 2:8-10 — For it is by grace you have been saved, through faith — not by works, so that no one can boast. For we are God's workmanship, created in Christ Jesus to do good works, which God prepared in advance for us to do.

Here all three concepts of human deeds converge in two sentences. Salvation is not payment for works we have done, the kind man can boast about. (And wear us out.) Salvation is God's gift received by our faith. The result of the transaction is that we yield to God's design for our lives. We are like a piece of heirloom furniture, a thousand times more valuable than the wood we're

176

made of. He designed us to lovingly perform deeds of service to Him and His creatures. The "ordinary" aspects of Christian living like Bible reading, prayer, witnessing, and sharing become extraordinarily exciting.

II Corinthians 8:24 — Therefore show these men the proof of your love and the reason for our pride in you, so that the churches can see it.

II Corinthians 8 and 9 contain a surprising approach to a project undertaken by Paul. In his desire to provide financial assistance to Christians in Jerusalem, he conducted a kind of contest pitting the churches of Macedonia against the church at Corinth. It was a win-win-win-win kind of contest. God would win the glory (II Cor. 9:12-15); the Jerusalem church would be the winner financially and in thanksgiving (v. 12), and congregations in Macedonia (Philippi, Thessalonica, and Berea) and Corinth would enjoy the special benefits of giving. In this context they are enjoying: "overflowing joy" (8:2); "enthusiasm" (9:2) ; "generous reaping" (9:6-11); and praise for their generosity (9:13-14).

Paul is careful not to *command* giving in this instance: "I am not commanding you, but I want to test the sincerity of your love by comparing it with the earnestness of others" (II Cor. 8:8; cf. 9:7). His approach had already worked with the Macedonians: "For I testify that they gave as much as they were able, and even beyond their ability. Entirely on their own, they urgently pleaded with us for the privilege of sharing in this service to the saints" (8:3-4). I Corinthians 8 and 9 deserve a detailed study and search for the kind of excitement that derives from giving, not as a command, but because we love God. If our people really understood the excitement of love the Sunday collection time would pulsate with energy instead of throbbing with torpidity.

I Corinthians 15:10 — But by the grace of God I am what I am, and his grace to me was not without effect. No, I worked harder than all of them — yet not I, but the grace of God that was with me.

I reserved this passage until the very end of Part One because there may not be a better single verse to convey the beauty and power of grace than it. Justification by grace stands at the head. Next comes Paul's response to grace. He reached out to possess the gift. Once he pulled it to his bosom, it became like an implanted energy cell. He obeyed better than any other apostle and his service surpassed theirs. But it was not Paul doing it! He only yielded in faith. From beginning to end it was God giving to him and through him. This is grace as God planned it.

Endnote

1. James Montgomery Boice, *Foundations of the Christian Faith*, Inter-Varsity Press, Downers Grove, IL, 1986, p. 367.

PART TWO

GRACE
LIVING

INTRODUCTION

This is really two books in one. Part One is theology and Part Two is practicality. I had several approaches in mind in constructing it that way. Hopefully, the theology is not so complicated that only theologians will read it. Average disciples can understand it. Evangelists, pastors and teachers should have no problem. Nor should small group Bible study leaders.

But once Part One has been digested, it is hoped that leaders will want to put it to use in their own lives and in the lives of those who look to them for direction. That's what Part Two is designed to do. Let me explain that design more fully.

Thirteen Chapters. Suitable for a one or two quarter lesson series.

Practical Subjects. These get down to where people live to make grace the chassis on which the daily Christian life rolls.

Repetition. There is some repetition in these lessons, for which I make no apology. My experience has been that learning the lessons of grace is a lifelong task. Some of the key issues I have inserted in more than one chapter.

What Do You Think? This is a series of thought and/or discussion questions that are keyed to points made in the chapter. They are flagged in the text itself using the [a], [b], [c] symbols. Immediately following the chapter are the corresponding questions. These will work well as a class assignment (along with reading the chapter, of course), or as a basis for class discussion. Or the teacher may answer them him or herself and use them as the basis for his or her classroom or small group presentation.

Into the Life. These are suggestions for making the learning become a part of the student's daily life. They are challenges, strategies, or suggestions. The real benefit of the study and/or class time is determined by the use one makes of these.

May God bless you, dear reader, teacher, or disciple as His Holy Spirit animates your life with grace!

W.P.

7

A GREATER GRASP OF GRACE

The theme of God's Word is grace. "For God so loved the world that he gave . . . ." Grace is the New Testament word that describes the giving nature of God. It refers primarily to His gift of His one and only Son as payment for our sins. It was a gift that was totally undeserved by us, given without reference to our response to it, yet given with no strings attached. In the broader sense grace refers to all that God gives us: the ability to receive His gift and respond to it in love; the multitudinous spiritual and material blessings that make life liveable; and finally the eternal bliss of heaven. Grace is in the first verse of Genesis and the last verse of Revelation.

Genesis 1:1 — In the beginning God created . . . .
Revelation 22:21 — The grace of the Lord Jesus be with God's people. Amen. [a]

But grace was never meant to be a vague theological term to

Christians. It was meant to be understood, appreciated, appropriated, and lived daily. It was meant to be as prominent in our spiritual lives as the sun is in our physical lives. It was meant to illuminate our hearts, to warm us, and to make us grow. God wanted the word on the lips of every Christian, in every conversation, in every prayer, in every song. He wanted us to be people of grace, saved by it, preserved by it, loving it, shaped by it, walking in it, valuing it, living and dying in it, and dying for it if necessary.

But let me tell you about three friends of mine: Clyde, Millie, and Brian. All three are Christians, saved by grace (whether they know it or not), members of the church. But there the similarities end.

Clyde came to Christ as a teenager after having attended church for as long as he could remember with his mother and sisters. He was carefully led by his Bible class teacher through the five steps of the plan of salvation (hearing, believing, repenting, confessing, being baptized), though he would admit that he can't remember too well what sins he repented of. He would tell you it was probably taking some candy from the corner grocery once, lying to his mother a few times, and looking at a classmate's answers during a test in Algebra I. Oh yes, he had found some pornographic pictures once in an alley and he looked at them. The baptism part he remembers well. The baptismal heaters hadn't been turned on and it was November. Brrrr.

He matured as a person and as a Christian. He was a very scrupulous Christian. Very careful to live right, to be a good example, to be faithful, to live on the safe side. He was a great Bible student and he seldom missed an assembly of the church. And he led several people to Christ during his own spiritual childhood. True, his prayers began sounding all the same, but maybe that was because he prayed so much.

But lately he's grown judgmental. He likes to sit in church and imagine why so-and-so isn't there. And critical. People just aren't doing what they ought to. Why can't people be like him? His patience and compassion wear thin. He's grown negative. The only

184

good preaching to him is preaching against someone or something. And he feeds on catastrophic expectations about people and programs. ("She'll never make it," and "We never did it that way before" are two favorite phrases of his.) He's like a pastdate carton of milk. Sour. He seems happiest when he is unhappiest. He is more anxious to straighten out someone than to hear him out. Hypocrites especially sunburn his soul. Problem Christians get strange treatment from him. If they are doing well he greets them warmly as brothers. If not, if he greets them he'll call them Mr. or Mrs. He draws a circle of God's faithful people periodically. Inside the circle are the saved (including himself of course). Outside are the lost. As the years have passed the circle gets smaller and smaller. And he seems to be enjoying it! He has become less and less interested in bringing people to Christ because most of them wouldn't have what it takes to be Christians anyhow. But he doesn't have to worry. His neighbors and work mates aren't interested in his faith anyhow.

And then there is Millie, the daughter of an elder. She was a really straight arrow for Jesus until she returned from college. Then she became one of the people who bothered Clyde so much. She only came to church when she felt like it. Missed the Lord's Supper more often than not. People generally felt her job as a flight attendant was a big part of her problem. And then there was her boyfriend who was not a Christian. The people she ran with from the airline were pretty wild. And she didn't hide the fact that she drank with them. Her boyfriend was into water skiing on Sundays, so he never came with her.

Don't worry, people have talked to Millie about her faithfulness to Jesus (or lack of). But she shoots back that she has been freed from rules and regulations. She is a Christian, not an Israelite under the Law of Moses, she says. She intends to be a happy, liberated Christian, not a grump like Clyde. (Yes, she used him as an example of what *not* to be.) None of her friends ever come to church. Few know she is a Christian. She once tried to help a girlfriend who thought she might have AIDS, but when

Jesus and church came up, the girl told her that she was just as much a Christian as Millie anyway.

And then there is Brian. He's in love. With Jesus. He is as enthusiastic today, eight years later, as he was the day of his new birth. Maybe more. He is for everything. And everybody. He lights up the room. But one thing he does is paradoxical. As great a Christian as he is he constantly talks about how God is delivering from this sin and that sin. He's not trying to impress you with himself, but with God. He's got so much patience with struggling souls. He says it's because he struggles too. About the only time he misses Christian assemblies is when he's sitting up with a sick friend, or out trying to talk someone into coming with him. I guess he just forgets the time.

What a believer Brian is! Not only in Jesus, but in people. I can grow just standing next to him. And I've been saved a lot longer than he. He doesn't know the Bible quite as well as Clyde, and I think he's made some errors in judgment as a Christian, but what he has is contagious. I can count ten or twelve people he's led to Christ for salvation in the last couple of years.

What's the difference?

Grace.

Neither Clyde nor Millie understands grace. Brian lives it. To the extent that Clyde or Millie reminds us of ourselves, neither do we understand grace. [b] We need a greater grasp of grace. Wouldn't we really like to live the Christian life like Paul described it in Romans 5:1-2? "Therefore, since we have been justified through faith, we have peace with God through our Lord Jesus Christ, through whom we have gained access by faith into this grace in which we now stand. And we rejoice in the hope of the glory of God." [c]

1. A GREATER GRASP OF GRACE BEGINS WITH A GREATER GRASP OF SIN.

A. *In true conversion the enormity of sin is generally felt.*

186

They sure felt it on the day of Pentecost (Acts 2:36-37). Saul did (Acts 9:4-5; 22:4-10). The jailer at Philippi did (Acts 16:25-34). [d]

B. *But the mature Christian's view of his own sin often gets warped.* Let's slip into prayer meeting quietly, unnoticed if possible. What are we hearing? "And Lord, forgive my weaknesses." "If I have sinned this week . . . ." Imperfections, failures, mistakes, shortcomings, human frailities — those are the terms being used. Whatever happened to sin? Or Sin? Or SIN? "Oh Dear Father, please be laughing at us. Don't get angry. We've forgotten how to say the word." [e]

C. *The funny things we Christians do with our sins.* Sometimes we try to ignore them (like Cain did, Gen. 4:9). Or euphemize them like the illustration above. Some of us have invented a Sin Scale by which to judge ourselves favorably. Oh sure you know how it works. We number it 1 to 10. The really abominable sins (mass murder, mutilation, rape, sexual abuse of children, etc.) we rate a 10. Armed robbery, gross immorality, abortion, murder, etc. rate 8 or 9. Embezzlement, homosexual behavior, hardcore pornography, abandoning children, theft, etc. get a 7. Black lies, attending X-rated movies, cheating the IRS, extramarital affairs, etc. get a 5 or 6. Robbing God of tithes, wasting money on the lottery (unless of course you win, at which time it falls clear off the bottom of the scale), stealing from your company, lustful thoughts, "soft" pornography, etc. get a 3 or 4. Sins of omission like failing to spend time alone with God, not studying your Bible lesson, or attending R-rated movies, white lies, greed, pride, hypocrisy, and gossip, are in the 1 or 2 category. Of course, we can make up our own scales to suit ourselves, but the trick is to stay in the 1 to 4 range and everything will be OK. And if all else fails we can always point the finger at someone who is a worse sinner than we are. [f]

D. *All this hocus-pocus makes repentance unnecessary.* And this is no new ploy by Satan. Luke 13:1-5 describes people who didn't want to face their own sins and repent of them. They were anxious to point the finger at others. How much hard-nosed repenting does the average Christian do weekly? How much is James 5:16 practiced in your fellowship? [g]

E. *The worst result of this warped view of our own sins is that we feel little need for grace.* Paul could say that he was the worst sinner of all (I Tim. 1:15-16) because he understood and trusted God's grace. [h]

2. LET'S GRASP THE NEW TESTAMENT TEACHING OF SALVATION BY GRACE THROUGH FAITH.

A. *Our sins must either be paid for by us or by someone else.* We have all sinned (Rom. 3:9-23) and sin results in spiritual death, which is separation from God forever (Rom. 6:23). However, our sins can be taken away by God's perfect sacrifice, Jesus Christ (John 1:29,35).

B. *Scripture says it absolutely: We cannot pay for our sins or earn our salvation.* That was the decision that came out of the council on circumcision (Acts 15:11). Paul used the example of Abraham to explain that justification (being forgiven, declared righteous) is by gift, not merit in Romans 4. II Corinthians 8:9 and Ephesians 2:8-9 affirm this too. [i]

C. *This gift of justification is received by faith.* Romans 5:1 is a stopping point in Paul's lengthy discussion of grace in Romans. It begins, "Therefore, since we have been justified through faith . . . ." Exactly how that justifying faith works is illustrated in the life of Abraham in Romans 4:16-25. [j] Acts of the Apostles illustrates justifying faith in the lives of scores who came to Christ. Their stories may be read in Acts 2:36-45; 8:4-13; 8:26-39; 16:25-35; 18:7-8; 19:1-7; 22:1-16. [k] This faith was not just intellectual belief in Jesus. It was faith that acted. But in no way did faith earn salvation.

D. *Then we live our Christian lives in God's grace.* Eternal life is not payment for Christian living and service (I Pet. 1:13-16).

188

Christian living becomes love-motivated, not fear-motivated (John 14:15; 15:9-10; I John 4:16-21). [l] Christians will still sin, but sin is no longer our lifestyle (Rom. 6:15-23), and when we do sin, God is anxious to forgive (I John 1:6-10). [m]

3. NOW WATCH US GROW IN GRACE!

Several things happen in Christians' lives when they begin to understand that they aren't going to heaven because they've been good, or good enough, or done enough good deeds, but rather because God is good and has given them eternal life. Let's get the one negative out of the way first.

A. *Some grow careless in their love.* That's the risk God took when He decided to love and give. The Millies among us cheapen grace by taking it for granted. Pretty soon they are living the same old worldly life as before, but they have a new problem: they believe their relationship to God is indestructible. Now that is dangerous. They lose their peace (Rom. 5:1; Phil. 4:4-7), their power over sin (Heb. 3:12-19), their godly testimony (Matt. 5:13-16), and ultimately they lose the gift itself (Heb. 12:15-29; II Pet. 2:20-22). [n]

Obviously, this was not God's design for grace. But it's the risk He took for all the potential good that might come. The good looks like this:

B. *Through grace we can look at ourselves honestly.* On the one hand we can admit that we are sinners because it's true, and because there is a remedy. We can admit that no matter how hard we try, we fail. We can really repent, and really change. On the other hand we can see our true value in God's eyes. Grace teaches us that we are worth God's utmost, His one and only Son. Up, up, up goes our self-image and our hope. [o]

C. *Grace enhances our appreciation of our salvation.* That great passage in Ephesians 1:3-14 really comes to life when we realize that the salvation we enjoy is "to the praise of his glorious grace, which he has freely given us in the One he loves" (v. 6). [p]

D. *Grace improves our empathy for the lost.* When we understand God's patience with us, ours with others improves. We're no longer on a self-righteous pedestal. We can really get down where sinners are because we are sinners too. [q]

E. *We can live more relaxed Christian lives.* We can quit living with "eternal insecurity." [r] We can believe in the Holy Spirit for who He is and what He represents in our lives. "Having believed, you were marked in him with a seal, the promised Holy Spirit, who is a deposit guaranteeing our inheritance until the redemption of those who are God's possession — to the praise of his glory" (Eph. 1:13b-14). We can quit working *for* God and start working *with* Him, as partners (I Cor. 3:9). [s]

F. *Grace can change our congregations.* Our fellowships can be places of openness and honesty — qualities often missing from churches. They can become hospitals for the sin-sick instead of museums for the display of perfect specimens. We won't have the reputation of being self-righteous. People will know us by our love, not our rightness on every issue. We can practice James 5:13-20. [t]

I have heard the story of the loss of life that occurred during the building of the Golden Gate bridge in San Francisco Bay during the 1930's. The losses became so great that engineers, safety experts, and civic authorities met to seek a solution. The work had fallen hopelessly behind schedule because of fear encountered by the workmen. Costs were soaring. Bond-holders were fearful of losing large sums if the work was not completed on schedule. Finally the suggestion was made that a large net be hung under the bridge to catch any workers who might fall. But the cost was nearly prohibitive. But what about the cost in lost time and lives? Finally the net was seen as the only solution. It was obtained and hung and work resumed. Workers were skeptical until one day a worker fell from the span into the net and was rescued. Form that day forward confidence was restored, the

190

work moved more quickly than ever. And I'm told the bridge was completed ahead of schedule.

That's grace — the net of God's love which relaxes us to serve Him in love.

(The foregoing was taken from a sermon by the same title preached by the author at Nationwide Youth Roundup, Sedalia, Colorado on August 5, 1976.)

WHAT DO YOU THINK?

(The following questions are keyed to sections in the preceding chapter. Refer to the section for full understanding of the question.)

[a] Where is grace in these two passages?
[b] What is wrong with Clyde's approach to the Christian life?
[c] At this point in the study do you believe Clyde has peace? Does Millie? Explain your answers.
[d] Discuss what must have been going through their minds.
[e] Why do you think it is hard for Christians to speak of their own sins by name?
[f] Do Christians really do this?
[g] Answer these questions. Why are we so soft on ourselves?
[h] Did Paul really mean this or was he just being dramatic? Would it be hard for you to say this and mean it?
[i] Does this mean that God doesn't weigh our good deeds against our bad and judge us accordingly? Explain.
[j] Explain exactly how Abraham's faith worked.
[k] How is faith demonstrated in these stories?
[l] What does this kind of Christian living look like?
[m] What keeps us from becoming outlaws like Millie?
[n] Can careless or rebellious Christians lose their gift of eternal life?
[o] How will this view of ourselves improve our self-image?
[p] What words and phrases in that passage reveal the value of our salvation?
[q] What good might come from this?

[r]   What does this expression mean?

[s]   Is relaxed Christian living really right? Explain.

[t]   How does your congregation measure up in these areas now? Can a greater grasp of grace really help?

INTO THE LIFE

1.   Make a list of sins you are currently committing. Write a description of each one. Describe how you think God must feel about each one.

2.   In your daily prayers include confession of these sins — by name. Find Bible verses that discuss them. Ask God to help you feel the sting. Ask Him to remove all self-righteousness and pride. Beg for forgiveness. Chart your progress.

3.   Leader, give your class or congregation a grace test. Formulate a brief quiz that will determine their views on the subject. Use this to plan future teaching and preaching emphasis.

8

GRACE AND GRAMMAR

Many years ago when I married my wife one of my first tasks was to learn to talk. Oh, I wasn't that young when we married! I knew how to talk well enough to pop the question. She understood, said yes, and the rest is history.

But I still needed to learn how to talk. To talk married talk. You know — "our car" instead of "my car;" "our bank account" instead of "my bank account;" "we're going to do such and such" instead of "I'm going to do such and such." The ceremony that evening in June didn't instantly teach me married talk. The minister said, "I now pronounce you husband and wife," but it took me weeks to know how to pronounce "us," "we," and "our."

The same phenomenon occurs with the great transaction of grace. In a split second at the ceremony of baptism we receive God's gift of eternal life. But it takes us weeks (months? years?) to learn how to talk grace. God is patient with us, no doubt. He may even chuckle as we learn. We had a few chuckles during our early days as wife and husband. I'm reminded of the story (told to me as true) of the brand new Christian who lived in the backwoods. His hair was hardly dry when he was encouraged to offer his first prayer as a new child of God. Now that his own future was secure his thoughts went to his buddies who were still lost. So he prayed for them. "And dear God, don't let my friends go to hell. They're too green to burn." Pointed, if not very polished.

The Apostle Paul knew we would have trouble transitioning from dead in sin to alive in Jesus, so he wrote: "In the same way, count yourselves dead to sin but alive to God in Christ Jesus" (Rom. 6:11). "Reckon," "consider," and "regard" are used in other translations in place of "count." There is a time and thought lapse for us between the transaction and the reality of it. "Count yourselves" is Paul's way of saying, "Learn the reality of grace. Learn the language of grace. Walk and talk like the new creature you are, even before it comes naturally." [a]

Talking grace talk is not some religious gimmick. I am referring to putting into our everyday speech the truths of our new relationship with God. We are justified, counted righteous, qualified for heaven, all because of Jesus. Talking about grace has the very special benefit of helping grace become real and natural to us. We may be able to define the term ("the unmerited favor of God"), but that's a pretty short conversation. A hopeless world needs to hear more. And when we do speak we ". . . should do it as one speaking the very words of God" (I Pet. 4:11). [b]

D.H. Kehl, an English professor from Arizona State University, more than fifteen years ago wrote an article in *Christianity Today* entitled, "The Grammar of Grace." In it he pressed the need for a fundamental overhaul of our grammar if we are going to enjoy personally, and effectively share this marvelous standing we have with God. I couldn't say it any better, so with proper acknowledgements to Dr. Kehl, let me summarize and elaborate upon some of his points. I will add one point at the end that is especially important for us who are heirs of the Restoration Movement.

1. THE PRONOUNS OF GRACE

Come on, don't you remember your English grammar? A pronoun is a word that stands for a noun. The pronouns of grace are "He," "Him," and "His" instead of "I," "me," and "mine." Paul had his grammar right: "I have been crucified with Christ and I no longer live, but Christ lives in me. The life I live in the body, I live by faith in the Son of God, who loved me and gave himself for me. I do not set aside the grace of God . . ." (Gal. 2:20-21a). [c]

Romans 7 and 8 are an interesting study in these pronouns. In chapter seven "I" occurs many times. [d] And the chapter winds down with Paul's desperate cry, "What a wretched man I am!" (v. 24). "A man wrapped up in himself makes a very small package." Finally, in the last verse, he finds his salvation in "Him." The eighth chapter then is about being "in Jesus," a phrase that describes grace. This chapter might be called Paul's Declaration of Dependence. When "I" is replaced with "He" in our thinking and in our talk, His Spirit inspires us to live the grace life. [e]

2. THE NUMBER OF GRACE

Come on, English students. Number refers to whether a noun or pronoun is singular or plural. The number of grace is plural. God and we make a majority! ". . . The one who is in you is greater than the one who is in the world" (I John 4:4b). Grace means we are no longer alone! I Corinthians 3:5-9 and II Corinthians 5:17-20 show that we are God's partners, not slaves or even employees. [f]

195

Do you know what this means? The success of our personal lives no longer depends on our struggle alone. The success of the church doesn't either. When people reject Christ they haven't rejected us. "We're in this together, Lord. When I fail, we fail together. When the church isn't what it ought to be, it doesn't depend solely on me to make it right." [g]

3. THE TENSE OF GRACE

Now we're into verbs — past, present or future. Grace living is very much present tense, not so much past or even future. Grace erases guilt for past sins. We don't have to grieve over them any more. Grace doesn't make us long to be out of this world so we can enjoy heaven. Grace makes living here and now wonderful! We can live grace-fully! [h]

Paul's direction was "Forgetting what is behind and straining toward what is ahead, I press on toward the goal to win the prize for which God has called me heavenward in Christ Jesus" (Phil. 3:13b-14). The past was totally out of the picture, the goal was future, but the "straining" and "pressing on" were present tense. No sitting in a rocking chair waiting for His return. Places to go, things to do, people to see for Jesus. "For the grace of God that brings salvation has appeared to all men. It teaches us to say 'No' to ungodliness and worldly passions, and to live self-controlled, upright, and godly lives in this present age, while we wait for the blessed hope — the glorious appearing of our great God and Savior, Jesus Christ" (Titus 2:11-13). [i]

4. THE VOICE OF GRACE

You remember: active, where the verb does the acting, or passive, where the action is done to it. You don't remember? So what. The voice of grace is active. God acted on our behalf while we were "powerless," "sinners," and "God's enemies," according to Romans 5:6-11. He acted while we were at best "Christians in prospect" (I John 4:10). He loved us before we loved Him (I John 4:19). He loads us with benefits every day, according to the King James translation of Psalm 68:19. [j]

Grace-indued Christians are also active. John gave us unmistakably clear lessons on making grace an active force in our lives in I John 3:16-18. The gift we have received is not meant to reside in us, but to flow through us to others. It will never run out (Luke 6:38). We can go into the dens of iniquity and solicit candidates for God's mercy. We can't hang a sign in front of a squeaky-clean chruch building and bemoan the fact that drunks, pimps and prostitutes, drug addicts and pushers, homosexuals and the like don't come to church. We can't wag our heads at the world going to hell in a handbasket. We can at least get into the handbasket and try to pull some willing people out (Jude 22-23). [k]

5. THE MODE OR MOOD OF GRACE

Here's where most of our English grammar fails us. The indicative mood of a verb expresses fact or certainty, and the subjunctive expresses doubt or something contrary to fact. In Mark 9:22-23 Jesus corrected the grammar of the father who brought his demon-possessed son to Him for healing. "But if you can do anything . . ." the father implored. " 'If you can?' " Jesus protested. "Everything is possible for him who believes," He added, placing the doubt (if there was any) on the man, not on himself. [l]

In a day when uncertainty oozes from almost everyone's pores, Christians who have received God's grace, and have been declared righteous, and know it, can speak in the indicative mood, with certainty. "Yet I am not ashamed, because I know whom I have believed . . ." (II Tim. 1:12a). "And we know that

197

in all things God works for the good of those who love him, who have been called according to his purpose" (Rom. 8:28). "And my God will meet all your needs according to his glorious riches in Christ Jesus" (Phil. 4:19). [m] We don't speak arrogantly, just confidently. And our confidence is rooted in what God did for us at Calvary.

6. THE PREPOSITIONS OF GRACE

Prepositions are those little connecting words like in, with, for, against, among, etc. Some are negative, some are positive. The prepositions of grace are all positive. We are "in Christ," Ephesians 1:1 says. [n] And Christ is "in" us, Colossians 1:27. [o]

"In this work we work with God," the Phillips translation of I Corinthians 3:9 reads. "Fellow-workers" is how other translations render it. We don't even work *for* God, we work *with* Him, as partners in his marvelous work of reconciling the world to himself. "If God is for us, who can be against us?" Romans 8:31 asks. There the prepositions say that God is not trying to find a way to condemn us, but to save us. He is so much for us that no other power can come between us and Him unless we allow it. The succeeding verses in Romans 8 describe how much He is for us [p]

7. THE CONJUNCTIONS OF GRACE

Like prepositions, conjunctions are little words that join (or separate) other words or phrases: either, or, neither, nor, both, and. When it comes to justification, it is *either* by grace *or* by works. The New Testament makes clear that it is by grace (Eph. 2:4-5, 8-10). [q]

It is not by grace *and* good works, *and* obedience, as though they all three cooperated together in our salvation. Some have the concept that Christians obey and work to the best of their

198

ability and God's grace makes up the difference between our best effort and God's least standard. But that's not what Paul taught with the case of Abraham in Romans 4. He taught that rightousness (right standing with God) was "credited" to him as a gift, not paid to him as wages. [r] Eternal life is a gift, not wages paid for work done, according to Romans 6:23. [s] [t]

Since words relate directly to concepts, let us get our words in line with the concepts of Scripture and speak the grammar of grace. Thinking about grace and learning the language will surely translate into concrete grace-full living that will draw our friends and loved ones to our Jesus!

WHAT DO YOU THINK?

(The following questions are keyed to sections in the preceding chapter. Refer to the section for full understanding of the questions.)

[a] What was the most difficult for you to get accustomed to when you first became a Christian?
[b] How do you currently explain your salvation and Christian life to others?
[c] Exactly what did Paul mean in this passage?
[d] How many times?
[e] From Romans 8 how would you describe the grace-life?
[f] Explain how this partnership works.
[g] How can this outlook impact our Christian lives and service?
[h] Is there anything wrong with living in the past or future?
[i] Specifically, what are some things we ought to be doing while we live in grace?
[j] List ten benefits you presently enjoy from the Father.
[k] How does grace help us in such active outreach?
[l] How does the Bible say grace is received by us in the first place? (Eph. 2:8)
[m] Where is grace in these passages?
[n] Locate as many other times as you can where that phrase is

used in Ephesians.

[o]   What exactly does this expression mean?

[p]   Just exactly how much is God for us?

[q]   What are the works mentioned in verse 10?

[r]   Put your understanding of this chapter in words for your personal use or for class discussion.

[s]   How is eternal death earned?

[t]   Are there some other parts of speech that might help us understand and talk about grace in a better way?

INTO THE LIFE

1.   Locate and mark as many grace passages in the Bible as you can. Use a transparent felt-tip marker or indicate them by placing the letter "G" in the margin.

2.   Begin to daily thank God for some aspect of His grace. You may want to "pray through" one of the passages you marked. Think of it like this: God is speaking to you in that passage. Isn't it appropriate that you respond? So, talk about the passage to Him, telling Him how you feel about it. Try this refreshing kind of prayer.

3.   With a Bible study group, prayer group, prayer or disciple partner discuss how you can put grace at the center of your Christian lives, making it a matter of daily thought, conversation, and prayer. You may even devise a game where you reward any mention of grace or fine any failure. Use the money for your own practice of the grace of giving.

4.   Since by grace we were "created in Christ Jesus for good works," initiate plans for personal or group good works you can perform as a loving response to God's grace.

9

GRACE AND JOY

"For the kingdom of God is not a matter of eating and drinking, but of righteousness, peace and joy in the Holy Spirit" (Rom. 14:17).

How are things where you go to church? Are you going more and enjoying it less? Or going less and enjoying it more? Or going less and enjoying it less?

Can people feel the joy that is in your church? Do visitors come back because they are drawn magnetically by joy? Does the song leader have to badger people to get them to sing? Does the Lord's Supper seem more like a wake than a celebration? Do people eagerly listen to the message, following along in their Bibles, maybe taking notes? Do they seem to be having fun? Do people exit afterwards like they were fire drilling? Are you really filled at assemblies? Or drained? [a]

When a group of believers discovers that grace is the basis of their standing with God, joy breaks out all over. It actually oozes from the pores of the body of Christ. A marvelous metamorphosis occurs when Christians really believe that their standing with God is not based on performance, but on grace. The Christian life becomes a party given by God to celebrate our return home (Luke 15:6,9,22-24). We can enjoy it. We can wear smiles, not shmurgks (those are a combination of shirks, smurks, and shrugs, the demeanor of many Christians). And we can wear them home and spread them around the community.

And guess what? When joy improves, so does performance. Performance, you know — nose to the grindstone, hand on the wheel, eyes on the road, sucked up and bucked up. Performance — the hard taskmaster by which we judge ourselves and everyone else (everyone else a bit harder than ourselves). Improved performance via grace and joy. Maybe God knew all the time that if He gave us a clean past and a guaranteed future we would love Him to death (our own). We would love and serve Him with an intensity that commandments, or threats, or guilt could never produce. I'm sure He knew what He was doing. [b]

HERE'S HOW GRACE WORKS
RULE: Sin must be punished, Romans 6:23.

PROBLEM: Man sins and must be punished, Romans 3:23.

SOLUTION: God will give His Son who will take our punishment, thereby satisfying the demands of his own justice, and crediting us with God's righteousness, Romans 3:21-26.

SALVATION: God's gift of righteousness is received by us through faith, Romans 5:1-2.

STANDING: Forgiven Christians live in that grace, enjoying it every day, Romans 5:2 [c]

Oooooooo, how the understanding and appreciation of grace will unleash joy on you and your congregation!

1. GRACE RELAXES US IN SPIRITUAL SECURITY.

Enough of this "eternal insecurity." Listen to the Word: "Consider the incredible love that the Father has shown us in allowing us to be called 'children of God' — and that is not just what we are called, but what we are. Our heredity on the Godward side is no mere figure of speech" (I John 3:1-2a, Phillips Translation). [d] "Being confident of this, that he who began a good work in you will carry it on to completion until the day of Christ Jesus" (Phil. 1:6). [e]

God is at least as smart as an employer who, instead of standing over an employee issuing dire warnings and threats in case of failure, believes in us, exudes confidence, hands out compliments and sticks with us even when we fail. [f]

"But isn't there the danger that we will get *too relaxed* in our Christian lives if we rely too much on grace?" someone wisely asks. Complacency is a problem for every Christian, regardless of his understanding of grace, so we can neutralize that part of the question. It really comes down to a Biblical question: Are we secure in our standing with God or aren't we? What does the Book say? If it says we are then we can relax as much as God allows us. Here's what it says:

> *Matthew 18:4* — God is not willing that any of these little ones should perish.
> *John 3:16-17* — God's love which resulted in the gift of His one and only Son was aimed at our preservation, not our perishing.
> *John 6:37* — Jesus will never drive away those who come to Him.
> *Romans 8:31-39* — Nothing can separate us from the love of God which is in Christ Jesus.
> *I John 5:11* — God has given us eternal life. It is spoken of as a present possession of the Christian. [g]

These verses are God's viewpoint. He didn't save us to lose us. We are absolutely secure so far as He is concerned. Isn't that relaxing! [h] Can you see how much more joyously we can go about our Christian lives? We struggle to be all we can, then relax in His grace. When we lose, we win when He is for us!

2. GRACE TELLS US: IT'S OK IF YOU MAKE MISTAKES.

I know Christians who are afraid to make mistakes. I mean *really afraid*. Therefore they don't do much of anything. They make them anyway, but they alibi or hide them because they don't know what to do with them. They rationalize that they aren't as bad as others. And they live under a little grey cloud of self-delusion. They can't admit that they are sinners because sinners are going to hell. [i]

Enter grace. It doesn't tell us to deliberately sin, but it acknowledges that we do. It tells us that we can live by faith, we can try things that don't work, we can fall, we can admit our sins, we can enjoy more adventuresome, exciting lives, because grace isn't a one-shot gift. For those who live in grace, forgiveness is always available when we repent (I John 1:8-10). God and Jesus are in the forgiving business, not the condemning business (John 3:17). Sure, those who reject Him will be condemned, but those who want Him as their Lord and Savior will be forgiven. [j]

Isn't it nice to know that your mistakes aren't fatal? And you can call them sins. You can admit, right alongside one of God's greatest servants, that you are "the worst" of sinners (I Tim. 1:15). You can even confess them to others (James 5:16). Doesn't that sound like a great way to live? [k]

3. THROUGH GRACE WE SEE SALVATION AS A RELATIONSHIP.

From the vantage point of grace John 3:16 has a whole new look. I always saw it as a statement of Christian doctrine, or maybe a preview of the gospel. It may be both of those, but I now know that it is about relationships, which is really what makes the world go 'round. Let's take a walk through it relationally.

"For God so loved the world" — That's the first relationship.

204

God and the world, with God's love holding it together.

"That he gave his one and only Son" — There's the second relationship. God and Jesus, both of them giving.

"That whoever believes in him shall not perish but have eternal life" — There's the third relationship. It is stated potentially here. All it lacks is our believing that the first two relationships exist to make it happen. [l]

And maybe the glue that holds these relationships together should be looked at more closely: loving, giving, believing. What risks God took! He loved and gave, two of the most dangerous acts we can imagine. We might not receive either. We might not reciprocate. Oh, how the heart of God could be crushed. But He took the risks. Then He asked that we take a risk commensurate with His. Believe. Get all the evidence we can about Jesus, and then believe that he is truly the Father's loving gift. Is that too much to ask? We think not.

And so we enjoy a relationship with God. It's a relationship of loving and giving and believing. A religion of relationship is one of joy. He is greater than we are, He owns us, we serve Him, we are accountable to Him, we will be rewarded or punished by Him, but underlying all these Biblical truths is the fact that we are related to Him. He is our Father, Jesus is our Savior, the Holy Spirit is our comforter. God loves us like children. He is anxious to forgive, to receive us back, to enjoy our fellowship. The story of the prodigal son illustrates the joy of relationship that God's grace brings us (Luke 15:11-32). [m] That story ends in a joyous celebration.

4. GRACE ALLOWS US TO LOVE OURSELVES APPROPRIATELY.

Grace says we are OK because Jesus is OK and we belong to Him (I Cor. 3:23). God feels good about us, and for us to feel any differently would be inappropriate. Matthew 5:48 may sound impossible to us unless we understand grace. There Jesus calls us to "Be perfect, therefore, as your heavenly Father is perfect." That sounds like a big order. Too big. But I don't believe He was asking us to be God, or as good as God, but to be complete, all we were designed to be. That's what God is — complete. And that is the meaning of the Greek word Jesus used. [n]

None of this popular self-glorification that is advocated by pop-psychologists. Grace says we have been given God's righteousness. We didn't earn it. We didn't get our heads on straight and it happened. We are not Christians because we keep all the rules, but because the rule-maker is our Father. And one of the rules He has made is that when His children sin and repent He forgives them. He doesn't love us because our performance is perfect, but because we are His. We are children of God because we have a relationship with Him that was paid for by His only Son. If we can't love someone who was (and is) loved that much by the Creator, then our love for the Creator is in question. [o]

Back up. Take a look in the mirror of grace. Now isn't that a fine specimen of God's handiwork? Go ahead, enjoy.

5. GRACE RELIEVES US FROM BEING PHARISEES.

Pharisees were religious folk who thought God loved them especially because they were so good. The truth of the matter is that God loved them *in spite of* their goodness. Because their goodness was often self-contrived, or selective, or hypocritical or dishonest. [p]

One of their self-appointed jobs was to keep religion pure. Their role in God's work was to find fault with others, hold themselves up as examples of purity, and then demand that others shape up (Matt. 9:10-11; 12:1-2; 15:1-2; 23:1-36). That's exhausting work, as Jesus acknowledged in Matthew 23. And it's really not much fun. It makes life a drag. I'm sure they were a dour bunch. "Imperfection is everywhere. What a drag." Their offspring are still around. [q]

The worst part about being a Pharisee is that you won't be saved (Matt. 23:15), not because Pharisees weren't good, but because they trusted in their goodness to save them (Luke 18:9). Under grace you don't have to "look down on everybody else" like they did. You can look up to Jesus and invite others to do the same.

When we quit being Pharisees, the wrinkles on our souls relax, and a grin of joy spreads across our faces. People don't run when we come around. They want to know what we're grinning about. Shall we tell them? [r]

6. GRACE SENDS US BACK INTO THE WORLD.

Most every Christian is aware that we are under the Great Commission which commands us to "make disciples of all the nations" (Matt. 28:19). [s] But let's don't go back into the world out of which we have been saved unless we go with a message of grace. Let's not make disciples like the Pharisees did. Jesus said theirs ended up "twice as much a son of hell as you are" (Matt. 23:15b). Let's don't offer people a drab, dull, melancholy faith. That's not the religion of Jesus. Why would anybody want to exchange one dreary, depressed lifestyle for another one — one that is going to last forever? [t]

We all need two conversions: one out of the world, and another back into it. We came out of the world of sin with dirt all over us, bent and broken, bloody from encounters with Satan, barely able to slump into the arms of Jesus. But He has cleaned us up, stood us on our feet, lifted our heads, straightened our backs, taken the wobble out of our legs, lovingly pressed a smile on our faces and lighted our eyes with a twinkle of joy. The makeover cost us nothing of value. What we have is the best we've ever had. The prospects of an even brighter future abound in God's Word. [u] And it was all free.

I think the world is ready for us. Let's go back to those ugly haunts from which we came. Here we come world, this time with grace and joy! It's free and it's fun!

Everybody is searching for joy somewhere — in drugs, but they kill. In sexual immorality, but there's AIDS. In drink, but when you sober up nothing has changed. In religion, but much of it is cold and depressing. Some have given up on joy and settled for happiness. [v] But that's often expensive and short-lived. If our Christianity consists of "going to church," and we are in the same lines as everyone else trying to buy happiness, we don't have anything to offer either. Let's discover grace personally. Congregationally. Let's live in it, let it ooze from every pore, spread it around. God won't run out.

WHAT DO YOU THINK?

(The following questions are keyed to sections in the preceding chapter. Refer to the section for full understanding of the questions.)

[a] Answer all these questions. Honestly.

[b] How do you think the younger son in Luke 15 performed after he was reinstated in the family?

[c] Is this your understanding of grace? If not, where do you disagree?

[d] What is John saying?

[e] What will this confidence do for us?

[f] Can you name the New Testament character who Jesus believed in, complimented, and stuck with (despite many failures), who later became a pillar of the church?

[g] From these passages explain in your own words the security we have in our salvation from God's viewpoint.

[h] Do we have any say in our security? Can we ruin our chances?

[i] Do you know anyone like this?

[j] Aren't we encouraging loose living here? Discuss.

[k] What kind of church would this approach to grace make?

[l] Is that a new view of John 3:16 to you? Does it seem valid?

[m] In the story how did the son's relationship benefit him?
[n] Can you find other passages that use this word to mean "complete"?
[o] How does appropriate self-love manifest itself in a Christian?
[p] What all do you know about the Pharisees? Discuss.
[q] Do you know any?
[r] Who do you know who is a grace-filled, non-Pharisee Christian? Describe.
[s] Does that verse apply to every Christian?
[t] Do non-Christians see Christianity this way sometimes?
[u] What is the future of the Christian?
[v] What is the difference between joy and happiness?

INTO THE LIFE
1. Place the section entitled "Here's How Grace Works" in the fly leaf of your Bible so you can use it easily with non-Christians.
2. Visit some other congregations and assess their joy-level. Try to identify the source of their joy.
3. Next Sunday pretend you are a first-time visitor to your own group or congregation. Look for joy. Write a brief report on what you found.
4. With your class or group, decide some ways your congregation can be more grace-oriented. Then, delegate two or three to go to the leaders of your congregation with specific suggestions of how grace can be more prominent in the life of the body.
5. Discuss among your group the techniques you use for sharing your faith. How prominent is joy in them? How grace-oriented are they? Discover ways to elevate the grace and joy level.

10

GRACE AND ANGER

Ever been involved in a church fight? You didn't know such things happened? Welcome to the real world. I grew up on them. I have the yellowed clipping from a childhood church experience I remember vividly. The headline reads, "Police Called to Quell Riot at Church." As headlines go, that was a little overkill. But it was ugly and unchristian in many respects. As a 14-year-old rascal I thought it was kind of fun. (We didn't have television in those days.) I'm sure God was displeased.

There were no doctrinal issues involved, really. But what was involved was anger. It was the catalyst that accelerated it from some minor dispute into a local holy war. Anger that had been simmering for years, I suspect. Then came the dispute (whatever it was), and issues were soon buried beneath tons of stored up anger. [a] This is the scenario that causes churches to split over what appear to be eternally unimportant issues: size and design of a church building, handling of church funds, standards of dress

211

and adornment, selection of leaders, communion practices, church music, support of missionaries, support of para-church organizations, etc., ad nauseum.

How about anger in your personal life? In your family life? Some of us are fumers. We don't say much but we're steamed. We just drag our feet. Others of us overreact to fairly insignificant events or situations. This is called gunnysacking, or collecting trading stamps, which is storing up hurts and disappointments and then dumping the whole bag or redeeming the whole book all at one time. Dads who come home and kick the cat, slam the door, and scream at the wife and kids are often taking out stored up anger at the boss. Some of us are supreme negativists. Be advised, anger is part and parcel of negativism. Our fellow Christians aren't what they ought to be, neither are our leaders, neither is our family, nor the U.S.A., nor the world, nor the universe, for that matter. Nothing is right. I call it omni-anger, when people seem to be angry about everything and everybody. We can't see the silver lining for the cloud. And furthermore we're depressed. Sometimes anger is so far underground that we don't consider it anger at all. "It's just the way I am," we explain. But don't worry, we'll keep our teeth tightly clenched so no smile can find a place to land. And then there's the meanest anger of all, the passive aggressive. He or she appears to get along well with everyone, never even shows any appropriate anger. They don't get angry, they get even. In sly, sabotaging, nonverbal ways. [b]

One of the most popular forms of anger among Americans today is ridicule, according to psychologists. Popular television series live on it. It is considered enjoyable repartee in good families. The "up" use it to keep the "down" down. The "down" use it to pull the "up" down. Often the barbs get so sharp that blood spurts. It is the common denominator of most racial slurs and jokes, no matter how much we deny it. Ridicule even slips behind the pulpit sometimes. It's an acceptable substitute for frontal attack. But it is still mean. There are razor sharp teeth behind the smile. [c]

The jury is still out on the interplay between anger and physical health. A classic work in this field, and with a spiritual dimension, is S.I. McMillen's *None of These Diseases*. In it he has a lengthy list of illnesses that are known or suspected to be caused or exacerbated by anger. Tim LaHaye's more recent work entitled *Anger Is a Choice*, has an entire chapter on anger and health. [d]

Grace to the rescue! Yes, there is something in our appreciation of God's giving nature, and our living in it that can take the ugly out of anger. Most of the abuses of anger can be traced to (1) our sense of spiritual insecurity, (2) our views of probationary Christianity, or (3) our need of perfect performance to gain God's favor. Get these issues settled and anger diminishes to its proper proportions. [e] It serves us. We are no longer its slaves.

1. ANGER: POWERFUL, BUT NOT ALL BAD.

The pages of the Bible are stained with the blood of people who were killed by anger. Usually someone else's. Usually unjustified. Genesis 4:4 notes that anger killed Abel. Pharaoh's angry disposition killed thousands of Egyptians (Ex. 10:28). Anger killed King Saul after torturing him for several years. It numbers among its victims: Naboth, Ahab, Jezebel, Asa, Uzziah, Ahasuerus, Haman, and scores of male babies in Bethlehem. [f] Others were stretched on the rack of anger and tortured by it. Anger cost them dearly. I speak of Moses, Naaman, Jonah, and Jesus' hometown buddies (Luke 4:28). [g]

But, as you have suspected, the Bible doesn't cast anger in a totally negative light. The anger of Jacob's sons in Genesis 34:7 is not construed negatively, even though lives were lost because of it. Jacob had appropriate anger toward Rachel in Genesis 30:2. Moses was often angry, usually for the right reasons (Ex. 11:8; 32:19). Samson's anger is depicted positively in Judges 14:19. So is Nehemiah's in Nehemiah 13:17,25. "He looked around at them in anger and, deeply distressed at their stubborn hearts, said to the man . . ." (Mark 3:5). There anger is attributed to Jesus, so it had to be righteous. So was Paul's in Acts 17:16. [h]

Instructions in the New Testament regarding anger fit nicely with the above examples. Here are the main passages:

> *Matthew 5:22* — But I tell you that anyone who is angry with his brother will be subject to judgment. Again, anyone who says to his brother, "Raca," is answerable to the Sanhedrin. But anyone who says, "You fool!" will be in danger of the fire of hell."
>
> *Galatians 5:19-20* — The acts of the sinful nature are obvious: . . . hatred, discord, jealousy, fits of rage . . . dissensions, factions and envy."
>
> *Ephesians 4:26-27* — "In your anger do not sin": Do not let the sun go down while you are still angry, and do not give the devil a foothold.
>
> *Ephesians 4:31* — Get rid of all bitterness, rage and anger, brawling and slander, along with every form of malice.
>
> *Colossians 3:8* — But now you must rid yourselves of all such things as these: anger, rage, malice, slander, and filthy language from your lips.
>
> *I Timothy 2:8* — I want men everywhere to lift up holy hands in prayer, without anger or disputing.
>
> *James 1:19-20* — My dear brothers, take note of this: Everyone should be quick to listen, slow to speak and slow to become angry, for man's anger does not bring about the righteous life that God desires. [i]

These passages use one of two Greek words for anger. *Orge*, which W.E. Vine defines as "originally any natural impulse, or desire, or disposition, come to signify anger, as the strongest of all passions," or *thumos*, which he defines as "wrath (not translated 'anger'), is to be distinguished from *orge*, in this respect, that *thumos* indicates a more agitated condition of the feelings, an outburst of wrath from inward indignation, while *orge* suggests a more settled or abiding condition of mind, frequently with a view to taking revenge. *Orge* is less sudden in its rise than *thumos*, but more lasting in its nature. *Thumos* expresses the inward feeling, *orge* the more active emotion. *Thumos* may issue in revenge, though it does not necessarily include it. It is characteristic that it quickly blazes up and quickly subsides, though it is not necessarily implied in each case."[1] The New Testament writers were talking about an emotion well-known to Christians.

2. HOLY SPIRIT, WHAT ARE YOU TELLING US ABOUT ANGER?

The passages exemplifying or teaching about anger that the Holy Spirit has placed in the Bible give us a balanced view of this subject. They say that:

A. *Some anger is irrational, or unjustified.* A classic example is Ahab. I Kings 21 tells the story of this childish king who wanted a piece of land owned by Naboth. Naboth refused to sell because it was his family inheritance. Scripture says, "So Ahab went home, sullen and angry because Naboth the Jezreelite had said, 'I will not give you the inheritance of my fathers.' He lay on his bed sulking and refused to eat" (I Kings 21:4). His wife, Jezebel, found him in that condition, asked what was the matter, scolded him like the child he was, and offered to get the property for him herself. The rest of the story is how one man's irrational anger resulted in the death of another. Naboth ended up dead, Ahab got his land, but ended up incurring the justified wrath of God. [j] Other examples of this kind of anger would be found in King Saul's relationship to David and the Pharisees' to Jesus. In each case they needed to examine their anger carefully and see the character flaws behind it.

B. *Some anger is misdirected.* Cain's certainly was. Abel had done nothing whatsoever to him, yet Cain murdered him, the innocent victim of misdirected anger. (Read the story fully in Genesis 4:1-16). With whom was he really angry? With God, of course. Careful students of the saga of Jonah discover that he too was really angry with God. He was unwilling to go to Nineveh not so much because he loathed Ninevites (Assyrians), but they were enemies of God's people, and to bring them to repentance would make them a greater threat to Israel. Undoubtedly Jonah couldn't understand God's motives, so he became angry. His prayer of despair in 4:2-3 makes it pretty obvious that he was angry with God. Jonah's and Cain's modern counterparts are parents who direct their anger against each other toward innocent children. In child abuse cases seldom is the victim the real object of anger, at least not initially. People who suffer personal tragedies, physical handicaps, or financial losses sometimes misdirect their anger. [k]

C. *Some anger is justified.* It is obvious that God has given us this emotional response for some good reason. From many Bible case histories anger can be seen as a proper response to pain, suffering, or injustice done to ourselves or others. The several cases mentioned earlier (Jacob, Jacob's sons, Moses, Samson, Nehemiah, Jesus and Paul) have that in common. We may assume that the way it was handled in each case was acceptable with God.

D. *All anger should be faced immediately and handled appropriately.* That is what the Ephesians passages and James 1:19-20 are all about. Anger never justifies sinful actions. It is to be processed appropriately, always using honesty, compassion, and forgiveness, never revenge. Ephesians 4:26-27 acknowledges that anger itself is not necessarily sinful. Some may be. Some may be handled badly and become sin. Speed in handling anger is important because it is such a high-geared emotion. Jonah's problem was "the burning of anger," according to Jonah 4:1. God's judgment fell on the king of Edom "because his anger raged continually and his fury flamed unchecked" (Amos 1:11b). If allowed to simmer in one's heart it may turn into bitterness, resentment, rage, brawling or slander. That's why God jumped so quickly into the situation between Cain and Abel (Gen. 4). [l]

James said to put the brakes on anger ahead of time. He suggested that being "quick to listen," and "slow to speak" might slow down anger. [m] "Man's anger," without the intervention of the Holy Spirit, "does not bring about the righteous life that God desires."

But with all these points aren't we only dealing with a human emotion? Isn't it just a matter of learning how to channel it constructively? What does grace have to do with it?

3. GRACE ADDS LIGHT TO THE HEAT OF ANGER.

A. First, grace gives us a view of God that is ennobling. His act of grace in giving His one and only Son to obtain forgiveness for us tells us that we have a good and giving God to deal with. He isn't angry at His creatures. He loves them. He doesn't sit in heaven with a giant magnifying glass and fly swatter trying to "get us." Sin is what He is angry with, and He has every right to be. Sin is what has come between us and Him (Isa. 59:1ff). His jaw is set to destroy sin and Satan. John's Revelation tells of the victory of God's people over Satan in chapter 12:10-12, and God's final victory over him in chapter 20:10.

God is for us! "What, then, shall we say in response to this? If God is for us, who can be against us? He who did not spare his own Son, but gave him up for us all — how will he not also, along with him, graciously give us all things?" (Rom. 8:31-32.) [n]

People who view God otherwise live in the fear of His displeasure. And prolonged fear leads to anger. Some people's religious beliefs lead them to actually resent God. "If He's so demanding, and we can never measure up, then why has he made us so? Are we little Kewpie dolls in whom He sticks pins? I don't think I like a God like that!" some people seem to be saying. [o]

B. Secondly, grace says that our standing with God is secure. We were given righteousness. We didn't earn it by handling our anger or other emotions correctly. And when we handle them incorrectly, God doesn't quit loving us. We don't lose our standing except by choosing to move away from God. "And this is the testimony: God has given us eternal life, and this life is in his Son. He who has the Son has life . . ." (I John 5:11-12a). [p]

Grace saves us from a lifetime of insecurity. "All that the Father gives me will come to me, and whoever comes to me I will never drive away. For I have come down from heaven not to do my will but to do the will of him who sent me. And this is the will of him who sent me, that I shall lose none of all that he has given me, but raise them up at the last day. For my Father's will is that everyone who looks to the Son and believes in him shall have eternal life, and I will raise him up in the last day" (John 6:37-40). [q] This means that we can relax in the Christian life, take things seriously, but not too seriously, because there is a safety net under us. It's called grace. God's disposition is to save us, not damn us. [r]

C. God gives grace to others too. Recently I was sitting in an assembly next to a well-dressed gentleman. When he crossed his leg I noticed that his sock was wrong-side-out. Strings from the embroidered logo (that should have been inside) were hanging out. I chuckled within myself, wondering how such a thing could happen. "Just careless," I thought. "So many people are careless these days. Why are people so persnickety about some things but careless about others?" After checking my own logo to see it was right-side out, I felt smug. Within the hour I was seated with another group. I crossed my leg confidently. It must have been a little better lighted now, because I was horrified to find the heel of my sock on the top of my ankle! An instant lesson in grace! Thank you, Jesus.

Whatever He's given us He's given every believer. Our Christian brothers and sisters live in grace too. When they stumble, like we do, He's gracious. When they're less than perfect, like we are, He's gracious. When they sometimes don't meet our expectations, like we sometimes don't meet theirs, He still loves them. When neither of us do, He still loves us. The little story Jesus told Simon in Luke 7:40-43 really applies here. Simon and his self-righteous friends weren't willing to grant grace to the prostitute who crashed their party to anoint Jesus' feet. Why wouldn't they? Because they didn't think they needed grace themselves. [s] Their anger is pretty obvious (v. 39,49).

There's no doubt about the anger of the 12-hour workers in Matthew 20:1-16. Workers who had worked less hours than they were receiving the same pay and they didn't like it one bit. What they failed to realize was that the opportunity to work itself was a gift from the landowner. People who don't realize that everyone needs grace (including themselves) are likely to get upset, grumble and complain. [t]

We have our problems with people who miss assemblies, don't we? With people who seem more in love with their jobs, or their families, or their pleasure than with God. People who are undisciplined. People who have body destroying habits they aren't quitting. And yet they're Christians. The problem is anger. I wonder whom we are really angry with? [u]

D. *Grace will enable us to cope better with anger.* First, we can quit playing God. If He chooses to grant grace to the best of us and worst of us, that's His business. We should be thankful that He has granted it to us. We can withhold judgments until He has spoken. Immediately passion softens. Spiritual reason can assert itself. We can begin to see things God's way. We can trust His love and good judgment. After all, isn't that what we want for ourselves? [v]

Secondly, we can examine our anger quietly and without fear. We've got at least until the sun goes down (Eph. 4:26). God isn't going to swat us down. After all, isn't anger itself a gift from God? [w] We can decide if it is justified. If it is, God is motivating us in it, and we can find direction in His Word for its proper use. It may call for confrontation. Or direct action. Or patience. Or forgiveness. It will never call for revenge (Rom. 12:17-21). [x] If our anger is misdirected or unjustified, God will be patient with us. He has given us a trio of gifts: prayer, the Word, and Christian counsel. [y]

219

And thirdly, we can deal with the pain beneath anger. Anger arises out of psychic injury. Our deepest esteem, sense of worth, and well-being have been attacked. Grace brings healing to that. Grace tells us that we are the most important thing in God's creation. "He who did not spare his own Son, but gave him up for us all — how will he not also, along with him, graciously give us all things?" Paul asked in Romans 8:32. God assures us that no matter how deep the pain, and how destroyed we feel, we are still loved. If that's true, nothing else matters. In grace God cuddles us in His arms, wipes away our tears, kisses our wounds, and comforts us. And which of us is too old to remember the magic healing powers of our mother's or father's arms?

E. Grace teaches us all there is to know about forgiveness. People who don't understand grace, don't understand forgiveness. If we have not embraced grace, forgiveness is a mechanical, tit-for-tat exercise. Forgiveness begins with grace, with realizing that we have been forgiven ourselves. "Therefore, as God's chosen people, holy and dearly loved, clothe yourselves with compassion, kindness, humility, gentleness and patience. Bear with each other and forgive whatever grievances you may have against one another. Forgive as the Lord forgave you" (Col. 3:12-13). Ephesians 4:32 says essentially the same thing. [z]

> People are strange,
> I cannot understand them.
> I had a sweetheart
> Who seemed to love me.
> I gave her roses, sweets, gems.
> I gave her all I had, my heart—
> And she broke it.
> I cannot forgive her.
>
> God had a world that should have loved Him.
> He gave it beauty, light and life.
> He gave it all He had, His Son,
> And it crucified Him.

People are strange,
I cannot understand them.
But God—
He loved them.

—Earl Marlatt

WHAT DO YOU THINK?

(The following questions are keyed to sections in the preceding chapter. Refer to the section for full understanding of the questions.)

[a]   Is it fair to say that most church fights are like this? Discuss.
[b]   Can you identify with any of these forms of anger?
[c]   Is this a fair assessment of ridicule? What are some other terms for ridicule?
[d]   Either from the works cited or from your own knowledge, what are some of the illnesses that you believe might be affected by anger?
[e]   What does each of these phrases mean?
[f]   Pick one of these names and research the story of their anger. Be ready to discuss.
[g]   Pick one of these names and research the story of their anger. Be ready to discuss.
[h]   Pick one of these names and research the story of their anger. Be ready to discuss.
[i]   How would you summarize these seven passages?
[j]   From I Kings 21 and 22 tell about the fate of Ahab.
[k]   Can you think of other examples of misdirected anger from Scripture or from life?
[l]   Do you know of cases where anger simmered into awful sins? Discuss.
[m]   How might these behaviors prevent the inappropriate handling of anger?
[n]   From memory, or with a concordance or topical index locate other passages that express how much God is for us.

[o] Are there religious beliefs that present God like this?

[p] What does this passage teach about our standing with God?

[q] Does this passage teach that we can never fall away? What does it teach?

[r] How does this reality impact the Christian life in general and anger specifically?

[s] Read that story. Try to recreate it. Do you believe they were angry?

[t] In both these stories who were the angry people really angry at?

[u] Answer that question.

[v] Exactly how do we want God to deal with our sins?

[w] Is it?

[x] What are some of the ways of dealing with justified anger taught here?

[y] How can these gifts help us with anger?

[z] Where is grace in these passages? What kind of disposition toward the sins of others does grace give us?

INTO THE LIFE

1. Make an Anger Inventory Form on a sheet of notebook paper. Divide it into three vertical columns, with the narrowest column in the middle. Head the left column *My Anger*, the middle column *Kind*, and the right column *Disposition*. Now, in the left column list the actions, circumstances, and people who make you angry. In the middle column write either *Justified, Unjustified,* or *Misdirected*, according to the differentiations set out earlier in this study. In the right column write how you have been handling that anger.

2. In each case where you have either misdirected your anger or handled it poorly, determine a better solution. Write the whole case, with the better solution, on a separate paper.

3. As a group project produce a similar inventory sheet for your congregation. Offer the results to leadership.

4. Write the story of (or discuss with a partner) your depression. Can you identify the anger in it?
5. Obtain and study Tim LaHaye's book *Anger Is a Choice*.

Endnote

1. *An Expository Dictionary of New Testament Words*, Fleming H. Revell Co., Old Tappan, NJ, 1940, pp. 55-56.

11

GRACE AND PERSONAL HOLINESS

It's hard to find anyone who is opposed to grace. Grace is right in there with motherhood and apple pie. The song "Amazing Grace" has been a favorite of the church for decades. There's even a pop version. It's hard to find a minister, teacher, or writer who won't at least give lip service to grace. But with some that's about as far as it goes. I've heard definitions and discussions that were about as skimpy as beachwear.

I think I know why. If we have come from any church background that sets standards for personal holiness for its members (and almost all do), we've probably heard more about modesty, ostentation, health habits, entertainment, and spiritual regimens than we have about grace. Grace is one thing, holiness is quite another. So when some "gracer" comes along talking about the security of believers, unconditional love, freedom from law, and judgment by relationship, not by performance alone, our hearts skip a few beats. [a] We have visions of the church being hit by a tornado and scattering our comfortable order all over the countryside. Or maybe we can see the church turning into a zoo. Worse than that — a zoo without fences so you can't tell the animals from the visitors. We've heard about congregations like this. Bizarre!

All those concerns are valid. God has them too. He is holiness personified. "Holy, holy, holy is the Lord God Almighty, who was, and is, and is to come," the living creatures chant continuously in Revelation 4:8. On the basis of His holiness He has called us to be holy. "But just as he who called you is holy, so be holy in all you do; for it is written, 'Be holy, because I am holy' " (I Pet. 1:15-16). God is more concerned about holiness than the most rigid, narrow-minded, uncompromising, scrupulous, monolithic, and indomitable board of elders who ever convened, deliberated and pontificated as guardians of godliness. Besides, He knows what holiness really is, and they only think they do. And He knows something else: If people really get grace into their hearts, holy living will come automatically, and it will come in a purer form than any legalistic prescription could ever accomplish.

Holy is the most common rendering of the Greek word *hagiasmos* and cognates. It can be defined as the state of separation God has designated for his people (*hagioi*, saints). The theological word *sanctification* has the same meaning.

Just how do grace and holiness fit together?

1. GOD GIVES US HOLINESS IN THE FIRST PLACE.

In baptism we are given new life (Rom. 6:4; Gal. 6:15). What is the nature of that new life? Colossians 1:21-23 says that part of our reconciliation to God includes being made "holy in his sight, without blemish and free from accusation." We were cleansed from a guilty conscience when we were baptized, according to Hebrews 10:22. Peter speaks of the gift of Christ on the cross acomplishing our death to sin and birth to righteousness (I Pet.

226

2:24). Perhaps the most specific passage in this vein is Hebrews 13:12, which says, "And so Jesus also suffered outside the city gate to make the people holy through his own blood." [b]

What was in God's mind? Obviously we can't maintain holiness at the same level He gave it to us at our conversions. So why start us off that way? There may be some deep theological reason rooted in the absolute righteousness of God, which is what was given us at conversion. But on a more practical level God must have felt that a higher level of true holiness would come from gifted people than from conscripted people. Making salvation a gift would touch hearts. And from holy hearts would come holy behavior. Confining holiness to behavior hadn't produced either holy hearts or holy lives in Old Testament Jews. It had only prepared people for the true holiness which would come through Jesus Christ. [c]

2. UNDER THE NEW COVENANT WE ARE CALLED TO HOLINESS AS A LOVING RELATIONSHIP WITHIN GOD'S GRACE.

Holy, pure living is never presented in the New Testament as an end in itself. That is, if we're holy enough we'll be accepted for eternal life. In the first place, we'll never be holy enough. In the second place, God has already given us eternal life (I John 5:11-12). So why be holy? Aren't the modern libertines right? Does it really matter how we live?

The better question is: Does it really matter how we love? Absolutely! God has shown us how to love with His own actions toward us (I John 4:7-21). And further, His inspired apostles have shown us how to love in their love letters. The Epistles are not catalogs of commands by which we merit salvation. They are teaching us a quality of love we've never known before. Passages in the Epistles looked at that way have a whole new impact on our lives. [d]

After reiterating some of the promises of God in II Corinthians 6 (that God will receive us, be a Father to us, and allow us to be His children), Paul called the Corinthians to "purify (them)selves from everything that contaminates body and spirit, perfecting holiness out of reverence for God" (II Cor. 7:1). Here's a two-pronged motivation for godly living: the promises of God and reverence for God. Aren't both of those rooted in love? [e]

The word "worthy" is one of the standards of a holy lifestyle to which Paul calls us in several of his letters. It provides interesting insights into this new kind of holiness.

> *Ephesians 4:1* — As a prisoner for the Lord, then, I urge you to live a life worthy of the calling you have received.
> *Philippians 1:27a* — Whatever happens, conduct yourselves in a manner worthy of the gospel of Christ.
> *Colossians 1:10* — And we pray this in order that you may live a life worthy of the Lord and may please him in every way: bearing fruit in every good work, growing in the knowledge of God.
> *I Thessalonians 2:11-12* — For you know that we dealt with each of you as a father deals with his own children, encouraging, comforting and urging you to live lives worthy of God, who calls you into his kingdom and glory.

Don't those provide an interesting call to godly living? They ask us first to decide the worth of the following:
—"the calling you have received,"
—"the gospel of Christ,"
—"the Lord," and
—"God."
What do you think? What are these worth? Our calling is our salvation; the gospel is the good news of the gift of eternal life; the Lord is Jesus; and God is God. Is there anything in this world even approaching these in value? [f] Paul never had any trouble deciding for himself (Phil. 3:7-11). [g]

Once we've determined true value on a spiritual basis, then Paul asks us to live accordingly, "Therefore, I urge you, brothers, in view of God's mercy, to offer your bodies as living sacrifices, holy and pleasing to God — which is your spiritual act of worship. Do not conform any longer to the pattern of this world, but be transformed by the renewing of your mind. Then you will be able to test and approve what God's will is — his good, pleasing and perfect will" (Rom. 12:1-2). With our values straight, living godly lives is much easier. Everything the world has to offer is laid alongside our calling, the gospel, our God and our Savior. The world comes in a poor second. It did for John (I John 2:15-17). [h] Then we ask ourselves, "What kind of conduct do these values demand?" Worldliness, by whatever definition you choose to give it, just isn't appropriate. [i] We don't have to have every detail spelled out for us. [j] "Don't talk about heaven and then live like hell," the apostles seem to be telling us.

An even stronger word is used in Titus 2:11-14 tying grace and holiness together. There Paul says that "It (grace) teaches us to say 'No' to ungodliness and worldly passions, and to live self-controlled, upright, and godly lives in this present age, while we wait for the blessed hope — the glorious appearing of our great God and Savior, Jesus Christ, who gave himself for us to redeem us from all wickedness and to purify for himself people that are his very own, eager to do what is good." Grace teaches us to be godly. People who understand grace will be godly. If they say Yes to ungodliness and worldly passions they aren't being taught by grace. That's what Paul said! [k]

And once we've gotten our values straight, and been taught, God still isn't finished with us.

3. FURTHERMORE, HE HAS GIVEN US HIS SPIRIT TO COACH US IN HOLINESS.

The gift of the Holy Spirit is one dimension of grace that is often overlooked. Little did the anguished souls in Acts 2 know what Peter was saying when he promised them the "gift of the

Holy Spirit" upon their repentance and baptism (Acts 2:38). What is important to us at this juncture is that having God's Spirit live within us is a gift. We don't deserve His presence because we have complied with some commands. He is not the payoff for work we have done. They were crying out for relief from the guilt of having crucified the Son of God, their Messiah (vv. 36-37). They were promised that — and the Holy Spirit was thrown in extra. He is frosting on the cake of salvation!

And just what kind of gift is he? "Having believed, you were marked in him with a seal, the promised Holy Spirit, who is a deposit guaranteeing our inheritance until the redemption of those who are God's possession — to the praise of his glory" (Eph. 1:13-14). The Holy Spirit as God's guarantee that He is in us and at work in us was a popular figure of speech for Paul. [l] He used it also in Ephesians 4:30; II Corinthians 1:22; and 5:5. "Seal" is the translation of a Greek word that was sometimes used for an engagement ring. Ladies who have had one slipped on their finger certainly know what it means!

Whatever else the Holy Spirit is doing in us, he is coaching us in holiness. In Ephesians 4:30 the context is holiness: "And do not grieve the Holy Spirit of God, with whom you were sealed for the day of redemption. Get rid of all bitterness, rage, ..." This is an ongoing project (Heb. 10:14). "The sanctifying work of the Spirit" is what Paul calls it in II Thessalonians 2:13. How is He accomplishing His work?

—*The Holy Spirit starts with our hearts.* "God has poured out his love into our hearts by the Holy Spirit, whom he has given us" (Rom. 5:5b). That's where holiness starts, isn't it? [m]

—*The Spirit produces the fruit of holiness in our attitudes, relationships, and lifestyles.* "Fruit of the Spirit" is what they are called in Galatians 5:22. [n] These are qualities of true holiness; they are above and beyond character traits that might be acquired or taught; they come from the work of the Spirit on our deepest spirits; they change our attitudes, relationships, and lifestyles; and they are acceptable in any culture or age. This kind of holiness doesn't need revising as morals, styles and lifestyles change. [o]

—*God's Spirit inhabits our physical bodies, because they have been consecrated as His temple.* In warning Christians at Corinth against sexual immorality Paul appeals to their knowledge of the Holy Spirit's part in their holiness. "Do you not know that your body is a temple of the Holy Spirit, who is in you, whom you have received from God? You are not your own; you were bought at a price. Therefore honor God with your body" (I Cor. 6:19-20). What a powerful motivation to live moral, honest, pure lives! Paul didn't have to anticipate and name all the forms of body abuse that Satan would ever invent to make this passage live into the twentieth century. He just reminds us that our bodies aren't ours to ruin; they were purchased with the blood of His Son as sacred dwelling places of His Spirit. Our response to such honor is to honor God with our bodies. Ephesians 2:22 says the same thing. [p]

—*God's Spirit adds dimensions of intimacy and power to our prayers.* Romans 8:1-27 discusses the difficulty we humans have relating to our all-powerful, all-knowing, eternal Heavenly Father. [q] We could be left with this struggle for a lifetime, but our Father's disposition is to give us whatever is necessary to make our relationship with Him intimate, mutually satisfying, and enriching. Once again His Spirit is the gift. In verses 26 and 27 Paul describes specifically the part He plays in prayer: "The Spirit of God not only maintains this hope within us, but helps us in our present limitations. For example, we do not know how to pray worthily as sons of God, but his Spirit within us is actually praying for us in those agonizing longings which never find words. And God who knows the heart's secrets understands, of course, the Spirit's intentions as he prays for those who love God" (Phillips Translation). If you have experienced the limitations of communication in the human realm, you know frustration with a capital F. If you have experienced the inexpressibility of some human emotions you know frustration with all capitals! [r] But God is so anxious to communicate with us that He has given us a

231

whole new communication system: Holy Spirit transmission. Through Him there are no inexpressible emotions. The Spirit feels emotions we hardly know are there. He carefully translates them into a heavenly language known only to the Godhead, and we have touched the throne of grace! God hears what we couldn't even speak; He feels what we feel. What a gift! [s]

—*The Spirit keeps the hope of perfect holiness alive in us.* "But by faith we eagerly await through the Spirit the righteousness for which we hope" (Gal. 5:5). No matter how well the Holy Spirit works in our lives we will never achieve perfect righteousness on earth. He will never finish His job. (I love the lapel pin I've seen a few times which reads: Please be patient, God is not finished with me yet.) Is this a discouragement? Never. His very presence is a reminder that in eternity we will actually be the righteous people God declared us to be when we believed. Righteousness was given us at our conversion (Rom. 3:21-22). But it was His, not ours. It was only credited to our account. [t] Someday, we will be genuinely righteous. In the meantime the Spirit keeps our hope eager.

"Make every effort to live in peace with all men and to be holy; without holiness no one will see the Lord. See to it that no one misses the grace of God . . ." (Heb. 12:14-15a). Grace and holiness — perfectly compatible to the writer of Hebrews.

WHAT DO YOU THINK?

(The following questions are keyed to sections in the preceding chapter. Refer to the section for full understanding of the questions.)

[a]   What do these four terms describe?

[b]   Would it be safe to say that at the moment of our new birth we are set aside to God's special service? Discuss.

[c]   How does the book of Malachi confirm this conclusion?

[d]   Take a few sample commands from the Epistles and view them this way. How do they feel? Would you be any less inclined to obey them?

[e] Are they? Explain.
[f] Can you describe in your own terms the value of these? Do so.
[g] Paul considered knowing Christ more valuable than what?
[h] What did John say about the world and its values?
[i] How do you define worldliness?
[j] Do you think that is really true? Discuss.
[k] Do you agree with that? Discuss.
[l] Explain the "seal" figure of speech.
[m] Do you agree? What are the implications of this truth?
[n] What are these fruits? How does each one express true holiness?
[o] Do these really make outward, observable changes in disciples?
[p] How does this knowledge motivate us to holiness?
[q] Besides prayer, what help from the Holy Spirit is discussed in these verses?
[r] Have you? Discuss.
[s] How can this gift help us with holiness?
[t] How does this knowledge motivate us to holiness?

INTO THE LIFE
1. What is your personal motivation for godly living? Are you motivated mostly by love for God? Or by rules and regulations of the church? Or by peer pressure? Evaluate your congregation the same way.
2. In what areas would Jesus say the world's values have encroached on your Christian life? Decide what a loving response to those problem areas would be. Set goals and timetables for making needed changes.
3. For discussion: What is there in the human spirit that longs for codes of conduct, rules for living, standards of dress, speech, entertainment, etc.? Which is the more mature approach — holiness through grace or holiness through rules?
4. Make a Fruit of the Spirit analysis chart based on Galatians

5:22-23 for yourself. Divide a sheet of notebook paper into four vertical columns, the first one narrower than the others. Head Col. 1 - Fruit; Col. 2 - Definition; Col. 3 - How Am I Doing?; and Col. 4 - How Can I Improve? If possible, get a partner, share charts. Exchange evaluations. Hold each other accountable. Review them every six months. Remember, this is not so much an effort on your part as *allowing* the Holy Spirit to produce His fruit in you. Just make yourself available to Him.

12

GRACE AND PERSONAL WITNESS

Several years ago I witnessed a presentation by a well-known evangelist on programmed Christian living that really impressed me. He had a stack of 8-track tapes labeled "Worship time," "prayer time," "work time," "sex time," and "soul-winning time." With great fanfare he inserted each tape into his mythical tape player at its appropriate time. He play-acted having a lost sinner meet the programmed Christian and ask how to be saved. "Oh, I'm sorry," said the Christian. "It's Wednesday, and soul-winning time is Thursday evenings at seven. Can you come back then?" Ouch.

An even greater tragedy is that many Christians don't have any soul-winning time period!

When you set the dismal personal witness record of the average Christian against the record of men like John the Baptist, Andrew and Philip, you realize that there is some missing ingredient in a lot of our lives. See if you can discover what it is.

John 1:29-37,40-49 — [29]The next day John saw Jesus coming toward him and said, "Look, the Lamb of God, who takes away the sin of the world! [30]This is the one I meant when I said, A man who comes after me has surpassed me because he was before me. [31]I myself did not know him, but the reason I came baptizing with water was that he might be revealed to Israel."

[32]Then John gave this testimony: "I saw the Spirit come down from heaven as a dove and remain on him. [33]I would not have known him, except that the one who sent me to baptize with water told me, the man on whom you see the Spirit come down and remain is he who will baptize with the Holy Spirit. [34]I have seen and I testify that this is the Son of God."

[35]The next day John was there again with two of his disciples. [36]When he saw Jesus passing by, he said, "Look, the Lamb of God!"

[37]When the two disciples heard him say this, they followed Jesus . . . .

[40]Andrew, Simon Peter's brother, was one of the two who had heard what John had said and who had followed Jesus. [41]The first thing Andrew did was to find his brother Simon and tell him, "We have found the Messiah" (that is, the Christ).

[42]Then he brought Simon to Jesus, who looked at him and said, "You are Simon son of John. You will be called Cephas" (which, when translated, is Peter).

[43]The next day Jesus decided to leave for Galilee. Finding Philip, he said to him, "Follow me."

[44]Philip, like Andrew and Peter, was from the town of Bethsaida. [45]Philip found Nathanael and told him, "We have found the one Moses wrote about in the Law, and about whom the prophets also wrote — Jesus of Nazareth, the son of Joseph."

[46]"Nazareth! Can anything good come from there?" Nathanael asked.

"Come and see," said Philip.

[47]When Jesus saw Nathanael approaching, he said of him, "Here is a true Israelite, in whom there is nothing false."

[48]"How do you know me?" Nathanael asked.

Jesus answered, "I saw you while you were still under the fig tree before Philip called you."

[49]Then Nathanael declared, "Rabbi, you are the Son of God; you are the king of Israel."

Why are many of us so different from these men? How can we be so reticent about sharing our faith? What's missing? The answer is: grace. Many of us are underwhelmed about the gift of forgiveness and eternal life we have received. We are not grace-full people. Knowing Jesus is not nearly so special to us as it was to these men. Meeting a movie star or sports hero excites us more. We have forgotten that Jesus is God, that all things were made by Him, that He is the true light, that He is God's one and only Son who is full of grace and truth (John 1:1-14). Consequently the excitement in knowing Jesus and the urgency to share Him has become as *unnatural* to us as it was *natural* to John, Andrew and Philip. [a]

When salvation as the absolute gift of God at the expense of His Son's life is actualized in our minds, driven deeply into our spirits, made such an obsession with us that we eat it, drink it, sleep it, sing it, pray it, go to sleep to it, wake up to it — then our hearts will explode like John's, Andrew's and Philip's did. To any who might question our obsession, we will reply with the apostles Peter and John, "For we cannot help speaking what we have seen and heard" (Acts 4:20). [b] We will share Paul's feeling of inner compulsion: "For Christ's love compels us, because we are convinced that one died for all, and therefore all died" (II Cor. 5:14).

On the other hand, if being a Christian is an inconvenience, a heavy burden, or no big deal, or even b-o-r-i-n-g, it is to be expected that we'll suffer in silence, or if our only testimony is a groan, people will ignore us. Seldom will people ask the cause of our depression, and if we tell them, they are likely to run the other way. Fast.

Grace to the rescue! Let's take another look at what we have. Let's count what it cost our Heavenly Father. Let's count our gain. Grace is like thinking you're broke and finding that folded up fifty dollar bill in the corner of your wallet. Someone has described grace alliteratively: **G**od's **R**iches **A**t **C**hrist's **E**xpense. A torrent of emotion breaks loose in the heart of any Christian who contemplates what grace means to him. And the grace that floods the heart spills onto the tongue.

1. LOOK AT THE EMOTIONS GRACE RELEASES IN OUR HEARTS.

Gratefulness. Tears trickled from her eyes and tumbled off her sunburned cheeks onto His dusty feet. Lovingly she cradled those feet in her arms and swabbed them with her tangled hair. She kissed them. More tear drops fell in puddles on His ankles and feet. She stroked them dry with her hair. That little vial of perfume she had been saving for some very special night, for some high-paying customer, she cracked open and poured onto his feet. Every last drop of it. A thin film of mud, made up of tears and expensive perfume coated His feet. The aroma enveloped the two of them. This was not your normal act of oriental hospitality. This was love. Not romantic love, but something deeper. Jesus may have been the first man she ever met who wasn't a customer. Who didn't come to get but to give. He may have been the first one with no demands. No expectations. She could wear her wrinkles, bruises, scars and browned, coarse skin. There were new ingredients in this relationship: the love and grace of God. It wasn't business. He was there to love and forgive her, two dreams she had never dared to dream.

The story is obviously the one told by Luke in 7:36-50. If anything in that story comes close to deserving equal billing with grace it is the gratefulness displayed by the woman. Just to be allowed in Jesus' presence so overwhelmed her that she wept and extravagantly anointed and kissed His feet. The possibility of being forgiven, of walking out of there unemployed, of starting over, of regaining her self-respect, of reviving her hope, of being loved for who she was, pierced a part of her heart she had almost forgotten was there. Gratefulness leaped to life. And what does gratefulness do to us? It dances out of us before we can shut off the music; it breaks down our inhibitions; it nearly makes fanatics out of us; it may even make us cry in front of people who will laugh at us. Though Scripture is silent, can you imagine this lady (and she is a lady when Jesus finishes with her), now made beautiful by grace, no longer a woman of the night, *not* telling people how it all came about? [c]

The prodigal son was the recipient of no higher quantity nor quality of grace than the best of us enjoys. [d] What was going through his mind as he enjoyed the celebration of his homecoming (Luke 15:22-27)? To be welcomed back to the family he had abandoned, to be forgiven his waste, to be given another chance — all were undeserved, unexpected, unbelievable, but they were true. If such an outpouring of grace doesn't produce thanksgiving in us, then our emotions are dead. It's doubtful that we have received the gift at all. His weren't, and neither are ours.

Humility. How could there be any pride in a righteousness so obviously not our own? [e] "All our righteous acts are like filthy rags," Isaiah declared (Isa. 64:6b). Even after we have it we still sin. And besides, we can't afford this salvation. It cost the life of the Son of God. We don't deserve it. We can't earn it no matter how hard we work. It's a gift. [f] Pride and self-righteousness wither in its presence.

Excitement and Enthusiasm. John the Baptist, Andrew and Philip weren't unique in their excitement over Jesus. They were the norm. Consider the case of the Samaritan woman in John 4. Once Jesus identified himself (v. 26) her fuse was lighted. The water she had come to draw from Jacob's well was forgotten, and so was the pot. She hot-footed it back to town. She didn't write a book about her experience with the Messiah. We can imagine her yelling and screaming with excitement as she cleared city limits. She exploded. "Come, see a man who told me everything I ever did. Could this be the Christ?" (v. 29). And people paid attention. "They came out of the town and made their way toward him . . . . Many of the Samaritans from that town believed in him because of the woman's testimony" (vv. 30,39a). Sure, it was an intellectual response on their part, but her enthusiasm is what first caught their attention.

If enthusiasm derives from the Greek *en theos*, meaning *God within*, God is never more within us than when we receive His grace. If people in general can get excited over the beauty of God's creation, surely we Christians can get more excited over the beauty of His re-creation. [g]

Reconciliation. That's a pleasant word, isn't it? God has given us the privilege of standing between himself and lost sinners, announcing that despite their rebellion they can be reconciled, returned to friendship and fellowship with God.

> *II Corinthians 5:17-21* — Therefore, if anyone is in Christ, he is a new creation; the old has gone, the new has come! All this is from God, who reconciled us to himself through Christ, not counting men's sins against them. And he has committed to us the message of reconciliation. We are therefore Christ's ambassadors, as though God were making his appeal through us. We implore you on Christ's behalf: Be reconciled to God. God made him who had no sin to be sin for us, so that in him we might become the righteousness of God. [h]

Is there any more exciting opportunity than this? Is there any better news to bring to people? We think not.

Sorrow. Paul used a poignant illustration of the role we play in getting the message of grace to a lost world. It suggests the emotion of sorrow that Christians will sometimes have as we share our faith with others. Not all will hear us.

> *II Corinthians 2:14-17a* — But thanks be to God, who always leads us in triumphal procession in Christ and through us spreads everywhere the fragrance of the knowledge of him. For we are to God the aroma of Christ among those who are being saved and those who are perishing. To the one we are the smell of death; to the other, the fragrance of life. And who is equal to such a task?

Early Christians were very familiar with the sight of conquering generals returning home with their prisoners of war. The smell of torches which were lighted when they reached the capital city were an ominous reminder to the prisoners that some of them would soon be killed and some would be spared. We are the smell of those torches, Paul says, announcing life or death to prisoners of sin. [i] What a heavy responsibility! Some are going to reject our Savior. We find it nearly impossible to believe. We may take the rejection personally. We grieve.

But the very sorrow that rejection produces can be the catalyst to stronger efforts at personal evangelism, to more patience, to a wider outreach. "Those who sow in tears will reap with songs of joy," the Psalmist wrote in Psalm 126:5. Maybe we need more tears in our personal evangelism programs. [j] He continued, "He who goes out weeping, carrying seed to sow, will return with songs of joy, carrying sheaves with him." Though he wasn't talking about giving witness to our faith, the principle surely holds. [k]

Hope. When we realize how giving God is in this matter of forgiveness and eternal life, hope wells up within us. We believe that we are not alone in seeing the value of grace. Others are drawn to it, warmed by it, ready to hear about it from people who are already saved by grace. God is at work in them too. We can believe that He has been at work in their hearts long before we arrived. And He'll be there when we leave. The good news is really good.

Jews tended to think no one was interested in God but them. Perhaps His disciples thought even more narrowly when they asked, "Who then can be saved?" (Luke 18:26). [l] His answer inspired hope. "Jesus replied, 'What is impossible with men is possible with God' " (v. 27). Jesus meant to give them (and us) more hope when He declared, "I have other sheep which are not of this sheep pen. I must bring them also. They too will listen to my voice, and there shall be one flock and one shepherd" (John 10:16). [m] Grace can dispel our despair we feel when we think people really don't want our faith. A big gulp of grace will fill our hearts with hope. [n]

241

2. LOOK AT THE MESSAGE OF GRACE WE GET TO SHARE.

Our message is a Man. Not a system. Not theology. Not a regimen. Not even a church. "Come and see a man . . ." the Samaritan woman announced. And what a Man! Sinless, but willing to become sin "so that in him we might become the righteousness of God" (II Cor. 5:21). [o]

Our message is about a relationship with a Man. "Come, follow me, and I will make you fishers of men," He invited some fishermen. They followed and in three short years they had grown to know Him, love Him, and believe He was God's Messiah. Eventually they would be willing to die for Him. He was a great teacher, but greater than that He loved them. "Having loved his own who were in the world, he now showed them the full extent of his love" (John 13:1). This was John's way of saying that He was willing to be killed for them. That relationship was not just for them. We can be in Him and have Him in us, His apostles taught (Eph. 1:3, et al; Col. 1:27, et al.). For us too, it's a relationship of love to the ultimate. He died for us too. [p]

Our message is about a relationship with a man and His friends. Though Jesus left this earth He left His Spirit in His people. We can offer others the friendship of the best people on earth — Christians. The New Testament term is fellowship, which means a sharing of all aspects of our lives. Why, that's the very thing lonely, hurting, despairing, hopeless people are looking for, isn't it! It's just as warm as it was when the church first began (Acts 2:42-47). [q]

Our message is about a relationship with a Man and His friends that lasts forever. All other relationships are bound by time. This one isn't. Jesus didn't want His apostles to think their relationship would be ended by His death, so He said, "Do not let your hearts be troubled. Trust in God; trust also in me. In my Father's house are many rooms; if it were not so, I would have told you. I am going there to prepare a place for you. And if I go and prepare a place for you, I will come back and take you to be with me that you also may be where I am" (John 14:1-3). That house is for us too: ". . . we have a building from God, eternal in the heaven, not built by human hands" (II Cor. 5:1b). Do you think we can *give away* real estate like that? [r]

Once grace floods our hearts emotionally and intellectually, the Holy Spirit can move us into a world that is looking for exactly what we have found:

The Man, Christ Jesus;

A relationship with Christ Jesus;

A relationship with Christ Jesus and His followers;

A relationship with Christ Jesus and His followers that lasts forever.

And once they've found it they too will be

Grateful, and

Humble, and

Excited, and

Sorrowful, and

Hopeful.

They will share their faith too and the whole purpose for God loving the world will be realized.

WHAT DO YOU THINK?

(The following questions are keyed to sections in the preceding chapter. Refer to the section for full understanding of the questions.)

[a] Do modern Christians often cool down in their enthusiasm the longer they are Christians? If so, why do you think they do?

[b] What were the circumstances of their saying this?

[c] Can you? On the contrary, what do you think she did?

[d] What does that statement mean? Do you agree?

[e] Whose righteousness do we have? (Rom. 1:17; 3:21-22).

[f] Do you agree with those statements? Discuss.

[g] Do you agree? Discuss.

[h]   Explain the concept of reconciliation and our part in it from this passage.

[i]   How is this true?

[j]   Do you agree? Disagree? Discuss.

[k]   Do you think it holds?

[l]   What prompted such a question?

[m] Who were these "other sheep"?

[n]   Do hopelessness and fear of rejection ever afflict modern disciples? Can a better understanding of grace help? How?

[o]   How can we present the man, Jesus, to people?

[p]   How can we present the relationship aspect of our faith?

[q]   Is this really attractive to people? What are all the "Anonymous" groups in our society about?

[r]   Is talking about heaven a fair way to influence people to believe and obey Jesus? Discuss.

INTO THE LIFE

1.   Write the story of your life from the perspective of witnessing. Describe how important and exciting your own Christian life is. Describe how important sharing your faith is. Describe how often and in what ways you share your faith. Describe the results. Describe how you feel about people condemned to hell.

2.   If you are studying with a church class ask each member to interview three other members of the church on the issues contained in 1. Put them all together in a report and offer it to your leaders, along with suggestions for improvement.

3.   Make a list of steps you can take personally to (A) increase your appreciation for God's grace in your life; and (B) improve your outreach to the lost. Begin following them immediately.

13

GRACE AND GUILT

Here's one man's story about guilt. And relief from guilt.

I know that relief can come when you begin to understand grace: its breadth; its power; its healing, stabilizing effects. You see, I was one of those Christians who could give the dictionary definition of grace: the unmerited favor of God. And I was among those Christians who secretly struggled with guilt, constantly trying to prove to myself and to others by my works how good and clean I was. Frankly, I was afraid to admit I was a sinner. Others sinned; I had weaknesses, shortcomings, problems . . . but not sin. That was too harsh. I had not yet discovered grace.

My study of grace spread out over many months in rather extensive detail. I wanted to know, so I read every Bible verse that used the word "grace." I had heard in a public address that grace could resolve inner frustrations and even clear up my misconceptions about works. I guess I wanted to hear that, as confusing as it sounded. You see, I had been working my head off for the Lord, yet feeling strangely unfulfilled at the same time.

Other religious persuasions had bragged on grace, but not my circle. I bragged on what I did and didn't do. And without realizing it I was harvesting the fruits that kind of thinking. It's called guilt.

Gradually a few verses started soaking in: "By grace you have been saved through faith" (That really scared me at first.); "God gives grace to the humble" (That really scared me.); "My grace is sufficient for you" (That one confused me.).

To get an overview I took an old Bible and clipped out all the New Testament verses on grace. Laying them side by side on my desk I began arranging them in what seemed to be natural groupings. Never had I heard of anyone doing this, but it helped me. For the first time I began seeing God's wisdom about grace.

What about you?

Are you ready for some relief from guilt? I know how some of you feel. I felt the same way — dragging tons of inner frustrations, working but unfulfilled, active but empty.[1]

Well, what about you? Does his story sound familiar? Are you serving the "God of all grace" with guilt? Is your Christian life robbed of joy because you're never what you ought to be? Nor are your fellows? Do you still feel guilty after you've prayed for forgiveness? [a]

More than likely you've got a grace problem. Grace and guilt are related, you know. Guilt is a gift from God too. They work *together* for our salvation. But if Satan can corrupt them, the very means of our salvation can become the means of our condemnation. For some, grace can become license, their right to sin with impunity. For others, guilt can become such an obsession that they can't accept grace. They choose instead to live in misery while God's medicine sits nearby unopened, unused.

It's time we took a closer look at these two issues.

1. GRACE ACCENTUATES GUILT.

If the first half of Paul's letter to the Romans is about grace, why does he spend half of that half detailing the horrors of sin? Because grace (God's gift of forgiveness and eternal life to

246

undeserving sinners) will not be seen in all its beauty except against the backdrop of the repugnance of sin. Look at it this way. If you had the words "God is love" in bright white neon, nobody would pay much attention to it unless it was seen against a dark background. And the darker the background, the more the sign would stand out. [b]

Romans 1-3 provides that very dark background. Beginning in verse 18 of chapter one and continuing to the end of that chapter, Paul describes the sins of *pagans*: "godlessness" and "wickedness" for starters (v. 18). From there on it gets really ghastly. [c] These people had neither written nor oral communication from God, yet they were guilty "since what may be known about God is plain to them, because God has made it plain to them. For since the creation of the world God's invisible qualities — his eternal power and divine nature — have been clearly seen, being understood from what has been made, so that men are without excuse" (vv. 19-20). [d]

By contrast, Jews were recipients of both oral and written communication from Jehovah, yet they were unseemly sinners too. Chapter two details their sins, beginning with judgmentalism, which is the sin of passing judgment on others to cover up your own (v. 1). What a sin! Then Paul throws the book at them, suggesting that they aren't even really Jews (vv. 28-29). [e] All this, Paul writes in 3:1-8, in spite of their spiritual advantage. [f]

Just in case any reader of his work (then or now), should feel he or she has escaped God's wrath and Paul's indictments, in 3:9-20 he quotes from several Old Testament passages that make all humankind guilty of sin. [g] "For all have sinned and fall short of the glory of God" — that's the bottom line, says Paul (3:23).

Man has never seen the beauty of God's grace until he has been devastated by his own guilt. Psalm 51 is a heart-throbbing confession of sin and plea for mercy from David. It is believed to have been written after his sin with Bathsheba. If anything could make David hurt worse than the sin and its tragic outcome, it would be the conviction that seized his heart that he had done this awful thing to such a gracious and merciful God, a God of "un-failing love" and "great compassion" (Psa. 51:11). [h] "Against you, and you only, have I sinned and done what is evil in your sight," he moaned (v. 4a). Grace crushes the guilty heart. It inflames the guilty soul. David described it similarly in Psalm 38:4. "My guilt has overwhelmed me like a burden too heavy to bear." If God were just a cruel tyrant, perhaps there would be no guilt at all. [i] But He's not. He's the "God of all grace" (I Pet. 5:10). And His grace accentuates our guilt!

It was no different when Peter first publicly announced God's grace through His Son on Pentecost. The shrieks of the guilty described in Acts 2:37 were preceded by the arrow of conviction which Peter shot straight into their hearts in v. 36.

2. GRACE RELIEVES GUILT.

"Amazing Grace" is probably the number one favorite song of Christians right now. One verse has an interesting message:
" 'Twas grace that taught my heart to fear,
    and grace my fears relieved."
Grace lays heavy guilt on us, doesn't it? But it also relieves our guilt. Here's how.

A. *We receive forgiveness by grace.* "In him we have redemption through his blood, the forgiveness of sins, in accordance with the riches of God's grace that he lavished on us with all wisdom and understanding" (Eph. 1:7-8). There's our answer: forgiveness and redemption (being bought back from sin) are available to us through the gift of the blood of Jesus. [j]

Grace leaves us more than forgiven. It leaves us justified: "There is no difference, for all have sinned and fall short of the glory of God, and are justified freely by his grace through the redemption that came by Christ Jesus" (Rom. 3:22b-24). Justification is a legal term that means we have been declared just, or righteous. [k]

B. We receive forgiveness by grace through faith. "This righteousness from God comes through faith in Jesus Christ," Paul has already explained in Romans 3:22.

C. We receive forgiveness by grace through faith like Abraham had. Romans 4 tells us exactly what kind of faith enables us to receive God's grace. It is a faith that trusts (v. 5), that engages both mind and body in the pursuit of God, and God's will (vv. 18-22). [l]

Thus Paul could write triumphantly, "Therefore, since we have been justified through faith, we have peace with God through our Lord Jesus Christ" (Rom. 5:1). How do you spell relief from guilt? G-R-A-C-E!

3. GRACE KEEPS GUILT IN PERSPECTIVE FOR THE CHRISTIAN.

As wonderful a gift as guilt is, if it is unjustified (because we have not sinned), or not responded to properly, it can become cyanide to the soul of the Christian. So, we need some Biblical perspective.

A. Christians sin . . . and there is little advantage in denying or minimizing our sins. Calling them faults, weaknesses, short-comings, or failures only postpones the inevitable reality — that we are sinners. [m] We'll either learn it now and deal with our sins, or we'll learn it at the judgment and God will deal with them. I John 1:8, which was written to Christians, deals with the matter: "If we claim to be without sin, we deceive ourselves and the truth is not in us."

B. When Christians sin . . . we should feel the sting of guilt as much or more than we did before we were saved. If we don't we've really got problems! [n] Peter made sure the newly converted sorcerer in Acts 8 did. "May your money perish with you, because you thought you could buy the gift of God with money! You have no part or share in this ministry, because your heart is not right before God. Repent of this wickedness and pray to the Lord. Perhaps he will forgive you for having such a thought in your heart. For I see that you are full of bitterness and captive to sin" (vv. 20-23). Guilt swelled in his heart. "Then Simon answered, 'Pray to the Lord for me so that nothing you have said may happen to me' " (v. 24). [o]

C. *When we repent and confess our sins* . . . we are forgiven. No, we don't have to be rebaptized every time we sin. "If we confess our sins, he is faithful and just and will forgive us our sins and purify us from all unrighteousness" (I John 1:9). That's the divine antidote for guilt. [p]

D. *When our sins are forgiven* . . . we have to forgive ourselves. Forgiving ourselves is sometimes the hardest part of the process. But whatever it takes, we must, for to fail to do so is to deny grace. [q]

E. *When our sins are forgiven* . . . guilt is gone! To find ourselves wallowing in guilt, and overwhelmed by a sense of worthlessness may seem virtuous, but it really isn't. Again, to continue living in guilt when God has forgiven us is to deny grace.

F. *When our sins are forgiven* . . . and we fail (or refuse) to forgive ourselves and be free from guilt we may find it difficult to forgive others. If we hold ourselves to impossible standards, or deny ourselves God's forgiveness and release from guilt we may deny the same to our fellow Christians. And we will find ourselves uproariously unhappy. [r]

G. *When we haven't performed for God as well as we should* . . . guilt is inappropriate. Disappointment is appropriate. So is sorrow. But guilt is wrong because God's grace in our lives doesn't depend on perfect performance. God doesn't love us only so long as we do well. Guilt is wrong because our performance is not ours alone anyhow: "But by the grace of God I am what I am, and his grace to me was not without effect. No, I worked harder than all of them — yet not I, but the grace of God that was with me" (I Cor. 15:10). He was God's partner. When a partnership like this doesn't perform as well as it should it hardly seems right that one partner (and the junior one at that) should feel guilty. Furthermore, a Christian who takes this approach is doomed to live in guilt most of the time. [s]

H. *Guilt-ridden Christians are a menace . . .* to themselves and to the whole body of believers. They judge themselves too harshly. They can't forgive themselves. They are usually depressed. They make themselves sick. Often they are angry because they try so hard and still aren't perfect. And if that weren't enough they dump the same garbage on their Christian brothers and sisters and if they aren't checked, the whole body ends up judgmental, legalistic, unforgiving, depressed, and sick. [t]

I. *Gracious Christians live well . . .* with God, with themselves and with their fellow disciples. They feel loved by God and they love Him well in return. They offer a high level of obedience, not because they have to but because they want to. They are comfortable with themselves, neither proud nor self-debasing. Coming from their standing in grace they can agree with Paul when he wrote, "For by the grace given me I say to every one of you: Do not think of yourself more highly than you ought, but rather think of yourself with sober judgment, in accordance with the measure of faith God has given you" (Rom. 12:3). [u] They are the kind of Christians you want to be around. You come away from time spent with them feeling like a million dollars!

And guess who else is drawn to them? The same kind of people who were drawn to the Master. Hurting people. Lonely people. Searching people. People looking for abundant life. A church of grace-full, guilt-free Christians will be a growing church. [v]

WHAT DO YOU THINK?
(The following questions are keyed to sections in the preceding chapter. Refer to the section for full understanding of the question.)
[a] What are your feelings about guilt?
[b] Why do you think grace is not understood and appreciated

by Christians like it should be?

[c] What other descriptive words and phrases does Paul use in this passage?

[d] What does this passage mean?

[e] Of what other sins were the Jews guilty?

[f] What kind of silly argument does Paul anticipate and refute in those verses?

[g] What sins are mentioned here?

[h] Do you agree with this? Discuss.

[i] What do you think? Is our guilt compounded because God is so gracious? Discuss.

[j] What is the Biblical concept behind shedding blood for sin?

[k] Are we now actually righteous or just legally declared righteous? What's the difference?

[l] Don't verses 2-5 say that Abraham didn't work? How do you reconcile those verses with the fact that Abraham had to work to father a son when he and Sarah were both beyond child-bearing age (vv. 18-22)?

[m] Do we have a problem calling our sins by their real names?

[n] What kind of problems?

[o] Is it possible for Christians so quickly to fall so deeply into sin? Discuss.

[p] Is it that easy? Shouldn't there be some penance done? Discuss.

[q] Why is that true?

[r] That sounds like a contradiction in terms. What is meant by this?

[s] This may be a controversial paragraph. Do you agree with it? May this be the problem with some guilt-ridden Christians? Discuss.

[t] Does that really happen? Discuss.

[u] How does that verse deal with both extremes in self-concept (pride and self-debasement)?

[v] Is this to say that non-growing churches may not be gracefully dealing with guilt? Discuss.

INTO THE LIFE

1. Read II Samuel 11 and 12 and Psalm 51. Write a phrase by phrase commentary on Psalm 51 from David's viewpoint accentuating conviction of sin, guilt, repentance, forgiveness and restoration to God's favor. This should give you a good view of true guilt.

2. Do the same with the Jews who heard Peter's sermon in Acts 2.

3. With a disciple partner discuss your feelings about guilt, from childhood to the present. Then discuss your feelings about grace, forgiveness, and release of guilt. The two of you together should attempt to have a healthy view of grace and guilt.

4. Discuss with your partner any problems you may have in the following areas: hypercriticism of brethren, depression, judgmental attitudes, and anger that may arise from unresolved guilt.

5. If you struggle with forgiving yourself, write passages on God's forgiveness on 3 x 5 cards and converse with your Heavenly Father on one passage daily. Tell Him your feelings and struggles. Ask Him to help you accept forgiveness.

Endnote

1. Ron Carlson, "Grace and Guilt," *Good News*, 8/83, Los Angeles, California.

14

GRACE AND SELF-IMAGE

One of my favorite people is Sterling Lacy. We met several years ago on the common ground of grace. But we came different roads to get there. Being a psychologist he discovered grace as the basis of sound Christian psychology. People in his counseling rooms were crying for something, and it was grace. My own background of inner-city ministry can hardly be compared to his, except that my people's most basic need is grace too. The exciting reality of God's grace must touch the tap root of every sinner for damaged self-concept to begin to heal. Long before Dr. Lacy touched his first patient with grace, God touched him in a unique way. Listen to his story.

Chemistry class during my senior year of high school was almost my Waterloo. On the final day of the school year I had to pass a chemistry test to get a passing grade in the class and obtain enough credits to graduate. I had studied hard, but deep down inside I knew I was going to fail.

"Here goes nothing," I said to myself as I sat for the exam that day. When the bell had rung to open the class, the teacher made this announcement: "I have made a terrible mistake. As you know, I have two chemistry classes and you are my second class. I ran off only enough tests for one class. And I hold those finished tests in my hand. Here's what I'm going to do. I'm giving each of you a test completed by another student. Write your answers on a clean sheet of paper. I know the other student's answers will be on the test you will be using, but you have to make the decision as to whether you think their answer is correct."

He proceeded to hand out the used tests. Guess who got the valedictorian's test? Guess who didn't change very many answers on that test? Guess who passed the final exam with flying colors?

That, my friend, in a nutshell is God's grace. When I face God's final exam I am going to be graded by Jesus' test paper. Believe me, He passed! And so will I — by God's grace.[1]

"Graded by Jesus' test paper" — what an excellent picture of grace. [a] He passed the test, didn't He? With a perfect score.

A positive, optimistic view of oneself is a lifelong struggle for everyone. Yes, everyone. I used to think that only people with bad backgrounds, or handicaps, or poor people, or ethnic minorities had low self-esteem. But then I discovered that every human being who ever grows to maturity shares a common problem, and that problem erodes self-esteem. Let me tell you more about it.

Little babies are born without any self-concept. They're just here. And before any self-concept is formed they are loved by mother and family just because they are there. They may be wrinkled, or scrawny, or fat, or bald, or hairy, or ruddy, or pale, it doesn't really matter, they are loved. In a few months they sense that and respond with smiles and gurgles. If you could ask them how they feel about themselves, they would probably say, "Everybody seems to love me, and I love me too." Along the line they clash with this loving society into which they have been born. They feel displeasure coming from those who have loved them. Self-concept takes a little dip. When they comply with the demands of loved ones, they are positively stroked, pleasure returns and with it self-concept improves. This transaction is repeated hundreds of times during childhood. Hopefully their parents are wise enough to reinforce their basic goodness, to discipline them positively, and punish bad behavior instead of attacking their character ("You told a lie," not "You're nothing but a liar!"). With reasonable upbringing we all reach adolescence feeling fairly good about ourselves. We can probably handle the physical changes, the awkwardness, the acne, and the social struggles in stride.

But enter sin. While childhood misbehaviors are no reflection on our basic character, sin is. When we sin, we become sinners. Now we *are* liars. God says so. And we know so. The sting is sharp. Before long, no matter what else decent we are, we are sinners. We may be the best wide receiver on the team, or the Young Business Executive of the Year in our community; our own kids may hug us and look at us like we are God, but we know the truth. *We are sinners.* And if we know how God hates sin, we hate ourselves. [b] Down goes self-esteem, trampled under the feet of our accuser, Satan. [c] Successes in life may lift our esteem temporarily, but in the privacy of our hearts we know who we really are.

In this context grace shines gloriously.

1. THROUGH GRACE GOD ENTERS INTO A PERSONAL RELATIONSHIP WITH US.

Now if our human self-concept is so rooted in relationships (parents, siblings, extended family, teachers, employers and friends), it isn't surprising that the spiritual dimension is too. God isn't into systems as much as He's into people. He has always sought relationships with them.

"What is man that you make so much of him, that you give

him so much attention . . .?" Job asked in 7:17.

Isaiah 1 contains God's heart cry over Israel because that nation had nearly destroyed its relationship with God. In that chapter He describes them as rebellious children, but still he pleads, " 'Come now, let us reason together,' says the Lord. 'Though your sins are like scarlet, they shall be as white as snow; though they be red like crimson, they shall be like wool' " (v. 18).

Against Israel's cry of abandonment God says, " 'Can a mother forget the baby at her breast and have no compassion on the child she has borne? Though she may forget, I will not forget you!' " (Isa. 49:15).

"For God so loved the world that he gave his one and only Son, that whoever believes in him shall not perish but have eternal life" (John 3:16). As pointed out in an earlier chapter, this is a verse about relationships. [d]

"As God has said: 'I will live with them and walk among them, and I will be their God, and they will be my people' " (II Cor. 6:16b).

So many of Jesus' references to the kingdom were set in eating situations. Meals were sacred occasions to the ancients. They were celebrations of relationship. In the kingdom God eats with His people. See Matthew 8:10-12; 22:1-14; Luke 14:16-24; Revelation 19:9,17-18.

"And so we will be with the Lord forever," Paul said in describing the final outcome of Jesus' second coming (I Thess. 5:17b). [e]

But sin keeps getting in the way.

The good news is that "Where sin increased, grace increased all the more" (Rom. 5:20b). [f] What God did through grace was declare us righteous, or credit us with righteousness so that our relationship to Him could be restored. Our sins would be counted against us no more. That marvelous gift is first described in Genesis 15:6, with reference to Abraham. What was lacking in godliness in his life was provided for him by God himself so that their relationship could be secured. In Romans 4 Paul extends that gift beyond Abraham to us.

Romans 4:3,6-8,22-24 — What does the Scripture say?

"Abraham believed God, and it was credited to him as righteousness." David says the same things when he speaks of the blessedness of the man to whom God credits righteousness apart from works: "Blessed are they whose transgressions are forgiven, whose sins are covered. Blessed is the man whose sin the Lord will never count against him." The words "it was credited to him" were written not for him alone, but also for us, to whom God will credit righteousness — for us who believe in him who raised Jesus our Lord from the dead.

But this gift has to be received by us. No gift is real unless it is received. And how is this gift of credited righteousness, this gift of restored relationship with God received? Romans 4:3 said it: "Abraham believed God, and it was credited to him as righteousness." [g] Verse 24 puts it on the same basis for us — "believe in him who raised Jesus our Lord from the dead." Acts of Apostles records several stories of people receiving that gift (See Acts 2:36-41; 8:9-13; 8:30-39; 9:1-19; 10:34-48; 16:13-15; 16:25-34; 18:5-11; 19:1-7; 22:1-21). [h] We receive it today exactly the same way.

2. GRACE RELATIONSHIPS ARE DESIGNED BY GOD TO NOURISH OUR SELF-ESTEEM.

Not only is there the nearly incredible relationship we enjoy with God through His gift of eternal life, there are other relationships that go with it. There is a very powerful gift that God gives us at the moment of our conversion that seems aimed at restoring the good self-concept we lost when we became sinners. It's called fellowship, or *koinonia* in the Greek. Obviously, it has several purposes, and the nourishment of self-esteem is a prominent one. The very first people to be baptized into Christ for the forgiveness of their sins "devoted themselves to . . . fellowship" (Acts 2:42). The word simply means the sharing of lives on every level (love, time, resources, etc.). John explained later that this fellowship arises out of our fellowship with God (I John 1:3-7). When you read in Acts and the epistles how this fellowship worked, it is not hard to see how it helped people see their real value even though they had been at one time nearly ruined by sin. [i]

As Paul neared the end of his treatise on grace in Romans he couldn't resist illustrating just how important we are to God. He did it by showing how worthless we were as lost sinners when Christ died for us. Yet He died. He must have seen value that the blinders of sin had kept us from seeing.

> *Romans 5:6-11* — You see, at just the right time, when we were still powerless, Christ died for the ungodly. Very rarely will anyone die for a righteous man, though for a good man someone might possibly dare to die. But God demonstrates his own love for us in this: While we were still sinners, Christ died for us.
>
> Since we have now been justified by his blood, how much more shall we be saved from God's wrath through him! For if, when we were God's enemies, we were reconciled to him through the death of his Son, how much more, having been reconciled, shall we be saved through his life! Not only is this so, but we also rejoice in God through our Lord Jesus Christ, through whom we have now received reconciliation.

Reconciliation — having our relationship with God restored. And it's all God's gift. In that passage can you see our value going down so long as we lived in sin? Can you see what God has done for us to restore that value? [j]

Ephesians has several sections that were obviously inspired by the Spirit to lift our self-esteem. And all of them are rooted in grace.

> *Ephesians 1:3-14* — Praise be to the God and Father of our Lord Jesus Christ, who has blessed us in the heavenly realms with every spiritual blessing in Christ. For he chose us in him before the creation of the world to be holy and blameless in his sight. In love he predestined us to be adopted as his sons through Jesus Christ, in accordance with his pleasure and will — to the praise of his

glorious grace, which he has freely given us in the One he loves. In him we have redemption through his blood, the forgiveness of sins, in accordance with the riches of God's grace that he lavished on us with all wisdom and understanding. And he made known to us the mystery of his will according to his good pleasure, which he purposed in Christ, to be put into effect when the times will have reached their fulfillment — to bring all things in heaven and on earth together under one head, even Christ.

In him we were also chosen, having been predestined according to the plan of him who works out everything in conformity with the purpose of his will, in order that we, who were the first to hope in Christ, might be for the praise of his glory. And you also were included in Christ when you heard the word of truth, the gospel of your salvation. Having believed, you were marked in him with a seal, the promised Holy Spirit, who is a deposit guaranteeing our inheritance until the redemption of those who are God's possession — to the praise of his glory.

The relationship in that passage is between us and our Heavenly Father. Just take note of the esteem-building truths contained in those verses: "who has blessed us in the heavenly realms;" "For he chose us in him;" "In love he predestined us to be adopted as his sons." [k] And it is rooted in grace: "to the praise of his glorious grace" (v. 7). Grace tells us that we are of inestimable value to the Father.

Ephesians 2:11-18 — Therefore, remember that formerly you who are Gentiles by birth and called "uncircumcised" by those who call themselves "the circumcision" (that done in the body by the hands of men) — remember that at that time you were separate from Christ, excluded from citizenship in Israel and foreigners to the covenants of the promise, without hope and without God in the world. But now in Christ Jesus you who once were far away have been brought near through the blood of Christ.

For he himself is our peace, who has made the two one and has destroyed the barrier, the dividing wall of hostility, by abolishing in his flesh the law with its commandments and regulations. His purpose was to create in himself one new man out of the two, thus making peace, and in this one body to reconcile both of them to God through the cross, by which he put to death their hostility. He came and preached peace to you who were far away and peace to those who were near. For through him we both have access to the Father by one Spirit.

Racial prejudice deals the worst of blows to self-esteem. William Barclay, in commenting on this passage, describes the prejudice Jews had against Gentiles: "The Jew had an immense contempt for the Gentile. They said that the Gentiles were created by God to be fuel for the fires of Hell; that God loved only Israel of all the nations that he had made; that the best of serpents should be crushed, the best of Gentiles killed. It was not even lawful to render help to a Gentile woman in childbirth, for that would be to bring another Gentile into the world. The barrier between Jew and Gentile was absolute. If a Jew married a Gentile, the funeral of that Jew was carried out. Such contact with a Gentile was equivalent of death; even to go into a Gentile house rendered a Jew unclean."[2]

Racial prejudice denigrates both the hated and the hateful. The hated is made to appear less than he is (and he ultimately believes it), and though the hater may feel more valuable, in the quiet of his heart he begins to doubt his own worth, and that doubt is validated by a public which generally despises those who depreciate others solely for racial reasons. [l] Perhaps an even worse tragedy is that the two are denied the relationship that would undoubtedly improve both their self-concepts. [m]

But look how God has enriched us through the gift of relationship! First, the relationship with God was established (v. 13,16); then, relationships with our estranged fellow men (v. 14); we are made "one new man" (v. 15), which describes our newness and our unity; now we can live together peaceably (v. 15-17); and finally, we share a common Holy Spirit (v. 18). We've gone from enemies to best of friends! This trip builds our self-esteem enormously. [n]

Our earliest and perhaps best development of an adequate

self-image comes through domestic relationships. Ephesians 5:21-6:9 gives detailed instructions for personal enhancement within the framework of marriage and home.

Ephesians 5:21-6:9 — Submit to one another out of reverence for Christ.

Wives, submit to your husbands as to the Lord. For the husband is the head of the wife as Christ is the head of the church, his body, of which he is the Savior. Now as the church submits to Christ, so also wives should submit to their husbands in everything.

Husbands, love your wives, just as Christ loved the church and gave himself up for her to make her holy, cleansing her by the washing with water through the word, and to present her to himself as a radiant church, without stain or wrinkle or any other blemish, but holy and blameless. In the same way, husbands ought to love their wives as their own bodies. He who loves his wife loves himself. After all, no one ever hated his own body, but he feeds and cares for it, just as Christ does the church — for we are members of his body. "For this reason a man will leave his father and mother and be united to his wife, and the two will become one flesh." This is a profound mystery — but I am talking about Christ and the church. However, each one of you also must love his wife as he loves himself, and the wife must respect her husband.

Children, obey your parents in the Lord, for this is right. "Honor your father and mother" — which is the first commandment with a promise — "that it may go well with you and that you may enjoy long life on the earth."

Fathers, do not exasperate your children; instead, bring them up in the training and instruction of the Lord.

Slaves, obey your earthly masters with respect and fear, and with sincerity of heart, just as you would obey Christ. Obey them not only to win their favor when their eye is on you, but like slaves of Christ, doing the will of God from your heart. Serve wholeheartedly, as if you were serving the Lord, not men, because you know that the Lord will reward everyone for whatever good he does, whether he is slave or free.

And masters, treat your slaves in the same way. Do not threaten them, since you know that he who is both their Master and yours is in heaven, and there is no favoritism with him.

Some of the ingredients may be a bit surprising, but we can trust the wisdom of God as it is conferred through the Holy Spirit. Take a closer look.

Submission is a key word. A general spirit of submission is commanded in verse 21. Submission of wife to husband, children to parents, and slaves to masters is taught here. [o]

Reverence, respect and honor are also ingredients. Reverence for God and respect for husbands, parents and masters is commanded. [p]

Love is an obvious ingredient of good self-image. Someone has observed that the greatest gift a father can give his children is to love their mother. And Paul commands it. [q]

Obedience is emphasized in several places in this passage. Obedience "with respect and fear, and with sincerity of heart, just as you would obey Christ" (6:5). Wholehearted obedience. [r]

Training and instruction of children improves their self-esteem, especially when it is done patiently by a father. [s]

How's that for heavenly nourishment of our self-image? Grace gives us a relationship with God, and then enhances all our other relationships. We even end up at peace with our enemies!

3. WHEN WE'RE CHILDREN OF THE KING, RELATED TO THE BEST PEOPLE ON EARTH, AND WE KNOW IT, WE ACT LIKE IT.

I John 3:1-3 is a beautiful celebration of who we are in Christ and how that affects our living.

> How great is the love the Father has lavished on us, that we should be called children of God! And that is what we are! The reason the world does not know us is that it did not know him. Dear friends, now we are children of God, and what we will be has not yet been made known. But we know that when he appears, we shall be like him, for we shall see him as he is. Everyone who has this hope in him purifies himself, just as he is pure.

By God's loving grace we have become His children. That's who we are. No doubt about it. Regardless of all the discounts this world puts on us. [t] All that awaits is the manifestation of His Son. Then everyone will know. In the meantime we feel good about ourselves. We grieve deeply when we sin. After all, we have presumed on grace and trampled on love. We fall to our knees begging forgiveness and love. We discover His love has never left, and forgiveness awaits only our repentance. [u] We are forgiven. We know our standing was never in jeopardy with God. We long to be finally delivered from sin. We know we shall be. Our hope to one day be like Jesus — sinless, pushes us to purity. When we do well we feel good about ourselves because we know God is at work in us. When we don't do well, our self-esteem doesn't need to plunge, since we have not been loved because we have done well, but because we are children of God. [v]

WHAT DO YOU THINK?

(The following questions are keyed to sections in the preceding chapter. Refer to the section for full understanding of the question.)

[a] Do you agree? Discuss.

[b] How does God feel about sin? Does the Bible say He actually hates it? Does that mean He hates sinners?

[c] Is Satan actually called the accuser in Scripture? What is the meaning behind that term?

[d] What did that chapter bring out about this verse? (See Chapter Three.)

[e] When we put all these verses together how can we say God feels about us?

[f] What does that verse mean?

[g] What was the evidence of Abraham's faith that is cited in Romans 4?

[h] Summarize what those people did to receive the gift of salvation.

[i]   Of what did this fellowship consist? How could it improve people's self-image?
[j]   Answer those questions.
[k]   List all similar phrases and discuss how each one addresses our self-concept positively.
[l]   Do you agree with that? Discuss.
[m]   What does that mean? Can you compare the Jew/Gentile situation with racial prejudice in our society?
[n]   How does it?
[o]   How does submission impact self-image?
[p]   How do reverence and respect impact self-image?
[q]   How does love impact self-image?
[r]   How does learning to obey impact self-image?
[s]   How does training impact self-image?
[t]   To what discounts is the Christian susceptible?
[u]   Is this true, or is there more required of us?
[v]   Is this a true picture of the way we should look at our own sins?

INTO THE LIFE

1.   Leader, this study provides an excellent forum for improving relationships. Set up the mechanics for discussions of their own self-image by class members. Perhaps one-to-one would work well. Whatever method is used, make sure people talk about how they feel about themselves.
2.   The Bible has scores of passages that contribute to positive self-concept in Christians. Locate a large group of these. Decide what each one means and how it contributes to self-esteem. Memorize key verses that can be used as daily affirmations of your true worth to God.

Endnotes

1. Sterling Lacy, "Grace and Self-Image," *Good News* , 7/83, Los Angeles, California.

2. *The Daily Bible Study Series: The Letters to the Galatians and Ephesians*, Revised Edition, The Westminster Press, Philadelphia, PA, 1976.

15

GRACE AND APOSTASY

"For God did not appoint us to suffer wrath but to receive salvation through our Lord Jesus Christ" (I Thess. 5:9). An underlying motivation of grace is God's unwillingness that His creation, fallen though it has become, should be eternally lost. "The Lord is not slow in keeping his promise, as some understand slowness. He is patient with you, not wanting anyone to perish, but everyone to come to repentance (II Pet. 3:9). God's aim is our salvation — from Genesis 3:15 to John 3:16-17 to Revelation 22:17. [a] One hundred percent of His efforts are aimed at that.

In Southern California there is a termite extermination company whose logo is a pint-sized English-dressed gentleman holding a mallet behind his back as he stalks an unsuspecting termite. He's not far from depicting many people's view of our

Creator. They see Him stalking us sinners, waiting to catch us in the act so He can zap us. I feel sorry for those who live with that view. It's not the gracious picture of God the Bible paints.

God has made His choice with regard to our salvation: "He is . . . not wanting anyone to perish." The Bible makes it clear that we are given freedom of the final decision in matters moral and spiritual. [b] If we have the freedom to choose Christ as our Savior, we are also free not to choose Him, or to repudiate an original choice of Him. The latter choice is called apostasy, or backsliding, in our contemporary vernacular. The condition is spoken of numerous times in both the Old and New Testaments. Jesus described it with the picture of a farmer grabbing a plow handle and then looking backwards (Luke 9:62). Peter described it with two gross illustrations: a pig that is washed returning to the muck of the pigpen, and a sick dog which vomits and then returns to remasticate the vomit (II Pet. 2:20-22).

Apostasy is warned against repeatedly in Scripture: Matthew 5:13; Matthew 10:33; Matthew 13:20-21; Galatians 5:7; II Thessalonians 2:13-17; I Timothy 1:19; I Timothy 5:15; etc. [c]

There is a popular doctrine among some evangelical groups today called "Eternal Security," or "Once Saved Always Saved." It is a remnant of John Calvin's 16th century theology. It really teaches that God, not man, has the ultimate choice in who will be saved and who will not. It denies that God has made us mortals autonomous. In essence it teaches that God has chosen that no one who has ever been saved will be lost. Several popular media evangelists/teachers espouse this view. Calvin and his modern counterparts no doubt feel that they are exalting grace, making it even more gracious. But you can never exalt one part of Scripture by denying another. [d] God's grace is exalted in His love for backsliders, His anxiousness to receive apostate Christians back into His presence, and His willingness to grant them full pardons. Grace and backsliding are not antagonistic at all. Backsliding merely causes God to swing into a different kind of action, but grace is still the motivation.

1. FOUR APOSTASY PASSAGES THAT MENTION GRACE

Galatians 5:4 — You who are trying to be justified by law have been alienated from Christ; you have fallen away from grace.

Here is a passage so unmistakably clear that Eternal Security proponents have wrestled with it for centuries. Paul is speaking of Christians, people who can be said to have been "in grace." But now they are alienated and fallen away. A past relationship is now gone. They had been invaded by Judaizers, i.e., people who taught that one had to keep the law of Moses as well as believe in Jesus Christ to be saved. [e] This idea was so foreign to the doctrine of grace that it needed to be opposed strongly. It was more than a misconception. It was misdirection. It annihilated grace. It was salvation by deeds, not as God's gift. It was an affront to the Creator! Any person who taught this, believed this, or relied on it was "fallen away from grace." [f]

And what of the fate of such a person? If one is fallen away from the only means of salvation, he is lost. [g]

Calvinists can only handle this verse by trivializing Paul's concern. "You can see it has no reference to a saved person becoming lost. 'You are fallen from grace' here means 'you have departed from God's plan of salvation by grace; you have fallen into false doctrine.' "[1] He makes it sound like falling into false doctrine is no big deal. Or that falling into this particular false doctrine is no big deal. I'd hate to have my eternal hope centered on grace and then fall out of it! Wouldn't you?

This passage is an unmistakable warning against a special kind of backsliding — relying on law-keeping for salvation. [h] It's a sure way to be lost.

Hebrews 6:4-6 — It is impossible for those who have once been enlightened, who have tasted the heavenly gift, who have shared in the Holy Spirit, who have tasted the powers of the coming age, if they fall away, to be brought back to repentance, because to their loss they are crucifying the Son of God all over again and

271

subjecting him to public disgrace.

"The heavenly gift." What else could that be but the gift of Jesus Christ for our salvation? [i] Several phrases in verses 4 and 5 describe a Christian. [j] "If they fall away" (v. 6), describes apostasy. And they are lost, and cannot be granted repentance so long as they remain in that apostate condition. [k] Teachers of the Eternal Security doctrine are forced to admit from verses like these that Christians can backslide, but they deny that they can backslide far enough to be lost. But this passage paints a hopeless picture for backsliders.

> *Hebrews 10:26-31* — If we deliberately keep on sinning after we have received the knowledge of the truth, no sacrifice for sins is left, but only a fearful expectation of judgment and of raging fire that will consume the enemies of God. Anyone who rejected the law of Moses died without mercy on the testimony of two or three witnesses. How much more severely do you think a man deserves to be punished who has trampled the Son of God under foot, who has treated as an unholy thing the blood of the covenant that sanctified him, and who has insulted the Spirit of grace? For we know him who said, "It is mine to avenge, I will repay," and again, "The Lord will judge his people." It is a dreadful thing to fall into the hands of the living God.

"Insulted the Spirit of grace." That's a serious act! How does one do that? Does he shake his fist at God's Holy Spirit and defy His lordship? Perhaps. But more likely he does what is described as "deliberately keep(s) on sinning," that is, he determinedly rejects the very Christ he once accepted as God's gift for his salvation. [l] And there can be no doubt that the person here described is a backslidden Christian. Verses 26 and 29 are unmistakably clear. [m]

This passage suggests that since salvation through Jesus is such a beautiful gift that anyone who receives it and then treats it contemptibly will suffer a more severe punishment than Mosaic lawbreakers did (vv. 28-29). [n]

> Hebrews 12:14-15 — Make every effort to live in peace with all
> men and to be holy; without holiness no one will see the Lord.
> See to it that no one misses the grace of God and that no bitter
> root grows up to cause trouble and defile many.

The phrase "See to it that no one misses the grace of God" is
the issue in this passage. Since the book of Hebrews is written to
Christians, the writer must be warning that some Christians might
miss the grace of God. The great gift given them at conversion
might slip through their fingers. [o] And how might this occur?
They might fail in their efforts at living peaceably, or they might
fail to live holy lives. [p]

2. THE ANATOMY OF AN APOSTASY

Kelly didn't rise from the waters of baptism, he catapulted,
like a Polaris missile. He was very excited about his new birth. He
had no doubts that eternal life was a gift, that he didn't deserve it.
After all, hadn't he lived his best years chasing wine, women and
song? Now he had presented himself as an empty vessel to Jesus,
and had been accepted, loved, and forgiven.

Things went well in Kelly's life for a couple of years, until,
driven by loneliness, he made friends with a young divorcee at his
work. The friendship was platonic at first, and he had hoped to
influence Jean toward his Lord. But romance began to win out
over spiritual influence. Love budded and blossomed.

But Jesus was still first in Kelly's life. At least that's what he
kept telling himself. His zeal for witnessing had waned a bit, and
they did spend a lot of evenings together so he missed some
evangelistic Bible studies he had formerly attended faithfully. He
was rationalizing a lot of things that used to be cut and dried in his
life. Jean wasn't budging spiritually. Why should she? She had
Kelly without having to accept his Savior. He had clearly com-

promised his love for Jesus Christ on behalf of the woman in his life.

Where was God all this time? Loving Kelly. Giving him His Holy Spirit to nudge him at first, and then to pinch him hard. And trying to move some Christians closer to him. God was far from giving up.

Nobody knew exactly what happened, but Kelly dropped out of the fellowship of the church. The truth was, Jean really didn't want his faith, and if he was going to have her, well . . . . Today Kelly is an ex-Christian. Oh, he would profess his love for God loudly, but there's no obedience, no worship, no service. If you could get him in a moment of quiet honesty, he would admit that the relationship is gone. By his own choice.

Now, where is God? Still loving him. Seeking him like the good shepherd. Standing by like the prodigal's father, letting him reap what he has sown, but anxious to forgive him and restore him to sonship. [q]

3. EVEN EXCOMMUNICATION IS GRACIOUS.

Both Jesus and Paul gave instructions for the withdrawal of fellowship by the church from certain apostate disciples. The following two passages give not only the mechanics for withdrawal, they assure us that withdrawal may be viewed as "God's other plan of salvation." It's as if God is saying: "By grace I brought them to me, but they left their first love. Now I'll give them something more. I'll love them enough to tell them that they are lost. I'll make them feel the pain of our broken relationship. I so desperately want them back that I'll do anything short of compromising with sin to get them back."

Matthew 18:15-20 — If your brother sins against you, go and show him his fault, just between the two of you. If he listens to you, you have won your brother over. But if he will not listen, take one or two others along, so that *every* matter may be established by the testimony of two or three witnesses. If he refuses to listen to them, tell it to the church; and if he refuses to listen to the church, treat him as you would a pagan or a tax collector.

I tell you the truth, whatever you bind on earth will be bound in heaven, and whatever you loose on earth will be loosed in heaven.

While we cannot be sure of the time frame of the gospel accounts, it is noteworthy that this section is set between the parables of the lost sheep and the unmerciful servant. Clearly Jesus' mood is forgiving, not destroying. Can't we view the procedure He outlined for dealing with a recalcitrant brother as being designed to win him back? And isn't that what grace is all about? [r] Gracious attitudes on the part of the offended one and the church are sure to accomplish more than if they approach the offender like they were God's avengers. [s]

I Corinthians 5:1-5,9-11 — It is actually reported that there is sexual immorality among you, and of a kind that does not occur even among pagans: A man has his father's wife. And you are proud! Shouldn't you rather have been filled with grief and have put out of your fellowship the man who did this? Even though I am not physically present, I am with you in spirit. And I have already passed judgment on the one who did this, just as if I were present. When you are assembled in the name of our Lord Jesus and I am with you in spirit, and the power of our Lord Jesus is present, hand this man over to Satan, so that the sinful nature may be destroyed and his spirit saved on the day of the Lord.

I have written you in my letter not to associate with sexually immoral people — not at all meaning the people of this world who are immoral, or the greedy and swindlers, or idolaters. In that case you would have to leave this world. But now I am writing you that you must not associate with anyone who calls himself a brother but is sexually immoral or greedy, an idolater or a slanderer, a drunkard or a swindler. With such a man do not even eat.

He was obviously apostate. Yet Paul's motivation is a

gracious one. He wanted the man saved in the end. [t] Some drastic measures had to be taken or he (and others) would be lost. Isn't this the same situation God faced when He decided to send His Son? If that act was gracious, so is this one. And with a little thought we can see grace in every step Paul outlined. [u] There is no suggestion that this offender be treated any way but graciously, despite the gravity of his sin. [v]

The two or three other passages dealing with disfellowship only confirm that it is a grace-motivated, grace-oriented act, designed to save one who has trampled on grace.

Yes, even after the wonderful gift is received, it can be carelessly dropped, or deliberately cast aside. But God isn't through giving. After all, grace is His very nature!

WHAT DO YOU THINK?

(The following questions are keyed to sections in the preceding chapter. Refer to the section for full understanding of the question.)

[a] What do these verses combine to say?

[b] What verses teach that we have freedom of choice?

[c] Read these verses and list the conditions they describe.

[d] Is this a fair representation of the Eternal Security view?

[e] What's wrong with this view?

[f] Read the context. Does this seem to be a fair explanation of this verse? Discuss.

[g] Is this a fair conclusion? Discuss.

[h] Are there people today who rely on law-keeping for salvation? Have they fallen from grace?

[i] Answer the question.

[j] What are they?

[k] Describe their apostate condition from verse 6.

[l] Is it possible for a Christian to do this? Discuss.

[m] What words or phrases convince you that this is describing a backslidden Christian?

[n] Is this what the writer is saying? Does it seem fair?

[o]   Is that a fair statement? Discuss.
[p]   How might these lead Christians to backsliding?
[q]   Is this a typical example of backsliding? At what point if Kelly had died would he actually have been lost? Can we really know the exact point?
[r]   Answer the questions.
[s]   Is withdrawal of fellowship (or excommunication) ever handled like that?
[t]   What parts of the passage verify that statement?
[u]   Give the passage thought and discover the acts of grace.
[v]   What about putting him out of the church (v. 2) and refusing to eat with him (v. 11)?

INTO THE LIFE

1.   List the names of people once in your fellowship who have fallen away from faithfulness. Discuss the circumstances of their backsliding. Are you convinced God still loves them, even after what they have done? To what extent are your feelings colored by what they did to you personally? Is there any anger in your feelings about them? Could you learn to have the heart of God for them? How? Discuss all these matters with your group.

2.   If your church doesn't have a Lost Sheep program or some other specific plan for extending the grace of God to backsliders, put one together. Submit it to your leaders. Offer to work in it.

3.   Write a script of a disfellowship action that would be completely grace-oriented. Offer it to your leaders for their study.

Endnote

1. John R. Rice, *Can a Saved Person Ever Be Lost?*, Sword of the Lord Publishers, Wheaton, IL, 1943.

16

GRACE AND CHURCH GROWTH

"But grow in grace . . ." (II Pet. 3:18).

Grace — the only way to grow!

Books on church growth abound in every Christian bookstore. They contain philosophies, strategies, mechanics, models and programs designed to make your church grow. Of course the truth is, only God can produce solid, spiritual and numerical growth. [a] He does it by His Spirit. Growth that is not Spirit-produced is not spiritual and will not last. [b]

This chapter offers a look at the dynamics, the spiritual underpinnings of church growth. It suggests that grace was the dynamic that produced the explosive growth of the church in the first century, and grace must be rediscovered in the twentieth century if we are to experience the kind of growth Jesus envisioned for us. Some of His parables make it clear that He envisioned a multiplying kingdom, not one that merely survived. [c] Not even the most beautifully scripted and executed plan of church growth will effect spiritual multiplication without the exaltation of grace.

There are certainly other dynamics that produce church growth. Fear, thought control, exclusivism, excitement, militarism, esprit de corps, and self-aggrandizement, to name a few. But they all pale alongside grace. And none have the blessings of heaven on them.

Stable, spiritual church growth occurs when an atmosphere of grace pervades the body of Christ, all else being equal. "Just exactly what is an atmosphere of grace?" you might ask. First, what it is not.

1. WHAT AN ATMOSPHERE OF GRACE IS NOT

A. *Softening the demands of Jesus.* The One who was "full of grace and truth," was also full of demands. Among them:

Matthew 5:21-26 — You have heard that it was said to the people long ago, "Do not murder, and anyone who murders will be subject to judgment." But I tell you that anyone who is angry with his brother will be subject to judgment. Again, anyone who says to his brother, "Raca," is answerable to the Sanhedrin. But anyone who says, "You fool!" will be in danger of the fire of hell. [d]

Therefore, if you are offering your gift at the altar and there remember that your brother has something against you, leave your gift there in front of the altar. First go and be reconciled to your brother; then come and offer your gift. [e]

Settle matters quickly with your adversary who is taking you to court. Do it while you are still with him on the way, or he may hand you over to the judge, and the judge may hand you over to the officer, and you may be thrown into prison. I tell you the truth, you will not get out until you have paid the last penny. [f]

Matthew 7:12-13 — Enter through the narrow gate. For wide is the gate and broad is the road that leads to destruction, and many enter through it. But small is the gate and narrow the road that leads to life, and only a few find it. [g]

Matthew 10:37-39 — Anyone who loves his father or mother

more than me is not worthy of me; anyone who loves his son or daughter more than me is not worthy of me; and anyone who does not take his cross and follow me is not worthy of me. Whoever finds his life will lose it, and whoever loses his life for my sake will find it. [h]

Luke 13:1-3 — Now there were some present at that time who told Jesus about the Galileans whose blood Pilate mixed with their sacrifices. Jesus answered, "Do you think that these Galileans were worse sinners than all the other Galileans because they suffered this way? I tell you, no! But unless you repent, you too will all perish." [i]

Luke 14:33 — In the same way, any of you who does not give up everything he has cannot be my disciple. [j]

Get the idea? Jesus wasn't soft. Grace isn't soft. We don't need to soften the demands of Jesus to have an atmosphere of grace. In fact, without them grace would be cheapened. A church that does not boom out demands of Jesus is a religious discount house. Grace doesn't need to be marked down fifty percent to sell.

B. Ignoring the evil, the ugly, or the negative. Again, the One "full of grace and truth" shows us the way. Listen to these negatives:

Matthew 11:20-21 — Then Jesus began to denounce the cities in which most of his miracles had been performed, because they did not repent. "Woe to you, Bethsaida! If the miracles that were performed in you had been performed in Tyre and Sidon, they would have repented long ago in sackcloth and ashes." [k]

Matthew 12:38-39 — Then some of the Pharisees and teachers of the law said to him, "Teacher, we want to see a miraculous sign from you." He answered, "A wicked and adulterous generation asks for a miraculous sign! But none will be given it except the sign of the prophet Jonah." [l]

Matthew 23:23-24 — "Woe to you, teachers of the law and Pharisees, you hypocrites! You give a tenth of your spices — mint, dill and cummin. But you have neglected the more important matters of the law — justice, mercy and faithfulness. You should have practiced the latter, without neglecting the former." [m]

281

An atmosphere of grace doesn't mean evil, hypocrisy, and the negatives of life can't be spoken about. They must be addressed because Jesus did.

C. *Permissiveness, lowering standards, compromising with Satan.* One of the best proofs of this is found in Jesus' dealing with the adulterous woman in John 8. You know the story. She was caught in the act and paraded to the temple grounds where her captors, the lawyers and Pharisees, planned to make a public spectacle of her while at the same time embarrassing Jesus. They knew His reputation for hob-nobbing with the worst of sinners (Mark 2:16), and even forgiving some particularly ugly ones (Luke 7:48). Here was a woman whom the law said deserved death. Would Jesus uphold the law, or would He compromise it? Only Jesus could get out of this one! You can decide which He did, but one thing He didn't do was wink at the woman's sin. [n] Her spirit of repentance was overwhelmingly obvious, so He granted forgiveness, and added, "Go now and leave your life of sin" (v. 11). Every disciple of His was to live a forgiven, regenerated life and she was no exception.

2. WHAT AN ATMOSPHERE OF GRACE IS

A. *Calling people to justification by grace through faith.* Churches today gain members by essentially two means: by grace, or by systems of rules-keeping. To be a Roman Catholic in good standing one must keep the rules of the church. The 16th century Reformation didn't change Catholicism, nor did it assure that all of Protestantism would believe the Biblical doctrine of justification by grace. Our own Restoration Movement that began in the last century gives lip service to grace, but we find it almost impossible to say with conviction, and without explanation, "For it is by grace you have been saved, through faith — and this is not from yourselves, it is the gift of God — not by works, so that no one can boast" (Eph. 2:8-9). We want to make sure people understand about baptism. [o]

If our problem were only doctrinal equivocation, it would be bad enough. But salvation by performance creates all sorts of deceptions and games-playing in a congregation. [p] And that kind of atmosphere produces Pharisees. Pharisees don't build churches, or for that matter godly lives.

Just look at the beauty of justification by grace through faith. "He has made us competent as ministers of a new covenant — not of the letter but of the Spirit; for the letter kills, but the Spirit gives life . . . . Now the Lord is the Spirit, and where the Spirit of the Lord is, there is liberty" (II Cor. 3:6,17). Grace brings life and liberty to a congregation. It grows like sunshine and rain grow daisies. [q]

B. Offering people the highest motivation to obedient service: love. People will work for God for all the wrong reasons, or at least not the highest reason if they aren't taught grace and love-motivated service. [r] But when they are, they grow personally and fruitfully.

Jesus asked for service from us on only one basis: love.

John 14:15,21,23 — "If you love me, you will obey what I command. . . . Whoever has my commands and obeys them, he is the one who loves me. He who loves me will be loved by my Father, and I too will love him and show myself to him." . . . Jesus replied, "If anyone loves me, he will obey my teaching. My Father will love him, and we will come to him and make our home with him."

If love is intact, obedience will be forthcoming. [s] [t]

Mark 12:28-34 — One of the teachers of the law came and heard them debating. Noticing that Jesus had given them a good answer, he asked him, "Of all the commandments, which is the most important?" "The most important one," answered Jesus, "is this: Hear O Israel, the Lord our God, the Lord is one. Love the Lord your God with all your heart and with all your soul and with all your mind and with all your strength. The second is this: Love your neighbor as yourself. There is no commandment greater than these." "Well said, teacher," the man replied. "You are right in saying that God is one and there is no other but him. To love him with all your heart, with all your understanding, and with all your strength, and to love your neighbor as yourself is more important than all burnt offerings and sacrifices." When Jesus saw that he had answered wisely, he said to him, "You are not far from the kingdom of God." And from then on no one dared ask him any more questions."

We might not have asked any more questions either! Though the two commandments Jesus labeled "most important" were first given in the Old Testament (Deut. 6:4-5; Lev. 19:18), they certainly never gained much prominence among Old Testament Jews. When the teacher questioned Jesus, it is doubtful he was expecting the answer Jesus gave him. "Love God" and "love your neighbor," and everything else will be fine, Jesus was saying. [u]

That kind of atmosphere in a congregation encourages growth. People who are outdoing one another in loving service are nice to be around. And wouldn't we all really rather serve from this motivation? [v]

C. *Encouraging genuine openness.* Grace makes it possible for us to be transparent. [w] "I am the worst of sinners," Paul could say because he understood grace (I Tim. 1:15b). Isn't that the basis on which all self-help organizations work? Alcoholics Anonymous and all its counterparts operate on complete openness. "My name is Joe and I'm an alcoholic . . ." is the way every talk begins. No wonder these groups are proliferating while churches are shrinking. Bruce Larson is right on target when he chides us, "Too often we have been under the impression that in becoming Christians we have somehow become like God: that is, perfect, correct, proper, and beyond criticism. If we fall into this trap we are really missing the Christian style and making ourselves unable to help others. The effective Christian is the one who has discovered that God's love is most understandable and easily transmitted at this point of vulnerability. All of us are drawn to the person who is vulnerable in his relationship with us . . . ."[1] [x]

D. Giving people the right to fail, and making it comfortable for them to repent, confess, be forgiven, and restored. Whew, those words sound heretical, don't they? "Giving people the right to fail?" And "making it comfortable for people to repent, and confess?" Sounds a little bit like Paul's proposal in Romans 6: that we sin more so God's grace will abound.

Fail we will. But will the church be able to handle it? Will we be able to admit it openly? Or would it be better to keep it quiet? Maybe just a private discussion with the elders would be best. If we "went forward" during a service could we really confess our sins, or would we be slipped into some side room to talk with elders or counselors who really don't want us to get too graphic? [y]

Grace lets us fail. Actually, God realizes we will, and He has decided to love us anyway. And forgive us (I John 1:9). Grace makes it safe to confess our sins, even to each other. "Therefore confess your sins to each other and pray for each other that you may be healed" (James 6:16a). Could this be the most ignored command in the New Testament? Maybe. [z] Only grace can make it comfortable, nothing else.

Grace purges the body of judgmentalism, one of the great impediments to confession, repentance and restoration. [aa] [bb] James condemns it (James 4:11-12), but it will become the personality of the congregation unless we understand grace. [cc] And who'd want to be a part of a group like that?

But consider the magnetism of a fellowship where we all admit that we are sinners (like Paul did), we believe that God is at work in all our brothers and sisters (like Paul said He is, Phil. 2:12-13), we can comfortably confess our sins (like James told us to), and we can be forgiven by God and restored by our Christian family (like Paul told us to, Gal. 6:1-2). [dd] Wouldn't you like to be part of a group like that? Who wouldn't?

E. *Rejecting legalism.* Strictly speaking, legalism is attaining justification by law-keeping, or salvation by works, as it is sometimes called. If only the concept itself were wrong, it would be bad enough. But the spirit of legalism is even worse. Legalists add other things to the gospel, and make them requirements for salvation also. The gospel *plus* doctrinal purity. The gospel *plus* perfect knowledge. The gospel *plus* perfect performance. The gospel *plus* proper worship. Once that spirit is turned loose in a congregation, forget church growth. How painfully I remember an encounter with a discontent denominationalist who was considering our church. Our guest speaker that day had just defined (Biblically, supposedly) what constituted modest apparel for women. At the meal following, my friend leaned over and said, "This isn't it." He could smell legalism whether he could spell it or not. [ee]

Read Galatians 2:11-16. Would you want to be part of a church that had people like Peter in it? [ff] I wish I could say legalistic churches don't grow. Sometimes they grow phenomenally. [gg] But the growth is unhealthy, and certainly not God-blessed.

F. *Celebrating joy.* That was the personality of the church of the first century. It was born in joy (Acts 2:46-47). When things went well, the family of God rejoiced (Acts 13:49-52). Joy is tantalizing. People can't resist it. They'll come just to find out what makes you tick. [hh]

Marvin Phillip's book, *The Joy Factor in Church Growth* (Howard Book House, West Monroe, LA, 1988) is joyful, easy reading. Marvin himself is living testimony to the part joy plays in personal and congregational growth.

G. *Practicing Gracious Evangelism.* No one would suggest for a moment that the church will grow if Christians don't evangelize. That's the nature of our faith — it's more caught than taught. Gracious evangelism not only features the beautiful story of God's grace, it is presented by people who enjoy that grace every moment of their lives. Theirs is not a doomsday message. It's good news! Someone died and left you a fortune! Congratulations, you've just won the grand prize! [ii] Congregations grow when their members share their gift daily in a heartfelt way.

WHAT DO YOU THINK?

(The following questions are keyed to sections in the preceding chapter. Refer to the section for full understanding of the question.)

[a]   Do you agree? Discuss.

[b]   Do you agree? Discuss.

[c]   Which parables deal with growth of the kingdom?

[d]   What is the demand Jesus made here?

[e]   What is the demand Jesus made here?

[f]   What is the demand Jesus made here?

[g]   What is the demand Jesus made here?

[h]   What is the demand Jesus made here?

[i]   What is the demand Jesus made here?

[j]   What is the demand Jesus made here?

[k]   What evil was Jesus denouncing here?

[l]   What evil was Jesus denouncing here?

[m]   What evil was Jesus denouncing here?

[n]   How do you justify what Jesus did for the woman?

[o]   Do you believe this is true? Why?

[p]   What are some of our deceptions and games?

[q]   Discuss how grace produces life and liberty in a group.

[r]   What are some wrong, or less than high motivations for Christian service?

[s]   Isn't Jesus saying that our love for Him is judged by our obedience? How can this be fair?

[t]   Do you agree with that statement? Discuss.

[u]   Weren't the Ten Commandments important? What was different about them and these two?

[v]   Would he?

[w]   What does "transparent" mean?

287

[x] Do you agree with Larson's point that vulnerability makes us more effective Christians? Discuss.

[y] Have you ever felt like this? Might others feel this way in your congregation?

[z] What is your experience with this command?

[aa] What is judgmentalism?

[bb] Do we ever feel reluctant to let some one be restored to the fellowship, as if it were ours to guard? Discuss.

[cc] Do you agree? Discuss.

[dd] Is this an accurate picture of a grace-conscious fellowship? Discuss.

[ee] What have been your experiences with legalism?

[ff] Would you? What exactly was going on with Peter?

[gg] Why would they?

[hh] Is joy really this powerful? Discuss.

[ii] Is this really an accurate portrayal of the message we have to share? Discuss.

INTO THE LIFE

1. What do you really feel about church growth? Is it really a priority in your life? Have you set goals to contribute personally to it? What do you do each week to help it grow? How much have you helped your group grow?

2. *Leader or teacher*, guide your class in preparing a growth pattern profile for your congregation (or class). Chart such things as gains by baptism, by transfer, losses by apostasy, by transfer. Include evangelistic methods, nurturing methods. Make a profile of the community in which the church works and the special needs that exist there.

3. With your class, group, or discipleship partner compare your congregation's atmosphere with what was described in this chapter.

4. Prepare a list of recommendations for your leaders that will help your congregation grow grace-fully. Pray about it, then ask for an opportunity to present it to them.

Endnote

1. Bruce Larson, *No Longer Strangers*, Word Books, Waco, TX, 1971, p. 57-58.

17

GRACE AND PRAYER

The privilege of addressing God as our Heavenly Father, petitioning Him to consider our wants and needs, and having Biblical confidence that we are heard and will be answered, is one of God's greatest gifts. It ranks only beneath the grace by which we are justified in the first place. Without that, there would be no reason to expect that we could communicate with God at all. So it's no surprise that people who have accepted the grace of justification are praying people.

"THE GOD OF ALL GRACE"

God's willingness to hear us is authenticated in dozens of places in the Bible. In each case, His hearing and answering us are not obligatory, but gracious. [a] True, He has bound Himself to hear and answer the cries of His children (II Chron. 7:14-15 for instance), but behind that is His acceptance of us as His children, His supreme act of grace. Even in Old Testament times He was famous for caring and hearing.

> *Exodus 22:22-23,27b* — Do not take advantage of a widow or an orphan. If you do and they cry out to me, I will certainly hear their cry. *(Speaking of the needy He added:)* When he cries out to me, I will hear, for I am compassionate.
> *Psalm 37:4* — Delight yourself in the Lord and he will give you the desires of your heart.
> *Psalm 50:15* — Call on me in the day of trouble; I will deliver you, and you will honor me.
> *Psalm 145:18-19* — The Lord is near to all who call on him, to all who call on him in truth. He fulfills the desires of those who fear him; and hears their cry and saves them.

No one knew better God's anxiousness to hear His children and lavish them with gifts than His own Son, who Himself was the recipient of God's goodness. "The Son can do nothing by himself," He declared in John 5:19a. He added, "For the Father loves the Son and shows him all he does. Yes, to your amazement he will show him even greater things than these," (v. 20). In His teaching on prayer He depicted a Heavenly Father who existed to give.

> *Matthew 7:7-11* — Ask and it will be given to you; seek and you will find; knock and the door will be opened to you. For everyone who asks receives; he who seeks finds; and to him who knocks, the door will be opened. Which of you, if his sons asks for bread, will give him a stone? Or if he asks for a fish, will give him a snake? If you, then, though you are evil, know how to give good gifts to your children, how much more will your Father in heaven give good gifts to those who ask him! *(This passage is as much a study of the nature of God as it is of prayer. God stands ready to say "Yes" more so than the best of parents. "How much more" describes His disposition.)* [b]
> *Matthew 18:19-20* — Again, I tell you that if two of you on earth agree about anything you ask for, it will be done for you by my Father in heaven. For where two or three come together in my

name, there am I with them. *(It doesn't take hosts of people pray-ing in order for God to move. It doesn't take a formal setting, either, like a church service. God is instantly on the scene when we pray.)* [c]

Luke 18:1-8 — Then Jesus told his disciples a parable to show them that they should always pray and not give up. He said, "In a certain town there was a judge who neither feared God nor cared about men. And there was a widow in that town who kept coming to him with the plea, "Grant me justice against my adversary." For some time he refused. But finally he said to himself, "Even though I don't fear God or care about men, yet because this widow keeps bothering me, I will see that she gets justice, so that she won't eventually wear me out with her coming!" And the Lord said, "Listen to what the unjust judge says. And will not God bring about justice for his chosen ones, who cry out to him day and night? Will he keep putting them off? I tell you, he will see that they get justice, and quickly. However, when the Son of Man comes, will he find faith on the earth?" [d] *(Here's an illustration by contrast of God's willingness to hear His children's prayers. And the contrasts are powerful.)* [e]

John 14:13-14 — "And I will do whatever you ask in my name, so that the Son may bring glory to the Father. You may ask me for anything in my name, and I will do it." [f] *(Here the Lord Jesus joins with His Father in assuring us of their willingness to grant gifts to us. He did just that according to Paul's words in Ephesians 4:7-8: "But to each one of us grace has been given as Christ apportioned it. This is why it says: 'When he ascended on high, he led captives in his train and gave gifts to men.' ")* [g]

The Apostles saw the same kind of gracious God on the other end of our prayers.

Romans 10:12 — For there is no difference between Jew and Gentile — the same Lord is Lord of all and richly blesses all who call on him.

II Corinthians 12:8-9 — Three times I pleaded with the Lord to take it away from me. But he said to me, "My grace is sufficient for you, for my power is made perfect in weakness." Therefore I will boast all the more gladly about my weaknesses, so that Christ's power may rest on me. *(This was an unexpected kind of graciousness that Paul received from God. His prayer was for the removal of some physical handicap he suffered, which he doubtless believed was hindering, or slowing down his ministry. Instead of the answer he requested he got an even greater one. He kept the handicap but got God's power in his life along with it. "For when I am weak, then I am strong," he said later (v. 10b). What a valuable gift!)* [h]

James 1:5 — If any of you lacks wisdom, he should ask God, who gives generously to all without finding fault, and it will be given to him. *("Generously." That's giving at its best. And the fact that God doesn't discount us for needing wisdom is its own special blessing.)* [i]

James 5:16b-18 — The prayer of a righteous man is powerful and effective. Elijah was a man just like us. He prayed earnestly that it would not rain, and it did not rain on the land for three and a half years. Again he prayed, and the heavens gave rain, and the earth produced its crop. [j] *(God was anxious to honor Elijah's request, both for punishment and for relief.)* [k]

I John 3:21-22 — Dear friends, if our hearts do not condemn us, we have confidence before God and receive from him anything we ask. *(John prayed confidently too, because he knew God's gracious disposition.)*

THE SAME KIND OF FAITH

If we've been saved by grace through faith, then prayer will come naturally. If we think we've been saved by works, then prayer is work, the hardest work of our entire Christian lives. God's way, salvation by grace through faith, is clearly the only way. The same kind of faith that brought the marvelous gift of salvation to us makes prayer come to life. In fact, without faith, we have neither justification nor answered prayer. Aside from praising God and presenting our requests, we are asked to bring nothing else but faith to prayer.

Matthew 21:21-22 — (The disciples had seen the words of Jesus wither the fig tree, and wondered how it happened.) Jesus replied, "I tell you the truth, if you have faith and do not doubt,

294

not only can you do what was done to the fig tree, but also you can say to this mountain, 'Go, throw yourself into the sea,' and it will be done. If you believe, you will receive whatever you ask for in prayer." [l]

James 1:5-7 — If any of you lacks wisdom, he should ask God, who gives generously to all without finding fault, and it will be given to him. But when he asks, he must believe and not doubt, because he who doubts is like a wave of the sea, blown and tossed by the wind. That man should not think he will receive anything from the Lord. *(Think of it — God is poised to pour wisdom into our minds, but we doubt we'll ever have it, and so He withdraws. Both of us are disappointed. [m] What a tragic possibility. But faith, not some herculean effort on our part, makes it all possible. Just the familiar leap into the arms of God.)*

But people who have accepted their salvation by grace are believers. Trusting God for daily needs, even for gigantic needs, for solutions to "impossible" problems — none of these is too hard for the God of grace.

PRAYER, THE LAST RESORT

Just as feelings that we can somehow earn salvation are the enemies of our understanding and love of grace, so are they the enemies of good prayer. Put another way, people who rely on their own performance for salvation, also tend to substitute performance for prayer. The unspoken attitude of many Christians (and leaders) is, "Well, we've tried everything else, we might as well pray." [n] No one has indicted our prayerlessness more than E.M. Bounds: "When we calmly reflect upon the fact that the progress of our Lord's kingdom is dependent upon prayer, it is sad to think that we give so little time to the holy exercise." [1] [o] Using Luther as a positive example, he wrote, "Martin Luther, when once asked what his plans for the following day were, answered, 'Work, work, from early until late. I have so much to do that I shall spend the first three hours in prayer.' " [2] [p]

GRACE-FULL PRAYING IS . . .

Regular communication between us and God. Like lovers. We talk and we listen. The talking is prayer, the listening is hearing the Word. How could we miss a day with the One we love? How could we just "wave as we go by," with little ditties before a meal, the 30-60 second prayers at a church gathering, the perfunctory prayers to begin church business meetings, etc.? [q] And then there's the great "Pray Without Ceasing Copout." Some sincere Christians confine their praying to "praying on the run." They pray while they are shaving, or curling their hair, or driving on the freeway, or balancing their checkbooks, or sitting in a boring seminar at work. Don't misunderstand — these are fine times to pray. They no doubt fit what Paul was talking about in I Thessalonians 5:17. But what about *quality time, undivided time* with your Lover? What about closet time? [r]

Let me explain the talking and listening aspect of grace-full prayer. The Navigators organization, in their "2:7 Personal Growth Series" teach a pattern of prayer that allows us to really communicate with the Father. It is so simple, and yet so effective — you'll wonder why it took you so long to learn it. They suggest that your prayer time consist in reading a passage from the Word and then discussing it with God in prayer. You can question it, argue about it, read it again, and finally understand it and/or submit to it. [s] It's not the only way to pray seriously, but it certainly opens up communication with God.

Praying first. Instead of last, when all human efforts have been fruitless. Because we know prayer is not an exercise in overcoming God's objections, but rather is appealing to His readiness, we can go there first. Because we know that human effort is insipid compared to God's power, we pray first. Out of that praying our efforts may be divinely directed and divinely empowered. [t]

Approaching the throne of grace with confidence. This is what we are invited to do in Hebrews 4:16. We can do it "because we have a great high priest who has gone through the

296

heavens, Jesus Christ the Son of God. (v. 14a). We can do it because He can "sympathize with our weaknesses" (v. 15b). God's wonderful act in sending His Son to this world tells us that it is never inappropriate to ask Him for anything. The door is always open. "Central's never busy," is the way the old gospel song said it. If we believe in grace we can pray boldly. [u]

Asking according to His will. "This is the assurance we have in approaching God: that if we ask anything according to his will, he hears us" (I John 5:14). There's spirit of giving on both ends of prayer. He's anxious to give, but we are willing to acquiesce to His will. [v]

Asking confidently. "Yes" is always on His lips. "For no matter how many promises God has made, they are 'Yes' in Christ. And so through him the 'Amen' is spoken by us to the glory of God" (II Cor. 1:20). Historically, Christians have struggled with this one. The church in Jerusalem was no monument to confidence when it prayed for Peter's release. God was more gracious than they were confident. When Peter was released, they couldn't believe it. The story is told in Acts 12:1-17. [w] If God could defy the powers of death in raising His Son to life and give us hope for our own resurrection to eternal life, we can be confident of His power and willingness to give no matter what we ask of Him. Confident praying is rooted in the basic nature of God: grace.

WHAT DO YOU THINK?

(The following questions are keyed to sections in the preceding chapter. Refer to the section for full understanding of the question.)

[a]   What does that mean?
[b]   How else would you describe it?
[c]   Does this make God seem unapproachable? Discuss.
[d]   What does that last question mean?
[e]   List some of the contrasts.
[f]   Is this the passage that teaches us to pray in Jesus' name?

[g]   Specifically, what were the gifts referred to here?

[h]   Have you or someone you know received this kind of gift in answer to prayer? If so, tell about it.

[i]   Explain this special kind of giving.

[j]   Where does the power of a righteous man's prayer reside?

[k]   Exactly what happened in this story about Elijah?

[l]   Can this passage be taken literally? If not, what does it mean?

[m]   Describe God's disappointment. Describe ours.

[n]   Do Christians actually act this way? Discuss.

[o]   Do you agree with Bounds? Discuss.

[p]   What do you think of Luther's practice? Is such a practice feasible today?

[q]   Does this describe your prayer life? How many minutes a day do you suppose it would occupy?

[r]   Is this a legitimate criticism? Discuss.

[s]   What can you see are some advantages in this way of praying?

[t]   Is prayer really this important? This powerful?

[u]   But shouldn't we also approach Him humbly? Harmonize these thoughts.

[v]   Does this seem fair? What Bible characters acquiesced?

[w]   Read that story in full and discuss how the church must have prayed and why they were so surprised when God answered their prayer.

INTO THE LIFE

1.   Write a history of your own prayer life from your conversion to now. Has it been grace-full?

2.   From your recent memory make a list of prayers that have been answered.

3.   Make a graph of three or four major spiritual projects in your life or the life of the congregation you attend charting how much time you (or the congregation) spend praying, how much time working, how much time scheming, how much

time worrying, etc.

4. Teacher, leader, discipleship partner, lead your group in a discussion of concrete ways you can add the dimension of grace to your prayers. Settle on a half-dozen ways, use them for a month, then evaluate them.

5. Try using the prayer communication technique taught by the Navigators for a month. Journal your discoveries. Evaluate the method as a permanent feature of your prayer life.

Endnote

1. *The Best of E.M. Bounds on Prayer*, Baker Book House, Grand Rapids, MI, 1981, p. 89.

2. Ibid.

18

GRACE AND UNITY

Therefore, since we have been justified through faith, we have peace with God through our Lord Jesus Christ, through whom we have gained access by faith into this grace in which we now stand (Rom. 5:1-2)

The implications of that passage are immense. It announces the restoration of peaceful fellowship with God that is available to every sinner. It says that fellowship was restored as a gift from God, available to everyone who believes. So far, so good.

But the "everyone" is what hangs us up. If that announcement is for this lost sinner, it is for every lost sinner. If I exercise Biblical faith and become God's child again, and other sinners do the same, and become the same, then that means we're *brothers*. If we're united with God, we're united with one another. Or at least we should be. Does our lack of recognition of that aspect of justification (unity with all other justified people) nullify it? Of course not. You'd think it did, the way many Christians posture themselves with regard to other justified folk. Christian unity isn't high priority on most people's agendas these days. [a]

But they're our brothers and sisters. Not step-brothers or half-sisters. If they were justified by the same grace we were, we're stuck (??) with them. If they believed the good news like we did, if they were convicted of sin like we were, if they repented like we did, if they counted the cost like we did, and were buried in a watery grave called baptism like we were, then we are members of the same family. [b] If we and they were "united with him . . . in his death" then we are united relationally and practically. [c]

Whatever happens, we're together. Well, almost whatever. One of us can renounce our relationship with God, or refuse to love Him, and our relationship with Him and each other is ended. My brother may err in understanding and applying Biblical doctrine (of course I never would), but he's still my brother. [d] He may miss some aspects of the New Testament pattern for personal living, or for the organization of the church, or his attitude may not be as good as it should be (I would never do any of those things either), but we're still united in Christ. [e] [f]

"Aren't you describing a rather loose kind of unity?" someone may ask. Yes. "Unity in diversity" was what the leaders of the 19th century Restoration Movement called it. They begged for unity on the fundamentals of our faith, while acknowledging that diversity was allowable in Scripture. Some of those passages will be studied below.

"But what about I Corinthians 1:10, where Paul appealed to a divided body of disciples in Corinth to 'agree with one another so that there may be no divisions among you and that you may be perfectly united in mind and thought,'?" our questioner might counter. Without consulting commentaries to make sure we understand that verse correctly, [g] all we have to do is read other places in Paul's writings where diversity of belief and practice is mentioned in not unfavorable terms.

Romans 14:1-2,5,13 — Accept him whose faith is weak, without passing judgment on disputable matters. One man's faith allows him to eat everything, but another man, whose faith is weak, eats only vegetables. One man considers one day more sacred than another; another man considers every day alike. Each one should be fully convinced in his own mind. Therefore let us stop passing judgment on one another. Instead, make up your mind not to put any stumbling block or obstacle in your brother's way." [h]

I Corinthians 8:1,4,7-9 — Now about food sacrificed to idols: We know that we all possess knowledge. Knowledge puffs up, but love builds up. So then, about eating food sacrificed to idols: We know that an idol is nothing at all in the world and that there is no God but one. But not everyone knows this. Some people are still so accustomed to idols that when they eat such food they think of it as having been sacrificed to an idol, and since their conscience is weak, it is defiled. But food does not bring us near to God; we are no worse if we do not eat, and no better if we do. Be careful, however, that the exercise of your freedom does not become a stumbling block to the weak." [i]

Colossians 2:16-17 — Therefore do not let anyone judge you by what you eat or drink, or with regard to a religious festival, a New Moon celebration or a Sabbath day. These are a shadow of the things that were to come; the reality, however, is found in Christ. [j] [k]

What is the recurring theme of these passages? Christians are not going to agree on everything, nor do they need to. All they need to do is honor each other's relationship to Christ. [l]

"But what we have in Christianity today isn't like that," our questioner protests. True. What we have is a hopelessly divided world of professing Christians. Not diverse, but divided. Hostile to each other in some instances. Warring in a few instances. The prayer for the unity of all believers that Jesus prayed at the close of His ministry is not being answered. The world is not believing like He prayed it would (John 17:21).

Is there no healing for these ugly lacerations on Christ's body? Are there no solutions to our division problems? Yes, there is hope. Is it too naive to believe that what it took to restore us to

God's household, the grace of God, will also bring all God's family members together? We think not. We believe in a "grace that is greater than all our sins."

WHY THE DIVISION BETWEEN JESUS' FOLLOWERS?

In a word: sin. At the center of all separation between men and God and between men and men is sin. "Surely the arm of the Lord is not too short to save, nor his ear too dull to hear. But your iniquities have separated you from your God; your sins have hidden his face from you, so that he will not hear" (Isa. 49:1-2). Sin separated Adam and Eve from the Creator. Sin drove Cain to kill Abel. Sin split Old Testament Israel into two warring nations. Sin separated Judas from the rest of his brethren and from His Master. The sin of hypocrisy nearly divided Paul and Peter (Gal. 2:11-16), and the sin surrounding the whole Jew/Gentile, circumcision/uncircumcision issue nearly divided the early church. And the rest is history. [m]

Without a doubt, sin is the father of division.

GRACE DEFEATS THE CULPRIT

So sin is the culprit! And what is God's remedy for sin? Grace. No other New Testament epistle explains the role grace plays in keeping Christians living, loving, and serving together like Ephesians does. Space prohibits a study of the whole book, but even a quick overview, plus a few close-ups will convince us that grace and unity are partners in God's great plan of reconciling the world to Himself. First, the overview.

The book divides itself naturally along these lines:

—What we have in the Lord Jesus is beautiful, Chapter 1.

—It came out of something ugly, called sin, Chapter 2:1-7.

—It came about through grace, Chapter 2:8-10.

—It brought all divided, warring people together in one body, Chapter 2:11-Chapter 3.

—This wonderful unity of the Spirit is ours to preserve, Chapter 4:1-16.

—Since sin is the greatest threat against it, reject sin, and choose in its place godly living, Chapter 4:17-Chapter 5:20.

—Submission within the one body will preserve it, Chapter 5:21-Chapter 6:9.

—Stand, fully armed, against sin, the destroyer of unity, Chapter 6:10-18. [n]

Isn't that a marvelous letter! The prayer of Jesus could be answered, according to Paul. A closer look at three passages in the book will reveal how grace melts people together into one body.

DEAD, BURIED, RISEN

The Ephesian Christians, Paul feared, might so enjoy their standing in God's grace that they would forget where they came from. So he reminds them.

Ephesians 2:1-10 — As for you, you were dead in your transgressions and sins, in which you used to live when you followed the ways of this world and of the ruler of the kingdom of the air, the spirit who is now at work in those who are disobedient. All of us also lived among them at one time, gratifying the cravings of our sinful nature and following its desires and thoughts. Like the rest, we were by nature objects of wrath. But because of his great love for us, God, who is rich in mercy, made us alive with Christ even when we were dead in transgressions — it is by grace you have been saved. And God raised us up with Christ and seated us with him in the heavenly realms in Christ Jesus, in order that in the coming ages he might show the incomparable riches of his grace, expressed in his kindness to us in Christ Jesus. For it is by grace you have been saved, through faith — and this not from yourselves, it is the gift of God — not by works, so that no one can boast. For we are God's workmanship, created in Christ Jesus to do good works, which God prepared in advance for us to do.

"Dead in your transgressions and sins" is the way Paul describes our lives before grace. "Dead even while she lives" is the way he described women who lived solely for fleshly pleasure (I Tim. 4:6b). [o] Living like that separated us from God, and it was our choice. Obviously, it separated us from godly people too. God made the first move toward reconciliation. He "made us alive with Christ even when we were dead in transgressions — it is by grace you have been saved" (v. 5). Because of the supreme efficacy of God's act, we were counted as alive even before we had responded to it. Once we did respond (through faith), we *were* alive, we were God's creatures again, the breach was bridged. [p]

FROM ENEMIES TO BROTHERS

As impossible as it might seem, two of the world's most hostile enemies, Jews and Gentiles, were united through the grace of God manifested in Christ.

Ephesians 2:11-22 — Therefore, remember that formerly you who are Gentiles by birth and called "uncircumcised" by those who call themselves "the circumcision" (that done in the body by the hands of men) — remember that at that time you were separate from Christ, excluded from citizenship in Israel and foreigners to the covenants of the promise, without hope and without God in the world. But now in Christ Jesus you who once were far away have been brought near through the blood of Christ.
For he himself is our peace, who has made the two one and has destroyed the barrier, the dividing wall of hostility, by abolishing in his flesh the law with its commandments and regulations. His purpose was to create in himself one new man out of the two, thus making peace, and in this one body to reconcile both of them to God through the cross, by which he put to death their hostility. He came and preached peace to you who were far

away and peace to those who were near. For through him we both have access to the Father by one Spirit.

Consequently, you are no longer foreigners and aliens, but fellow citizens with God's people and members of God's household, built on the foundation of the apostles and prophets, with Christ Jesus himself as the chief cornerstone. In him the whole building is joined together and rises to become a holy temple in the Lord. And in him you too are being built together to become a dwelling in which God lives by his Spirit.

If this could happen between Jews and Gentiles, then it can happen between any antagonists. [q] Jews thought they were God's children because they were circumcised. But circumcision meant nothing (Gal. 5:6). They were alienated from God because of that old culprit — sin, and didn't know it. Gentiles, on the other hand were guilty of sin in the first degree and had already pled guilty. The Jews constantly reminded them how godless and hopeless they were (v. 12). And both groups knew they didn't like each other. [r]

God didn't make Jews of Gentiles. He "made the two one," "one new man out of the two." And those new creatures, Christians, live in peace. Thus, two divided races, divided and hostile for centuries, were brought together peacefully by the death, burial and resurrection of Jesus. [s]

The end result of this is a beautiful family living in a beautiful house. (These are the pictures in vv. 19-22). It is a loving, united family, living in a well-built structure, all the parts of which are perfectly fitted together. There is such beautiful harmony in this family and perfection in the structure that God chooses to live therein, in the person of His Holy Spirit. [t]

All of this happened because "God so loved the world that he gave."

PRESERVE THIS PRECIOUS UNITY

Who would despoil this beautiful, peaceful, harmonious picture? Surely none of us who are part of it would, urges Paul.

> *Ephesians 4:1-7,11-16* — As a prisoner for the Lord, then, I urge you to live a life worthy of the calling you have received. Be completely humble and gentle; be patient, bearing with one another in love. Make every effort to keep the unity of the Spirit through the bond of peace. There is one body and one Spirit — just as you were called to one hope when you were called — one Lord, one faith, one baptism; one God and Father of all, who is over all and through all and in all.
> But to each of us grace has been given as Christ apportioned it. It was he who gave some to be apostles, some to be prophets, some to be evangelists, and some to be pastors and teachers, to prepare God's people for works of service, so that the body of Christ may be built up until we all reach unity in the faith and in the knowledge of the Son of God and become mature, attaining to the whole measure of the fullness of Christ.
> Then we will no longer be infants, tossed back and forth by the waves, and blown here and there by every wind of teaching and by the cunning and craftiness of men in their deceitful scheming. Instead, speaking the truth in love, we will in all things grow up into him who is the Head, that is, Christ. From him the whole body, joined and held together by every supporting ligament, grows and builds itself up in love, as each part does its work.

This isn't our unity. It's the "unity of the Spirit." If it were ours we might treat it carelessly. "Make every effort" to keep it, Paul urges. It's going to take humility, gentleness, patience, and loving forbearance. But above everything else it is going to take our firm conviction that unity is God's gift, a gift every bit as precious as the gift of our salvation. In fact, we go back to some questions suggested early in this chapter: Can I be united with my Lord if I'm separated from my brother? Can I have the Holy Spirit, the seal of my redemption (Eph. 1:13), without making "every effort to keep the unity of the Spirit"? [u]

As already noted, there is diversity in God's family. Here (vv. 11-13) the diversity is in function. Some are leaders, some led. All are to be committed to a kind of maturity where unity is real, and functional, and observable. This unity is every bit as essential as it is desirable. We are a "whole body," Paul says. And a body needs every part functioning wholly, providing the aspect of life that it alone can provide. This kind of unity flows from the Head (v. 15b). If we pull away from brothers and sisters, we also pull away from Jesus Christ. Thus, our determination to "keep the unity of the Spirit" is both Christ-serving and self-serving. If we want to be "in Christ" we must also be "in unity" with all Christians.

MAKING UNITY IN GRACE PRACTICAL

All the above is theory until it is lived in our congregations, and in the broader community of believers, on a daily basis. Following are some concrete suggestions that may help us:

1. Recognize that unity is a precious gift from God. Our keeping it was the dying wish of our Savior. Unity with God's children is never an option. [v]

2. Work at being united with all God's children with the same grace God showed us in salvation. It's a gigantic task, one that even most Christian leaders disdain. Finish the sentence: If God had worked to provide my salvation the way I work at Christian unity . . . . [w]

3. Love in all its dimensions. Unconditionally. "Accept one another, then, just as Christ accepted you, in order to bring praise to God" (I Cor. 15:7). [x] Love first. Build bridges, not walls. You can escape across your bridge if you've made a mistake, but if you erred in the other direction you may be too tired to tear down or climb the walls you built to keep "those people" out. [y] Communicate with everybody who speaks the language of love. And remember God gave you two ears and one mouth. Love "in spite of" when you have to. [z] Do whatever you can together. Maybe all you can do is smile together. That's a start. When you say, "Let's meet halfway," be planning to go three-quarters of the

309

way yourself. Compliment what you can. Always put the best construction on things, until you just can't any longer. [aa] Confront where you have to — but always in love. Make up your mind that no matter the outcome of trying to unite with brethren, you are committed to love. You'll be there when they're ready. Take the high road of the Savior: "Having loved his own who were in the world, he now showed them the full extent of his love" (John 13:1b). For Jesus, "the full extent of his love" meant dying for them. Let's love our brethren to the full extent — whatever that comes to mean. [bb]

WHAT DO YOU THINK?

[a] How would you describe the state of unity in Christendom today?
[b] Who are my Christian brothers?
[c] What does that statement mean? Do you agree?
[d] What situation does this statement suggest might occur?
[e] What situations does this statement suggest might occur?
[f] Are people like this still our brethren? Discuss.
[g] What do you think it means?
[h] Exactly what was the disagreement between Christians described in this passage?
[i] What was the disagreement here?
[j] What was the disagreement here?
[k] Could people with these disagreements all be Christian brothers?
[l] Can we do that on a practical level? Explain how.
[m] The separating, dividing aspect of sin is seldom discussed. Do you think it is valid? Discuss.
[n] Is unity really the theme of Ephesians? If not, how would you view it?
[o] What is there about sinful pleasure that makes the sinner "dead"?
[p] Precisely when does a dead sinner come alive?
[q] What do you know about the antagonism that existed be-

tween Jews and Gentiles? Discuss.

[r] Are there people in today's world who play these two roles? Who are they?

[s] What does this suggest might happen for divided Christians?

[t] Does this sound too good to be true? Does it allow for diversity? Discuss.

[u] Answer those questions.

[v] Do you agree? Do we treat it that way? Discuss.

[w] Finish it.

[x] How has Christ accepted us?

[y] What does this mean? So, what is the safe course?

[z] Can you suggest a situation where this might be necessary?

[aa] What does I Corinthians 13:5-7 say about this?

[bb] Is unity really this important? Discuss.

INTO THE LIFE

1. Leader, lead your group in a discussion of the following proposition: It is better to unite with brethren on issues of agreement than to insist on total agreement on every issue.

2. Make a Personal Unity Inventory. Let it include the following questions: What is my relationship with other Restoration Movement congregations in my area? How many people in them can I say I really know? How many could I say I really love? What are my differences with them? Have I ever discussed them? With what results?

3. Leader, ask your group to write a scenario showing how Christian unity could be achieved among all churches in your community that profess to follow Christ. From this lead them to formulate positive "action steps" that might make it come true.

4. Unity by compromise of Biblical teachings was never in Jesus' mind when He prayed for unity in John 17. Make a list of the Bible teachings you feel cannot be compromised in the interests of unity. When you finish, ask another trusted brother or sister if your list is realistic.

311

5. Set Unity Goals for your group. Decide on strategies that might help them come to pass. Chart the progress for one year.
6. Make a list of civic moral or spiritual projects in which you could cooperate with denominations in your community. Take steps to cooperate.

19

GRACE AND LIVING BY FAITH

What do you think about the following provocative paragraph?

Most of us leaped over all our doubts and fears to become Christians in the first place. We were believers in the truest sense of the word. We had very little knowledge but lots of faith. Then, once we are "in Christ," we seem to spend a lot of energy reducing the risks, insecurities, and uncertainties of the Christian life to as few as possible. The real believers among us are the freshly washed Christians. They live the Christian *faith*, we live the Christian *system*. They are people of faith, we are faithful. [a]

Is that the way things are?
Is there something really wrong with it?
Are we missing an important dimension of the Christian life?
Why are we like that?
It seems imperative initially to establish that the life of the

Christian is a life of faith. We call ours "the Christian faith," but is that how it is described in Scripture? It doesn't take much looking to find the answer.

> *Matthew 6:25-27,33* — Therefore I tell you, do not worry about your life, what you will eat or drink; or about your body, what you will wear. Is not life more important than food, and the body more important than clothes? Look at the birds of the air; they do not sow or reap or store away in barns, and yet your heavenly Father feeds them. Are you not much more valuable than they? Who of you by worrying can add a single hour to his life? But seek first his kingdom and his righteousness, and all these things will be given to you as well. [b]

This is Jesus' own call to trust God in the midst of the uncertainties of life. It was spoken to His disciples early in their relationship and this philosophy of faith was never rescinded.

> *Acts 4:32-35* — And all the believers were one in heart and mind. No one claimed that any of his possessions was his own, but they shared everything they had. With great power the apostles continued to testify to the resurrection of the Lord Jesus, and much grace was with them all. There were no needy persons among them. For from time to time those who owned lands or houses sold them, brought the money from the sales and put it at the apostles' feet, and it was distributed to anyone as he had need.

The early Christians are characterized here as "believers." Not as adherents, devotees, or church members. And when you take in the full impact of these verses, you realize that both the haves and the have nots were trusting folk. [c]

> *II Corinthians 4:8-14* — We are hard pressed on every side, but not crushed; perplexed, but not in despair; persecuted, but not abandoned; struck down, but not destroyed. We always carry around in our body the death of Jesus, so that the life of Jesus may also be revealed in our body. For we who are alive are always being given over to death for Jesus' sake, so that his life may be revealed in our mortal body. So then, death is at work in

us, but life is at work in you.

It is written: "I believed; therefore I have spoken.' With that same spirit of faith we also believe and therefore speak, because we know that the one who raised the Lord Jesus from the dead will also raise us with Jesus and present us with you in his presence.

Paul handled the pressures, perplexities, persecutions, and prostrations of his Christian life "with that same spirit of faith" that has always characterized God's heroes. [d] Living by faith was anything but secure and certain. In fact, his faith got him in trouble. [e] He described those troubles in more detail in II Corinthians 11:23-28.

II Corinthians 5:1-7 — Now we know that if the earthly tent we live in is destroyed, we have a building from God, an eternal house in heaven, not built by human hands. Meanwhile we groan, longing to be clothed with our heavenly dwelling, because when we are clothed, we will not be found naked. For while we are in this tent, we groan and are burdened, because we do not wish to be unclothed but to be clothed with our heavenly dwelling, so that what is mortal may be swallowed up by life. Now it is God who has made us for this very purpose and has given us the Spirit as a deposit, guaranteeing what is to come.

Therefore we are always confident and know that as long as we are at home in the body we are away from the Lord. We live by faith, not by sight. [f]

The confidence Paul had as a Christian didn't emanate from the physical realities of his life, but from his faith. That's pretty obvious, because his physical body wasn't in very good shape apparently. But he pushed on, fueled by faith.

BUT WHAT HAPPENS TO OUR FAITH?

Are we such average Christians that our lives are to be lived in dull monotony? Is the Christian life no more than shuffling in and out of a church building every week? When the baptistry heater caught on fire . . . was that the most excitement we've had at church in years? Must Christians find their fulfillment in life via the artificiality of sports, movies, the tabloids, the soaps — like the rest of the world? Must our children grow up feeling that TV is the real world and church is religious fantasy? Are missionaries the only Christians who live thrilling lives? [g]

Biblically, the answer is no. Hebrews 11 contains the stories of heroes, true, but it also chronicles stories of the nameless, ordinary believers "who through faith conquered kingdoms, administered justice, and gained what was promised; who shut the mouths of lions, quenched the fury of the flames, and escaped the edge of the sword; whose weakness was turned to strength; and who became powerful in battle and routed foreign enemies." Nor were these all men: "Women received back their dead, raised to life again." Nor did it always end well: "Others were tortured and refused to be released, so that they might gain a better resurrection. Some faced jeers and flogging, while still others were chained and put in prison. They were stoned; they were sawed in two; they were put to death by the sword." Nor did they always fare well materially: "They went about in sheepskins and goatskins, destitute, persecuted and mistreated — the world was not worthy of them. They wandered in deserts and mountains, and in caves and holes in the ground." (All the above is from Heb. 11:33-38).

That doesn't sound like members of any congregation we could name, does it? It doesn't even sound like modern Christians as a group. We might argue that times have changed, we live in a better world. Or that we work smarter. We might relegate all these Hebrews 11 descriptions to times of severe persecution, and since we don't have that today, we can't have the same kind of faith. Nonsense. [h]

WE'VE COME THIS FAR BY FAITH

They took no bigger leaps of faith than we are called to take in

316

the twentieth century. Their chasms were no broader, really. Our enemies may be different, but they are no less real, and no less ferocious. In an age of ubiquitous secularism we took the giant leap of faith that brought us the marvelous gift of eternal life. Our faith flew in the face of reason just as much as theirs did. We believed in redemption, reconciliation and propitiation before we could even pronounce the words, much less know what they meant.

But then something happened. We sat down to rest. We opened our Bibles and read the evidence behind what we believed. Before long we could pronounce (and even define) those words. Maybe we even read books about the Bible that confirmed the logic of our faith. We met lots of other people who believed the same things we did. We got comfortable with fellow believers. That was all well and good, but something insidious was happening.

We were losing the stretch in our faith. We are almost like the child who discovers that there is no Santa Claus. We go along with the charade, but we know better. We always keep one foot on the ground. We're a bit like some of the original disciples who kept their fishing nets handy in case this messiah/kingdom thing didn't work out (John 21:3). Occasionally a Christian or a Christian group will propose some heroic demonstration of faith but we let the air out of it with what we believe is a more "responsible," or "more spiritual" approach. Meanwhile churches spawn spiritual "couch potatoes" whose excitement level rises a couple of degrees on Sunday mornings at eleven when they hear about the brave men and women of faith, and then settles back down for the rest of the week. [i]

EXCITING FAITH AND AMAZING GRACE

Speaking of "couch potatoes" (perhaps "pew potatoes" for us), Paul wrote that "we have gained access by faith into this grace in which we now stand" (Rom. 5:2). Putting our full trust in

God got us here. We hail it as "Amazing Grace," and well it is. And notice that we "stand," not sit, in grace. We are to *live* in grace, not just read about it. And the life of grace is the life of faith. Grace was never meant to reduce the Christian life to a string of certainties. Paul explained it beautifully to Titus.

> *Titus 3:3-8* — At one time we too were foolish, disobedient, deceived and enslaved by all kinds of passions and pleasures. We lived in malice and envy, being hated and hating one another. But when the kindness and love of God our Savior appeared, he saved us, not because of righteous things we had done, but because of his mercy. He saved us through the washing of rebirth and renewal by the Holy Spirit, whom he poured out on us generously through Jesus Christ our Savior, so that, having been justified by his grace, we might become heirs having hope of eternal life. This is a trustworthy saying. And I want to stress these things, so that those who have trust in God may be careful to devote themselves to doing what is good. These things are excellent and profitable for everyone.

Our decision to believe delivered us from lives of the dull monotony of sin. Now, "having hope of eternal life," we "trust in God" to make our hope a reality. "We live by faith, not by sight" (II Cor. 5:7).

It's only fair that Scripture warns us that faith living is dangerous living. And it does in dozens of places and cases. Here are just a few of the dangers of faith living.

Living in grace by faith guarantees insecurity. Jan Johnson indicted most of us with her observation: "Many believers are 'rabbit hole' Christians. In the morning they pop out of their safe Christian homes, hold their breath at work, scurry home to their families and then off to their Bible studies, and finally end the day praying for the unbelievers they safely avoided all day" (*Moody Monthly*, 11/87). [j] Living by faith is living with the insecurity Daniel, Shadrach, Meshach, and Abednego lived with. Remember, it was their faith that got them there. And how about the ultimate insecurity of those described in Hebrews 11? "These were all commended for their faith, yet none of them received what had been promised" (v. 39). Can we relate to that? [k]

Living in grace by faith guarantees being misunderstood. Noah was. Abraham was. Moses was. It was their faith alone that got them musunderstood.

Living in grace by faith allows for failures. We don't intend to be wrong. It's just that people who leap sometimes don't land quite right. Grace says it OK to fail. Failure is never fatal to believers.

Living in grace by faith allows us to be wrong. Again, we don't intend to be wrong. But sometimes we miss God's leading. Sometimes we believe in people instead of God. Or in our own strength. That's bad business all right, but there's always repentance and forgiveness. Grace teaches us that playing it safe is playing. [l]

Living in grace by faith may mean suffering. It did for Joseph, and for Job. "My grace is sufficient for you," God told the suffering Paul (II Cor. 12:9). God's giving disposition is greater than any suffering our faith may cause us. Trust Him.

Living in grace by faith may cost us life itself. "Women received back their dead, raised to life again. Others were tortured and refused to be released, so that they might gain a better resurrection" (Heb. 11:35). What got them killed? Their faith.

Evangelical author Eugene Peterson has captured the intrinsic uncertainty and resultant insecurity of living by faith in the following paragraphs.

> Every once in a while, when I get tired of living by faith I drive twenty-five miles southwest to Memorial Stadium in Baltimore and watch the Orioles play baseball. For a couple of hours I am in a world that is defined by exactly measured lines and precise, geometric patterns. Every motion on the playing field is graceful and poised. Sloppy behavior is not tolerated. Complex physical feats are carried out with immense skill. Errors are instantly detected and their consequences immediately experienced. Rule infractions are punished directly. Unruly conduct is banished. The person who refused to play by the rules is ejected. Outstanding performance is recognized and applauded on the spot. While the

319

game is being played, people of widely divergent temperaments, moral values, religious commitments, and cultural backgrounds agree on a goal and the means for pursuing it. When the game is over, everyone knows who won and who lost. It is a world from which all uncertainty is banished, a world in which everything is clear and obvious. Afterward the entire experience is summarized in the starkly unambiguous vocabulary of numbers, exact to the third decimal point.

The world to which I return when the game is over contains all the elements that were visible in the stadium — elegance and sloppiness, grace and unruliness, victory and defeat, diversity and unity, reward and punishment, boundary and risk, indolence and excellence — but with a significant difference: instead of being sharply distinguished they are hopelessly muddled. What is going on at any particular time is almost never exactly clear. None of the lines are precise. The boundaries are not clear. Goals are not agreed upon. Means are in constant dispute. When I leave the world of brightly lighted geometric patterns, I pick my way through inkblots, trying to discern the significance of the shapes with all the help from Rorschach that I can get. My digital wrist watch, for all its technological accuracy, never tells me whether I am at the beginning or in the middle or near the end of an experience. At the end of the day — or the week, or the year — there is no agreement on who has won and who has lost.[1]

After reading those descriptions don't you get the feeling that all *real* living is faith living anyway? [m] And you'd just as well jump in? Do, the water's fine.

FAITH VS. FAITHFULNESS

Is it possible that we have tried to eliminate faith from our Christian faith and substitute faithfulness in its place? Or perhaps we have placed such a premium on faithfulness that faith seems like a second-class Christian virtue. [n] Jesus' encounter with the Roman centurion will shed some light on our dilemma.

Matthew 8:5-13 — When Jesus had entered Capernaum, a

centurion came to him, asking for help. "Lord," he said, "my servant lies at home paralyzed and in terrible suffering."

Jesus said to him, "I will go and heal him."

The centurion replied, "Lord, I do not deserve to have you come under my roof. But just say the word, and my servant will be healed. For I myself am a man under authority, with soldiers under me. I tell this one, 'Go,' and he goes; and that one 'Come,' and he comes. I say to my servant, 'Do this,' and he does it."

When Jesus heard this, he was astonished and said to those following him, "I tell you the truth, I have not found anyone in Israel with such great faith. I say to you that many will come from the east and the west, and will take their places at the feast with Abraham, Isaac and Jacob in the kingdom of heaven. But the subjects of the kingdom will be thrown outside, into the darkness, where there will be weeping and gnashing of teeth."

Then Jesus said to the centurion, "Go! It will be done just as you believed it would." And his servant was healed at that very hour.

The contrast between faith and faithfulness is clearly illustrated in the behavior of the centurion versus the behavior of the average Jew. A good Jew was the epitome of faithfulness, loyalty, dependability, and piety. But he wasn't much on faith (trust in, confidence in, reliance on, and dependence on God). And it's pretty obvious that Jesus valued faith as highly as, or more highly than faithfulness. In fact, faithful Israelites don't come off well at all in Jesus' word picture of the great feast with Abraham, Isaac, and Jacob. [o]

Don't misunderstand, faithfulness is a great Christian virtue. Timothy, Epaphras, Onesimus, Silas, Gaius, Paul, Antipas and Tychicus are called faithful men in the New Testament. It is faithful men and women who keep congregations going. They are the ones who keep the bills paid, the Bible taught, children trained, the gospel going out, people being born again. "Be faithful, even to the point of death, and I will give you the crown of life," the messenger to the Smyrnan church quotes Jesus as promising (Rev. 2:10b).

But so is faith a great virtue. And since it seems to be tougher

321

for us than its cousin, faithfulness, it deserves special notice here. [p] W.E. Vine's definition of this prominent New Testament word might be summarized like this:

—A firm conviction about God's truth;
—A personal surrender to God; and
—Conduct inspired by such surrender.

One whole New Testament chapter is devoted to illustrating this virtue: Hebrews 11. The attractive lives those valiant men and women lived are always preceded by the words "By faith." They're in the chapter for no other reason. Not because they were intelligent, or handsome, or beautiful, or strong, or wise, or even faithful (loyal, dependable, pious).

Alexander the Great caused great consternation in his army when he marched it across Asia Minor into virgin territory. Their consternation came because he was marching his men "off the map." And think of all the other maps that men and women of vision have marched off of. A clinical report of the final days of Charles II of England read: "A pint of blood was extracted from the royal right arm, and a half pint from the royal left shoulder, followed by an emitic. The royal head was shaved and a blister raised, then a sneezing powder, and a plaster of pitch on his feet. Finally forty drops of extract of human skull were given — after which His Majesty gave up the ghost." Aren't we thankful that medical science has moved into the unknowns?

But Hebrews 11 points us to the very first man to march off the map. "By faith Abraham . . . obeyed and went, even though he did not know where he was going." (Heb. 11:8). That's what faith living is — answering God's summons to the unknown.

As contradictory as it may sound, a congregation made up of faithful people who aren't also full of faith is not a faithful congregation. Why? We were not called just to be trustworthy. We were called to trust. A perfect illustration of the difference between faith and faithfulness is in the story of Jesus and Peter walking on water (Matt. 14:22-33). The eleven disciples who stayed in the boat were faithful, they were loyal, they had gotten in the boat like they were supposed to. But Peter was the one who was full of faith. He was convinced that Jesus could be trusted, he committed his very life to Him, and he stepped over the side — while the faithful ones watched. If Peter had been a baseball fan he would have explained it like this: "You can't steal second and keep your foot on first." [q]

When Paul sought to learn the spiritual vitality of the fledgling congregation at Thessalonica he sent Timothy to inquire of their faith. Not their orthodoxy. Not their organizational progress. Not their holiness. Not their evangelistic prowess. Not even their faithfulness. But their faith. He knew if they had firm conviction about Jesus, personally surrendered to Him, and acted on that surrender they would be OK. Read it:

I Thessalonians 3:1,2 — So when we could stand it no longer, we thought it best to be left by ourselves in Athens. We sent Timothy, who is our brother and God's fellow worker in spreading the gospel of Christ, to strengthen and encourage you in your faith.

I Thessalonians 3:5a — For this reason, when I could stand it no longer, I sent to find out about your faith.

I Thessalonians 3:6a — But Timothy has just now come to us from you and has brought good news about your faith and love.

I Thessalonians 3:7 — Therefore, brothers, in all our distress and persecution we were encouraged about you because of your faith.

I Thessalonians 3:10 — Night and day we pray most earnestly that we may see you again and supply what is lacking in your faith.

That's quite an emphasis on faith, isn't it! Are we as concerned today? [r]

FAITHFULNESS AND FAITH LIVING, GOD'S GREAT DUO

"Faith alone" won't save us, and neither will faithfulness

alone. It's not hard to see why faithfulness *plus* faith living are so vital to the future of God's church.

—We can be faithful to the Biblical pattern for the church but die for lack of vision. [s]

—We can be faithful in attendance, praying, giving, praising, etc., but die if we fail to believe in the Great Commission. [t]

—We can be holy, abstain from evil, refuse to compromise with evil, but if we cling to holiness for our security and fail to be great believers, great risk takers for Jesus, we'll die without the world really knowing we exist. [u]

—Urban congregations, even more than others, are dying because their leaders and members have opted for faithfulness over faith. Not very many are even "holding their own." And need we be reminded that "holding your own" was not looked upon very favorably by our Lord (Matt. 25:24-28)? [v]

Yes, faith is the missing dimension in many Christian lives. How can that be when we were saved by grace through faith in the first place? Now that we stand in grace, let us continue to walk by faith.

WHAT DO YOU THINK?

(The following questions are keyed to sections in the preceding chapter. Refer to the section for full understanding of the questions.)

[a] What is your reaction to that paragraph?

[b] The word "faith" doesn't appear in this passage. Is this a faith issue Jesus is talking about?

[c] Explain the faith they demonstrated.

[d] What is this "spirit of faith"?

[e] What does that mean?

[f] How would you characterize "living by faith"?

[g] Is this a fair assessment of many Christians' lives?

[h] Why do many Christians live dull lives?

[i] Is it fair to characterize the Christian life as exciting? Discuss.

[j] Is Johnson's description of some Christians accurate?

[k] Has the security tetish of the world invaded the church? Discuss.

[l] How can failure and sin be acceptable behavior for Christians?

[m] Is Peterson's description of "life as it really is" accurate? Discuss.

[n] Have we done this? Discuss.

[o] Is this a fair contrast between faith and faithfulness? Discuss.

[p] Is faith tougher to come by than faithfulness? Why?

[q] Do you agree that this story illustrates the difference between faith and faithfulness? Exactly what is the difference?

[r] What do we consider a faithful congregation today? Is our assessment Biblical?

[s] Does this ever happen? Discuss.

[t] Does this ever happen? Discuss.

[u] Does this ever happen? Discuss.

[v] Is this happening? Do you believe the lack of faith a major reason?

INTO THE LIFE

1. Do a Personal Self-Analysis. Is your Christian life characterized more by faith than faithfulness? List the evidences of each. Which is the driving force in your life?

2. Do a Personal Self-Motivation. Make a list of faith-steps you could make but haven't. (It could include such things as financial sacrifice for missions, a decision about personal ministry, bolder witnessing.) After each faith-step write an action-step to get yourself going. Date and sign your list. Put an evaluation date on your calendar 30 days later.

3. Do a Personal Self-Evaluation. After 30 days take another look at your faith-living. Mark progress, rejoice in it, and thank God. Make a new sheet for further faith-living.

4. Leader, write an in-depth evaluation of faith vs. faithfulness in your congregation, class or ministry. Devise a similar motivation and evaluation for the group you lead.

Endnote

1. Eugene Peterson, *Run with the Horses: The Quest for Life at Its Best,* InterVarsity Press, Downers Grove, IL, 1983.